MW00574738

Ghost Guns

Ghost Guns

Hobbyists, Hackers, and the Homemade Weapons Revolution

Mark A. Tallman

 PRAEGER®

An Imprint of ABC-CLIO, LLC

Santa Barbara, California • Denver, Colorado

Library of Congress Cataloging-in-Publication Data

Names: Tallman, Mark A., author.
Title: Ghost guns : hobbyists, hackers, and the homemade weapons revolution
 / Mark A. Tallman.
Description: Santa Barbara, California : Praeger, an imprint of ABC-CLIO,
 LLC, [2020] | Includes bibliographical references and index.
Identifiers: LCCN 2020006846 (print) | LCCN 2020006847 (ebook) | ISBN
 9781440865640 (hardcover) | ISBN 9781440865657 (ebook)
Subjects: LCSH: Firearms—Design and construction. | Gun control—United
 States.
Classification: LCC TS535 .T35 2020 (print) | LCC TS535 (ebook) | DDC
 683.4—dc23
LC record available at https://lccn.loc.gov/2020006846
LC ebook record available at https://lccn.loc.gov/2020006847

ISBN: 978-1-4408-6564-0 (print)
        978-1-4408-6565-7 (ebook)

24 23 22 21 20   1 2 3 4 5

This book is also available as an eBook.

Praeger
An Imprint of ABC-CLIO, LLC

ABC-CLIO, LLC
147 Castilian Drive
Santa Barbara, California 93117
www.abc-clio.com

This book is printed on acid-free paper ∞

Manufactured in the United States of America

Dedicated to the memory of Dr. Linn Freiwald,
a mentor not forgotten.

Contents

Tables and Figures

Tables

Figures

Acknowledgments

I'm indebted to Dr. Erica Chenoweth, Dr. Deborah Avant, Dr. Sam Kamin, Dr. Derigan Silver, and Prof. David Kopel for encouraging my exploration of this topic before many other academics took it seriously. Thanks to my family for considerable practical and intellectual support. Thanks to friends, colleagues, acquaintances, and respondents from academia, law enforcement, security, gun culture, and the maker culture, who are too numerous to name but whose feedback was essential to realistically understanding this complex issue.

Introduction: A Routine Shooting: Why Should We Care about Homemade Small Arms?

Attempting to control a technology is difficult, and not rarely impossible, because during its early stages, when it can be controlled, not enough can be known about its harmful social consequences to warrant controlling its development; but by the time these consequences are apparent, control has become costly and slow.

—David Collingridge (1982)

Man has created a grandiose world of technology, of which dread and fear are often the result. . . . Fortunately, events in the world and our way of life are not determined by technology alone.

—Karel Zeman (Muzeum Karla Zemana 2016)

On June 7, 2013, a psychologically disturbed Californian shot his father and brother, then set fire to the family residence. Emerging from the burning home, he commandeered a passing car. Forcing the driver at gunpoint, he shot at targets of opportunity en route to his final destination: the Santa Monica College Library. Students and staff scattered. The attacker searched for targets, but he'd picked an inauspicious day for a killing spree: local police were well staffed for a visit by President Obama. Officers entered the library seconds behind the shooter. After a brief gunfight, 23-year-old John Zawahri lay dead with a warm AR-15 at his feet.

In most respects, the shooting reflected the same macabre banalities that have become familiar. The spree lasted 14 minutes. Nine shot. Six dead. Zawahri fired 70 rounds in the library, but another 1,200 rounds in his magazines spoke to greater ambition. He'd dropped out of Santa Monica College three years earlier, becoming unemployed and withdrawn. Family were concerned about his mental health but didn't believe him capable of such a rampage. Each detail conformed to a frustratingly common pattern. It was a perfectly routine shooting spree.

Not quite as routine as a few details revealed later. Two years earlier, the Department of Justice had issued a letter denying Zawahri possession of firearms. This generated a disqualifying entry in the Federal Bureau of Investigation's (FBI) National Instant Background Check System (NICS). Zawahri couldn't pass a background check at retailers and would be arrested if found in possession of guns. Yet, he undertook a wild attack with an AR-15 in a state with some of the country's strictest gun laws. How did he get his weapon?

When guns are recovered at American crime scenes, detectives usually run queries in the eTrace system maintained by the Bureau of Alcohol, Tobacco, Firearms, and Explosives (BATFE). Functioning similarly (but not identically) to a registry, these records can often trace guns to their retail purchasers. Gun registries and tracing systems are premised on the assumption that all firearms begin as a unit of factory inventory. If we track every firearm produced, we can deduce how some of them end up at crime scenes. Tracing systems are reviewable records of a firearm's chain-of-custody from its factory origins, through brokers, wholesalers, and retailers, to its ultimate retail buyer. With these records, investigators can solve individual gun crimes, identify trafficking rings, and at least _attempt_ to reduce the flow of firearms from legal supplies to the illicit economy.

These systems bring some benefits, but they have vulnerabilities. Weapons tracing depends on a short string of alphanumeric characters. Licensed gunmakers stamp, engrave, or cast unique serial numbers on firearms at their point of manufacture. These alphanumeric strings are visible on the frame or lower receiver of almost all retail guns in America, and they've become the linchpin for firearm tracking.

If Zawahri stole his rifle, detectives could enter its serial number into eTrace, which would return information about the rifle's legal retailer. Then, detectives could review the retailer's records and identify whoever originally purchased it. Yet, this rifle had no serial, making it invisible to the tracing system. When a crime gun lacks traceable serials, this often indicates illicit trafficking (Braga et al. 2012). Traffickers use many tactics to acquire and resell weapons without a paper trail. One method is to _deface_ the serials, making guns untraceable even if police recover them.

This is illegal. Under the Gun Control Act of 1968 (GCA), defacement is prosecutable. Nevertheless, traffickers deface firearms to obscure evidence of their origins. Nowadays, forensic advancements enable recovery of many defaced serials; however, a thorough effort can obliterate them.

If Zawahri's rifle was defaced, this would leave a scar where the serial was scrubbed away. The gun might be untraceable, but the scar would indicate it was manufactured legally before being stolen or trafficked. Yet, this rifle had no scar: its smooth metal receiver spoke no tales. Zawahri wasn't incorrectly cleared by America's much-criticized background check system, and he hadn't stolen the gun. Instead, he had cobbled together a semiautomatic rifle using a hodgepodge of legally acquired parts. John Zawahri built himself a "ghost gun." Until the day of the shooting he was the only person that knew it existed.

Zawahri bought the rifle's lower receiver as a partially finished *blank*. Under federal law, blanks don't qualify as "firearms" until a sufficient proportion of work necessary to make it functional is completed. Before completion, blanks are legally indistinct from any object in the vague shape of a gun part. Blanks aren't serialized, require no background checks, and can be legally possessed by people who are prohibited from owning functional guns. Secondary components like slides, barrels, and fire controls also don't qualify as firearms. Every component of Zawahri's weapon could be purchased without a background check and completed at home. Detectives discovered Zawahri's workspace filled with inexpensive tools, unfinished parts, and a few more homemade guns.

Cases like these have fueled speculation about the security impacts of homemade, or "do-it-yourself (DIY)," weapons. Independent gunmaking may seem like a futuristic concept. In reality, guns have been made independently for a thousand years. Home gunmaking was a backwater for security research until the precipitous rise in media coverage following the first 3D-printed firearms. Before the 2010s, researchers often characterized homemade guns as a curiosity of the developing world, generally dismissing them as cheap, crude, and irrelevant substitutes for the *real thing*.

Today, there is growing concern that criminals and extremists are embracing homemade guns. Meanwhile, DIY firearms, accessories, and modifications have become popular among legitimate consumers in America. Research on homemade weapons has always been overshadowed by research on conventional firearms. This is justified. The sheer number of conventional firearms (and the magnitude of their social interactions) has always outstripped the criminal impact of homemade guns in the developed world. Consequently, we know comparatively little about the current status or future implications of DIY guns. Available information is a mash-up of nonstandardized sources: police reports, studies of *craft* weapons in developing countries, tabloid coverage, serious journalism vacillating between technical admiration and concern for public safety, sweeping generalizations by lobbyists and legislators, tutorials, reviews, and analyses by firearms journalists and small arms researchers, and expressions of schadenfreude by DIY provocateurs.

Because DIY gunmaking has only recently become a topic for mainstream research, many police agencies have not kept reliable records of homemade firearms they encounter. Some agencies have recently improved data collection, but many sources are incomplete, nonstandardized, inaccessible to the public, or cover a short period of time. The long-standing characterization of DIY firearms as a marginal counterpart to "real" guns has limited efforts to understand their implications. Regulatory proposals add up, but many are based on incomplete information.

What Is a Ghost Gun?

Independently fabricated small arms go by many names: "homemade," "DIY," "expedient," "improvised," "craft," "crypto," "80%," "component" builds, "knockoffs," "counterfeits," "zip" guns, and a variety of slang around the world. Yet, each of these terms is clearer than the one embraced by media: "ghost guns."

Homemade firearms have existed for a millennium, but the term "ghost gun" has more recent origins. The first media use of the term to reference actual firearms might be a 2001 article on plastic flare guns that the Real Irish Republican Army converted to fire live cartridges (Insall 2001). More recently, the term became popular after California senator Kevin de León held a press conference in 2014 where he displayed a homemade ghost gun, and promoted new regulations. De Leon's photo-op was well timed: it followed a spate of coverage on 3D-printed guns. Printable guns were promoted the two years prior by Cody Wilson, a Texas law student, flamboyant crypto-anarchist, and founder of the digital gunmaking firm Defense Distributed.

Articulate yet bombastically provocative, Wilson relished the over-blown fear of his single-shot 3D-printed *Liberator* handgun, which he described as his printed ghost gun as early as April 2013 (Camiel 2013). In the following years, Wilson undertook a promotional blitz, explaining to a pearl-clutching media how printable firearms portended the end of gun control. Google Trends reveals spikes in searches involving the terms "ghost gun," "homemade gun," and "3D-printed gun" between 2013 and

2020, coinciding with media reporting on Defense Distributed, its products, and legal battles. Defense Distributed and many independent gun-hackers have improved the engineering of digital firearms since.

Meanwhile, *frame builds* or *80% firearms* had quietly become popular for years. These are conventional firearms built from unfinished components. Many retailers and hobbyists rejected the term "ghost gun" as a sinister rebranding of a longstanding practice with little historic connection to crime. Other retailers embraced the hype as a marketing ploy. To the detriment of this book's promotion, the best URLs containing the term "ghost gun" are owned by build kit retailers. Mainstream journalists were unsettled by the untraceability of ghost guns, but this same quality played a role in their popularization. When commentators decried untraceable guns that users could build without registration or background checks, many Americans clicked purchase. In a wider sense, the popularization of the term "ghost gun" has laid bare its role as a promotional gimmick and rallying cry for advocates on both sides of America's toxic gun debate.

Context matters. If the primary concern about ghost guns is that they will not appear on registries, it may surprise some readers to know that ghost guns are *most* guns. *Small Arms Survey* estimates there are 857 million civilian-held firearms in global circulation, with 88 percent of that total unregistered (Karp 2018, 3). Perhaps a more relevant definition is that a ghost gun has no traceable serial numbers. Serialization may seem like a longstanding regulation, but it wasn't universally applied by American manufacturers until the 1968 GCA. Guns made before 1968, guns whose manufacturing or sales records are lost, defaced guns, and many foreign-made guns, may be untraceable (U.S. Department of Justice BATFE 2011, 3).

Lack of traceability fuels concern about homemade guns. Yet, most of the world's guns are unregistered, and many can't be traced through serials. Even with serial numbers, most crime guns are stolen or trafficked, ensuring that registries and tracing systems will finger the weapon's legal purchaser rather than its subsequent illegal user. In America alone, 250,000–500,000 guns are stolen annually, with 80 percent unrecovered after six months (U.S. Bureau of Justice Statistics 2012). The *New York Times* repeats a common estimate that approximately 50,000 guns are trafficked across state lines annually (Aisch and Keller 2015). These figures may underestimate the true scale of trafficking, yet they indicate an illicit supply many times larger than needed to generate all gun homicides per year.

Registries and serial numbers help police identify trafficked and stolen crime guns and monitor trends in theft and trafficking. However, numerous surveys indicate that most offenders don't purchase or possess their guns legally. Gun rights advocates question the role of firearm-tracking infrastructures in deterring gun crimes, as most offenses are committed by people who aren't identified in the gun's paper trail. Stolen guns, trafficked guns, defaced guns, and unregistered homemade guns are all invisible to tracking systems until recovered by police. In America, it's fairly easy to acquire guns in ways that separate them from their legal chains-of-custody. In that regard, homemade guns only complicate an existing problem.

A security-relevant definition of ghost guns might also include the vastly larger number of commercial firearms that are unregistered, untraceable, or circulating illicitly. It's not absurd to characterize most of the world's illicit guns as ghost guns insofar as no recordkeeping system will provide police with the gun's current whereabouts or the name of its illegal possessor. Nevertheless, when most people talk about ghost guns, they are clearly talking about *homemade* guns rather than many millions of conventional firearms that are nearly as difficult to track. Conversely, not all homemade guns are ghost guns. Some jurisdictions provide a regime for DIYers to serialize and register homemade firearms. These frameworks are controversial in America, but do represent an approach to reducing the *ghostly* character of homemade guns (provided sufficient public cooperation can be achieved). However, reaching the political agreement and public cooperation needed to make these laws effective, would require a strengthening of sociopolitical trust that has become elusive in American discourse.

Since many readers assume that homemade guns are synonymous with ghost guns, this book primarily focuses on the implications of homemade firearms as they interact with legacy regulatory regimes. Diversity of style, fabrication method, capability, and appeal are all factors for policy. Yet, the most basic definition of DIY products is that they're manufactured independently of licensed commerce. Conventional trafficking begins with theft and *diversion*: skimming commercial guns from legal supplies. DIY firearms involve fewer interactions with the commercial regulatory systems that have underpinned gun control for decades.

While vastly overshadowed by conventional products, DIY guns are catching on. Much DIY gunmaking has been legal under American law, and the vast majority of America's DIY gunmakers have no connection to crime. Yet crime is inevitable. In 2014, bank robbers used a homemade rifle in California. The following year, a Stanford student made a gun for a murder-suicide. Several active shootings have involved DIY products or modifications. Police periodically disrupt illegal gunmaking operations. Some cases are odd. In 2017, a Maryland honors student built a Glock and regularly brought it to high school, claiming fear of active shooters. In 2018, a Broadway puppeteer was caught printing a handgun at work. Weapons traces for DIY products have increased in the United States, but homemade weapons still appear to be responsible for a small proportion of America's overall gun crime. Much consternation emanates from jurisdictions with stricter laws. A new source of firearms may prove most disruptive in jurisdictions where illicit guns are harder to get.

Media coverage of the modern gunmaking phenomenon has occasionally approached hysteria, but some concerns have merit. Around the world, independent makers are improving their products. Even in countries with strict controls, DIY has become a source of illegal weapons largely untouched by legacy regulation. The traditional view of homemade weapons would place them in corrupt, economically disadvantaged, and conflict-ridden locales. This image still rings true. Homemade guns have been prevalent in developing nations. Since the earliest days of colonialism, local artisans reverse engineered *trade guns*. Much of today's illegal gunmaking (and violence) still reflects an economic and social welfare differential between global north and south.

DIY gunmakers have gained attention for their adoption of digital fabrication and nontraditional materials. Digital fabrication converts objects into cyber-physical goods existing on an uneasy continuum between information and physical thing. While digital manufacturing drives incredibly beneficial innovations and is increasingly integrated with mainstream industry, digitization of homemade guns struck some gun control advocates as an outrageous development. Meanwhile, DIY provocateurs cheer digital fabrication's seeming guarantee of firearm access irrespective of law. In that regard, DIY guns are among the early regulatory challenges brought to us by the emerging 4th Industrial and Open Source Revolutions.

DIY guns reflect a growing divide between industrial regulatory systems and the realities of an increasingly postindustrial world. Not only an emerging issue for politics and policing, they foreshadow a contest between the unknown necessities of twenty-first-century security and traditional safeguards for privacy, speech, and communication. Manufacturing capability has diffused since industrialization. More things can be made, and more people can make them. Digitization increasingly liberates manufacturing from traditional geographic, legal, and logistical constraints. We are only starting to grasp the implications, but postindustrialization is expected to transform society.

Gunmakers inevitably counted themselves among the early adopters. By modern manufacturing standards, guns are simple machines. Guns were invented centuries before industrialization, but the artisanal model had its drawbacks: productivity plateaued at the limits of labor efficiency, and precision plateaued at the limits of human performance. Eventually, governments wanted more and better guns than artisanry could provide. Modern factory techniques were incorporated into gunmaking before they were applied to most consumer goods. Yet, while guns were a catalyst of industrialization, industrial techniques have never been required to make them.

The principles behind firearms have been unchanged since the "fire lance" of tenth-century China. The fire lance was a tube attached to a pole. It launched projectiles similarly to a shotgun. There have been many innovations since, but despite sleek designs and precise manufacturing tolerances, most of today's firearms are mechanically similar to guns invented more than a century ago. The underlying concepts were conceived by innovative artisans who predated modern chemistry, physics, and factory methods by several centuries. What differs today is the accessibility of tools and information. The Digital Revolution, 4th Industrial Revolution, and Open Source Revolution are combining to facilitate independent design, manufacturing, and modification of firearms among many other products. American hobbyists and international gunhacking subcultures have driven innovation in homemade guns. Criminals and extremists are making them illicitly. The role of DIY is significant in some countries, yet the challenges it poses are only beginning to be understood. This book explores the security implications of DIY weapons, the practical aspects of making them, and the wider technological, legal, and civil liberties implications of recalibrating traditional gun controls to address modern DIY.

The Open Source Revolution's challenges will not be limited to guns. Chapters 1–2 describe a spectrum of manufacturing advancements that are applicable to home gunmaking. DIY gunmaking is often perceived as an emerging technology issue. Technology certainly plays a role. However, artisanal production was the norm until the nineteenth century. Historically, weapons regulation has reflected assumptions about how they're made.

Reliable data on DIY weapons is limited, but it's evident that they've improved and proliferated. What are the tricks of the illegal gunmaker's trade, and how do they challenge legacy regulation? Why would criminals or terrorists substitute DIY guns for conventional products? Chapters 3–5 explore these and other security implications.

How does DIY gunmaking interact with legacy law and political culture? Chapter 6 explores the sociopolitical dynamics of DIY gunmaking in the United States and provides limited comparisons to the experience of Australia: a nation superficially similar but vastly different on gun policy, culture, and outcomes. How might traffickers exploit each country's criminal incentives and regulatory vulnerabilities? The answers underscore the complexity of crime control in a postindustrial world.

Gunmaking is facilitated by a vast material-informational ecosystem. Much firearms information is open source and has traditionally been uncensored. As DIYers leverage information technology, proposals to combat them have reflected an expanding scope of surveillance and censorship. Some proposals are expansive enough to make bedfellows of gun rights, free speech, open source, and privacy advocates. What are the implications of controlling homemade weapons through controls on information and commerce? Chapters 7–8 explore that question—asserting that that the regulatory regimes necessary to stop homemade weapons may prove as socially transformative as the weapons themselves.

The world will be different if illegal gunmaking proliferates. It will also be different if we introduce expansive controls, and more different still if we implement expansive controls that don't work. How can liberal society adjust as technology makes it easier to produce weapons and contraband? We have options, but they require an honest assessment of risks and harms, and reconsideration of the binary logic that dominates gun politics. Chapter 9 lays out strategies to balance the legitimate values at stake.

More sociopolitical deconstruction than empirical criminology, this book examines the interactions of gunmaking technology, politics, and policy. This is a challenging task, and no book can fully do this issue justice. The underlying technologies and political developments have advanced too rapidly to pronounce their results in print. Further, weapons trafficking is a poorly tracked criminal subsector. How we describe gun trafficking, and the legal regimes best suited to minimize it, can vary considerably. Drawing policy-relevant connections is hard enough that some scholars have suggested evidentiary requirements for gun policy be lowered below the normative standards of social science. Referring to these difficulties, researchers Philip Cook and Jens Ludwig (2006) argued, "For many social policy applications we either must give up on the goal of evidence-based policy, or develop a broader conception of what counts as evidence" (694).

Analysis of weapons policy is always subjective to some degree. As Wright et al. (1983) observed decades ago, "Virtually all of the literature on these topics is polemical to some extent. . .," and any conclusion "does not depend at all on the numbers themselves, but on the implications one is willing to draw from them" (3–4). Political polarization ensures that even fair-minded research will be accused of bias.[1] This book derives from a range of sources that don't easily conform to the architecture of a standardized study. The book addresses security implications, but largely sidesteps suicide. In America, suicide is the most common form of firearm mortality. However, despite its greater toll, political psychology renders self-harm a less pressing issue for security or politics than criminal violence, a reality briefly addressed in chapter 6.

Guns are among the most politically coded issues in contemporary America. Battle lines are forming on DIY guns before we fully understand them. Criminologist and retired BATFE Program Manager William Vizzard described how factions are already forming: "You've got the libertarian side which coalesces with the gun rights folks, and the regulation proponents who coalesce with the 'I don't like guns' folks" (Interview 2016). An Australian criminologist lamented, "People go with their prejudices. What do you do when science is politicized?" (Interview 2016).

America's gun debate is nothing short of toxic. Several respondents cautioned that guns are a third rail in American politics. In a discourse characterized by shaming and misinformation, some respondents required confidentiality. One respondent from a gun control advocacy group warned that I might be threatened by "pro-gun extremists." During doctoral research on this topic, some faculty at a gunsmithing school agreed to participate in interviews. However, administrators nixed it because my university-mandated interview consent paperwork referred to firearms as "weapons." A few stakeholders from the firearm industry rebuffed invitations, assuming that I'm a "liberal antigun researcher," though others didn't jump to this conclusion after sufficient conversation.

Conversely, security studies professor and conventional weapons researcher Brett Steele cautioned: "You're actually doing something profoundly taboo in social science: you're trying to write in an objective manner about guns. When you try to sell this to mainstream academia, they'll dismiss you as a gun nut unless you have a critical bent" (Interview 2016). This warning might sound frivolous, but some research suggests university faculties harbor biases against applicants with perceived connections to gun rights advocacy (Yancey 2017, 57–69). The culture war over guns generates extensive media coverage, yet the tenor of that coverage may further fuel the conflict. Many gun rights supporters are distrustful of journalists and academics, assuming these liberal-dominated fields will never offer a positive depiction of gun culture. This perception plausibly contributes to declining trust in mainstream media and the rise of alt-media and populist politics. In 2018, *Gallup* found that 75 percent of U.S. independents, 66 percent of moderates, and 95 percent of conservatives reported their trust in mainstream media had declined in the last decade. One study suggests that relentlessly negative coverage toward gun rights advocacy may strengthen the National Rifle Association (NRA) and conservative media (Patrick 2013).

DIY gunmaking is increasingly relevant. Yet, it's impossible to understand its implications without relating homemade guns to the vastly larger role of commercial firearms, and the toxic politics and oft-disputed policies meant to regulate them. To hack through this jungle, I reviewed thousands of relevant documents, and interviewed (and in a few cases received written feedback from) 85 subject matter experts.[2] I spoke with current and retired law enforcement, security, counterterrorism, and cybersecurity specialists, legal scholars, political scientists, criminologists, prosecutors, elected officials, security screeners, industrial designers, makers, hackers, journalists, and advocates on both sides of the mandatory binary we call gun politics.

Gun policies and the research around them can be quantitatively incomplete, analytically subjective, politically contentious, economically impactful, emotionally laden, practically important, and politically charged. Whether modern DIY breaks or reinforces our preconceptions, the first step toward addressing an emerging challenge is to understand why it's a challenge at all. Technology contributes to modern DIY, and technologic anxieties drive much concern about homemade guns. It's impossible to understand DIY gunmaking without understanding the technology behind it. Ready or not, the Open Source Revolution is here.

Notes

1. Except for modest travel funds offered to all doctoral students at my PhD institution, I did not seek external funding for research on this topic. As a certified range safety officer, I've received NRA-approved training in safe shooting and range procedures, but have not sought or received any support whatsoever from the NRA, gun rights, or gun control/safety advocacy groups. I can't deny editorializing on this complex topic, nor can I deny that the most conscientious researchers are susceptible to motivated reasoning in favor of personal orientations. However, this book can't be accused of bias due to third-party patronage, because there was none.

2. Many, but not all, of which are directly quoted in this book.

CHAPTER ONE

Printing Pandora's Box: How the 4th Industrial Revolution Transforms Security

Blueprints are weapons, don't abuse them!
—World War II "Work Incentive" Poster (Duer 1942)

Do you honestly think you can understand what my code is? Regulators are gonna get killed by people who understand code!
—Anonymous machinist and software developer (Interview 2015)

The first gun I built was a Glock 26, or "Baby Glock." I ordered an 80 percent kit from a friendly online retailer. It arrived with all components: unfinished frame, nicely made barrel, slide, guide rod, spring, appropriately sized magazine under state law, and other parts. The frame came with a plastic jig that exposed the holes I'd need to drill and the polymer I'd need to remove. I worried about ruining the $150 frame. Thankfully, the retailer and DIY enthusiasts posted online tutorials.

Using a drill and a Dremel, I drilled the holes and removed the polymer. With hand files and sandpaper, I smoothed the cuts so the frame would accept the secondary components. It all assembled smoothly after some wet sanding. I cycled several magazines of dummy rounds, then cleaned the pistol and locked it up. The next day I went to my private property, mounted the pistol on a table vise and aimed it toward a berm. Donning eye and ear protection, I stood behind cover and pulled the string. The gun fired. A couple magazines later, I was fairly confident it would be safe to use. I felt a brief satisfaction familiar to millions of DIYers whether they build guns, cars, drones, or toys. I *built* something, and it worked!

To build an object is to engage it beyond the superficialities of consumption. We modern citizen-consumers spare little thought for the science, materials, and ingenuity that *make the world we buy*. To paraphrase Francis Bacon, knowledge is empowering. If I wanted to build another Glock, I felt I could do it faster and with fewer mistakes. Theoretically, I could enjoy target shooting or even defend my loved ones with this DIY pistol. Yet, I knew I'd rather trust a reputable manufacturer. This Glock was a fun build, but it would rarely see the outside of a locked safe.

I also had to admit that building it was much less technically impressive than it seemed. Everything about it was tailored for a novice. The metal components were precision machined. The polymer frame arrived partially complete: just below the legal threshold of a functional firearm. If the retailer had skimmed away a few more cubic centimeters of material, it would require a background check at a licensed dealer. This kit was not a gun, but it was as close to a gun as possible without technically buying one. It was also convenient that Glocks are designed around polymer frames. Metal-framed builds like the AR-15 or Colt 1911 would require more expensive tools. Today's DIY discourse is replete with concern about 3D-printed guns endowed with magical abilities to circumvent weapons screening. However, few outside the gun culture are aware that this controversy began decades ago—and it was Glock's plastic frame that started it.

Before the 1980s, most handguns were made of steel and wood. Glocks were different: their slides, barrels, and most moving parts were metal, but their frames were lightweight corrosion-resistant polymer. Glocks always contained enough metal to be detectable. They also use metal-cased ammunition, and their shape is unmistakably gunlike and difficult to miss in an X-ray or pat-down. Nevertheless, movies and TV shows implied that Glock's *plastic gun* was undetectable. Legislators soon passed the Undetectable Firearms Act of 1988 (UFA). The UFA prohibits guns without the equivalent of 3.7 ounces of detectable steel.

Today, many manufacturers use polymer frames. Industry adoption of polymers didn't result in mass marketing of undetectable guns, but did have another result: it made Glocks easy to complete from a ready-made kit. In building a Glock, I flouted two generations of gun policy backlash: the 1980s backlash over synthetic materials, and the last decade's backlash over DIY kits that can be completed easily (perhaps too easily, as some gun control advocates argue) by users with modest skill and simple tools.

How did it become so easy to make a firearm? Law plays a role, as do culture, politics, economics, and consumer demand. Yet the issue is not so simple as a few easily remedied loopholes. The story of ghost guns goes deeper: it's really a story of technology and social trust. How should we walk the treacherous line between decentralized innovation and the disruptions that accompany it? How do industries and consumers leverage technology in an era of political distrust? Ghost guns are only one foreshadowing as technology pulls us beyond the charted territory of industrial-era governance. Centuries of advancement in materials, tools, and information are coalescing. As tools improve and information proliferates, a wider range of items become producible outside of regulated supply chains. In the most ambitious scenarios posited by DIY provocateurs, all a maker would need is information about a desired product, and technology will make it so.

Open Source, Open Season: Challenges to Legacy Security

> **Inspector Kashyk:** Captain, why don't you join me? I've been looking forward to trying your replicator. . .
> **Captain Janeway:** I'm afraid that won't be possible. I had your replicator taken offline.
> **Inspector Kashyk:** In case I decided to replicate a weapon.
> **Captain Janeway:** A safety precaution, you understand.
> **Inspector Kashyk:** Better than anyone!
> —*Star Trek: Voyager*, "Counterpoint" (Landau 1998)

Optimistic sci-fi franchises like *Star Trek* imagine a postindustrial future where technology renders humanity smarter, healthier, more peaceful, and freer to pursue its highest aspirations. The marquee technologies behind this future are familiar to sci-fi fans. Faster-than-light propulsion, unlimited energy, and teleportation come to mind. Some of these technologies remain firmly in the realm of fiction. Yet, the *Star Trek* universe features another technology that is faster approaching: the *matter replicator*. The matter replicator converts energy to physical objects. *Star Trek* characters *replicate* whatever they need.

It's implied that replication created a postscarcity society where resource competition (and associated personal and tribal enmities) simply became irrelevant. Yet, among the visionary technologies in sci-fi, the replicator's social impacts are among the least explained. How did liberal societies prevent abuse of a technology offering mastery of physical production? On this question, Hollywood necessarily remains vague. Viewers must assume that replication ended material need, rendering humanity secure at the pinnacle of Maslow's hierarchy. But what if replicators came to a species irretrievably plagued by tribalism, envy, and conflict? Would replication solve these age-old problems, or make things worse?

We are just starting to develop technologies along these lines. Recent decades have seen rapid advances in digital fabrication. Digital fabrication combines the precision of industrial fabrication techniques, with the customizability of digital design and control systems. Obviously, it doesn't convert matter from pure energy, but digital fabrication does allow for small numbers of highly customizable digital tools to emulate the precision that once required extensive production lines of analog tools. The resulting 4th Industrial Revolution (4IR) promises incredible improvements to mainstream manufacturing, transportation, design, engineering, construction, crafts, and artistic trades. The Digital and 4th Industrial Revolutions also have a DIY counterpart: the Open Source Revolution. The Open Source Revolution reflects endlessly creative mashups of commercially available technologies. The fabrication techniques behind industrial products have been diffusing to user communities outside of the stereotypical factory environment.

Because today's replication technology remains in its infancy, its full sociopolitical impacts are speculative. Nevertheless, there is concern that these manufacturing revolutions will disrupt longstanding arrangements in security and governance. Writing for the RAND Corporation, Johnston, Smith, and Irwin (2018) argued that additive manufacturing (aka 3D-printing) has the "potential to dramatically disrupt the prevailing state system and international order," with potentially "dramatic effects on international conflict, violent extremism, and everyday crime" (2; 13). World Economic Forum Chairman Klaus Schwab (2016) argued that the 4IR will "profoundly impact the nature of national and international security." Writing for *Small Wars Journal*, Clint Arizmendi, Ben Pronk, and Jacob Choi (2014) contended that decentralized manufacturing may impact state security, legitimacy, and monopoly of force. Evaluating robotics in modern conflict, Peter Singer (2010) observed that private organizations, weaker states, and individuals can increasingly leverage DIY methods to challenge conventional power, a trend reflecting "the early stages of a new global redistribution of power"(266).

Decentralized manufacturing subverts *supply-side* regulation. Some types of contraband have been controllable only because they are hard to make. Referring to our cyber-physical world as the "Internet+," cryptographer and security theorist Bruce Schneier (2018) writes:

> Historically, we have often relied on scarcity for security. That is, we secure
> ourselves from the malicious uses of a thing by making that thing hard to

obtain. This has worked well for some things—polonium-210, the small-pox virus, and anti-tank missiles come to mind—and less well for others: alcohol, drugs, handguns. The Internet+ destroys that model. (204)

Supply-side tactics reflect this *security-through-scarcity* rationale. Supply-side controls attempt to disrupt the supply of contraband and minimize leakage (or *diversion*) of regulated goods to illicit channels. Supply-side measures attempt to control the distribution of a product to serve security, crime control, public health, revenue, or other sociopolitical objectives. In that sense, supply-side control isn't just regulation of physical goods: it's a form of social control. It's usually easier to implement supply-side controls on legal products. Legal commerce is accessible to authorities. Illicit commerce is clandestine, avoidant, adversarial, or corrupting of authorities. Industrialization created a regulatory contradiction. Centralized production and inventory tracking systems made it easier to trace products from their factory origins. However, industrialization vastly increased output, enabling diversified industries to circulate uncontrollable volumes of tools, materials, and products.

The 4IR and Open Source Revolutions are expanding what can be made outside of regulated infrastructures. Digital fabrication may undermine point-of-sale controls and "significantly accelerate weapons proliferation" (Johnston, Smith, and Irwin 2018, 13). Yet, DIY weapons are not new, nor is digital fabrication necessary to produce them. Armsmaking by violent nonstate actors (VNSAs) is longstanding. For decades, VNSAs improvised their own explosives and light weapons like mortars, mines, and recoilless rifles. The FBI is evaluating the viability of 3D-printers for bombmaking, and some analysts argue that a rise in DIY explosives and light weapons could prove more destabilizing than a popularization of illegal gunmaking (Tallman 2017, 235–36; Tirone and Gilley 2015). Gunrunners from America to Australia to Mexico and Canada have made firearms with digital tools. Analysts described the armsmaking of ISIS as "unlike anything we've ever seen" (Ismay, Gibbons-Neff, and Chivers 2017).

Kurdish militias, Mexican drug traffickers, and ISIS terrorists have produced their own armored vehicles. Occasionally, so have mechanically adept private citizens. In 2004, a disgruntled mechanic laid waste to the business district of Granby, Colorado, with his homemade combat bulldozer. Despite valiant efforts, local police were ill-equipped to stop the cleverly designed vehicle. Authorities considered deploying an antiarmor helicopter, but the attacker killed himself first.

DIY automation and robotics add complexity to this postindustrial security dynamic. Hackers can already control some automobiles remotely. Others have developed self-driving systems that can be retrofitted to cars for less than $1,000. Criminals smuggle contraband with aerial drones, while terrorists and hobbyists have mounted weapons on them. Even combat robots are falling within DIY capability. A U.S. military robot called SWORDS can remotely fire machine guns and 40mm grenades. However, years before SWORDS was deployed, engineer Graham Hawkes privately fabricated his own version using accessible components. He found that "within three minutes, my 80-year-old father-in-law was as deadly as a 30-year-old army captain" (Singer 2010, 368). Drug traffickers build submarines and dig tunnels with sophisticated mining equipment. Electronic surveillance and secure communication tools have diffused. Drug traffickers have built encrypted telecom infrastructures, while hackers build once-secretive surveillance tools from accessible components. During the 2006 Israel-Hezbollah conflict, Hezbollah became the first VNSA to use offensive drones, hacked into Israeli Defense Force (IDF) computers and radios, and eavesdropped on IDF officers' personal calls (264–65).

Mainstream security and governance institutions will surely seek countermeasures to this postindustrial diffusion of capability. Problematically, emerging technologies blur traditional regulatory lines. If more people can make more things using more tools and more materials, it seems that the scope of regulation must endlessly expand. If contraband can be made from more locations, traditional restraints on policing seem obstructive. If digital tools allow bad actors to make weapons, then broadened surveillance and censorship seem increasingly reasonable. Legacy players are tempted to control the information flows that facilitate disruptive innovation and empower new vectors of influence. This creates new tensions between liberal values and a broadening array of regulatory, surveillance, and censorship proposals.

Consider the drone. Some terrorists have weaponized them, but accidents probably pose greater short-term risk. There are 100+ unauthorized drone flights near airports every month (Federal Aviation Administration 2019). If civilian drones result in fatal incidents, to what degree should we regulate them? Will it suffice to expand flight restrictions and shoot-down authority near public facilities, as U.S. legislation now authorizes? In 2018, lawmakers reinstated a national drone registry within the National Defense Authorization Act despite a 2017 ruling against it in *Taylor v. Huerta.*

If most "crime drones" are homemade, will we censor information useful for building them, even if homemade drones are overwhelmingly used for legal purposes? Will we require background checks to purchase components? Laissez-faire advocates argue that there are many good reasons to use drones even near government facilities. Journalists and human rights campaigners use drones to document conditions at border facilities and refugee camps. They are used for disaster aid, firefighting, journalism, film, security, agriculture, research, delivery, hobby, and recreation. There are a million registered drones in America, and their users are almost entirely law-abiding. Writing for the antiregulation Heritage Foundation, Jason Snead and John-Michael Seibler (2016) criticize the drone registry as *security theater*, arguing that only low-risk users will register and serialize their drones as required.

If this sounds familiar, it should. Similar points are applicable to homemade guns. Like drone users, most of America's gunbuilders are nonmalicious. As with drones, legislators have proposed registration and serialization to track homemade guns, while gun rights advocates argue that these proposals invade privacy and will only gain compliance from low-risk users. DIYers can build guns and drones from a variety of components. Yet, improved tools, the diversity of components, and the proliferation of information make it difficult to totally stop homemade guns *or* drones through commercial regulations alone. Controlling technology is tempting, but only a stopgap. Technology diffusion occurs in closed societies and is critical to innovation in open ones. Diffusion favors upstarts because it extends a "free ride" on investments made by mainstream organizations (Singer 2010, 270–71). Hackers frequently defeat expensive security technologies. Worse, attackers can discard old methods if new ones are better, while defenders must invest in new countermeasures while maintaining preexisting ones.

These technologies bring inestimable benefits. However, as technology and trade empower wider populations, it becomes difficult to prevent small minorities of malicious actors from gaining disruptive capabilities. Meanwhile, emerging technologies promise transformative changes in economies and society. Some analysts believe robotics and IT are creating greater productivity gains than the steam engine (Bughin et al. 2018). Others forecast that 3D-printing alone will account for *half* of manufacturing within 20 years (Leering 2017). As mainstream industries integrate digital manufacture, the World Economic Forum forecasts 5 million job losses in 15 countries by 2022, and *Oxford Economics* predicts up to 20 million job losses by 2030. Johnston, Smith, and Irwin (2018) warn that "unemployment, isolation, and alienation of middle-and-low-skilled laborers could be exacerbated by additive manufacturing, potentially leading to societal unrest in both developed and developing countries" (16).

Into this backdrop comes the neoartisanal moment. This moment combines the decentralization of the artisanal age with the materials, tools, and precision of the industrial age. Importantly, today's makers have access to information learned through centuries and made accessible by the Print and Digital Revolutions. The neoartisanal moment reflects an accelerating diffusion of manufacturing capability. This diffusion will apply to many physical, electronic, artistic, biologic, chemical, robotic, and other items. By comparison, firearms are simple machines. It's harder to make iPhones than guns, and yet counterfeiters make fake iPhones by the thousands. It was only a matter of time until firearms escaped the half-hearted industrial controls introduced a few decades ago.

CHAPTER TWO

Teaching Iron to Fly: Artisanal, Industrial, and Neoartisanal Gunmaking

Guns 1.0: Armorers and Artisans

If you want to explain what's going on with DIY weapons today, you're going to have to get historical. You need to look back 2,000 years!

—Brett Steele, security and conventional weapons researcher (Interview 2016)

As if to bring death upon man with still greater rapidity, we have given wings to iron and taught it to fly.

—Pliny the Elder (Pliny and Rackham 1938, chap. 39)

Millennia before the gunpowder age, Judeo-Christian scripture describes the Philistines disarming ancient Hebrews by imposing prohibitions on blacksmithing:

Now there was no blacksmith to be found throughout all the land of Israel, for the Philistines said "Lest the Hebrews make swords or spears." But all the Israelites would go down to the Philistines to sharpen each man's plowshare, his mattock, his ax, and his sickle. (I Sam. 13: 19–20)

So it came about, on the day of battle, that there was neither sword nor spear found in the hand of any of the people who were with Saul and Jonathan. (I Sam. 13: 22)

Notwithstanding this example, effective control over arms production was unusual in antiquity. As historian Stanley Burstein described: "The technical simplicity of Ancient Near Eastern weaponry, primarily cutting and concussion weapons, and the general availability of the metallurgical technology and resources required to produce it, made it unlikely that such a ban could be effective for long" (Burns 1993, 552). Historian Udo Heyn observed that preindustrial weapons control focused on "the permissibility (rather than the availability) of arms" (569). Easily made weapons are difficult to control. Ancient societies focused on conflict deterrence, resolution, and social pressures, rather than supply-side arms control.

There were exceptions. At their zenith, the Athenians forced restive allies to dismantle their fleets and fortifications. Later, Sparta forced Athens to do the same. The Romans tried to declaw neighboring chiefdoms by restricting exports of bronze, iron, arms, and armor (560). In Machiavellian style, Rome forced Carthage to surrender huge quantities of weapons before revealing its final terms. When the Carthaginians realized their city would be destroyed and population enslaved, "the temples and public places were turned into workshops, in which the citizens worked night and day to manufacture new ones [weapons] out of the raw material which was to hand; 100 shields, 300 swords, 500 javelins were made every day, besides numerous catapults, for the cords of which the women offered their hair" (Warmington 1964, 248–51). This valiant effort failed. Carthage lacked enough resources to survive the subsequent siege.

Preindustrial regimes initially believed they could monopolize firearms. When guns arrived in Europe, longbows were the most effective battlefield projectile. In fact, longbows remained more effective for well over a century after firearms were introduced. Yet, mass longbow armies couldn't be trained quickly, and a monarch that wanted to harness them would risk populist rebellion with subjects trained in using a highly effective weapon. Economists Douglas Allen and Peter Leeson (2015) argue that mass longbow armies posed stability risks to medieval regimes. Hence, few medieval regimes encouraged their populations to train with longbows. More often, they relied on mercenaries and professional soldiers equipped with crossbows. Crossbows were easier to learn, costlier, and more difficult to make, and they could be kept in centralized armories. Firearms were the crossbow's political successor: fearsome yet exotic weapons that medieval regimes believed they could control.

Yet, from Europe to the Middle East and eventually the colonial sphere, guns escaped regime monopoly. Firearm diffusion weakened local nobility and strengthened centralized states that could afford gunpowder armies. This dynamic applied in Europe, the Ottoman Empire, the Safavid Empire, the Shaibanid Khanate, and the Mughal Empire (Khan 2006, 53–54). With the emergence of gunpowder armies, governments reduced their dependence on local aristocracy. However, firearm diffusion also came with risk of popular rebellion. Some regimes applied controls. For example, as handguns became more accessible, the sixteenth-century Ottomans imposed a firearms monopoly. However, like most such monopolies, it eventually weakened. Chemical engineer Asitesh Bhattacharya (2006) argues that elite interest within the Indian caste system slowed diffusion of gunpowder in Mughal India. In his words, gunpowder manuals were "guarded like treasures, and not communicated to the common people" (46–47). Nevertheless, the Mughal monopoly also weakened. Gun-toting peasants resisted taxes, and local aristocrats threatened the central regime with gunpowder forces. By the time the regime restricted blacksmithing, it was too late. The resulting fragmentation of power left India vulnerable to colonialism (Khan 2006, 61–63).

Japan's Tokugawa Shogunate imposed the most effective artisanal gun controls. This is extraordinary considering the backstory. Before prohibition, Japan's mastery of the gun was unparalleled. When Portuguese traders brought matchlocks in the 1540s, the warlords of Japan's Sengoku period reverse-engineered them (Lidin 2004, 4). Gunpowder weapons had already spread throughout Europe and Asia. Yet, only 20 years after learning about guns, Japan was the world's most prolific gunmaker. Japanese artisans improved matchlocks beyond European versions: their guns had better designs, metallurgy, reliability, and weather-resistance (Perrin 1979, 28).

In the late sixteenth century, Oda Nobunaga and his successor Hideyoshi harnessed gunpowder armies to subdue all warring factions, then promptly undertook a policy of disarmament. Guns had already worried the European warrior-nobility, but Europe's military class were around 1 percent of the population, and Europe's political diversity and sprawling geography made technology harder to contain. Conversely, Japan was isolated, and its warrior class was 7–10 percent of the population (Dyer 1985, 58). The Shogunate harnessed gunpowder armies but didn't want to disrupt longstanding sociopolitical hierarchies. Eliminating guns was conceivable for several reasons. First, Japan's nobility still held force supremacy. Under Hideyoshi's "sword hunt" decree, samurai seized weapons from peasants without exception (Kopel 1992, 30). If anyone resisted, samurai had "permission to kill and depart" (Warner and Draeger 1982, 34–35). Second, guns had only been in Japan for a few decades. Widening gun ownership was a source of urgency behind the political elite's disarmament plans (Khan 2006, 54), but gun ownership hadn't yet diffused as widely as in Europe.

Third, the Japanese mode of production was comparatively central-ized, and its logistics demanded elite resources. Salpeter and iron were expensive and mostly imported. Guns were initially made only by sword-smiths, so gunmaking skills did not widely diffuse. By 1625, an artisanal industry capable of equipping 40,000 musketeers for an invasion of Korea in 1592 made fewer than 400 muskets per year (Perrin 1979, 27). Eventu-ally, gunsmiths only repaired the remaining guns. In just 150 years, Japan massively equipped itself with artisanal firearms, then almost completely eliminated guns from circulation.

The Japanese case suggests that artisanal gunmaking can be sup-pressed. Yet, the case was unusual. Tokugawa Japan used authoritarian methods to suppress a comparatively centralized artisanal sector while maintaining isolation for more than a century. Similar conditions didn't exist elsewhere. Europe's style of adoption made diffusion inevitable. European arquebusiers produced and repaired guns in the field (Greener 2016, 58). Firearms concerned elites, but their destabilizing effects were initially limited to the battlefield. Basic metallurgy, woodworking, and smithing were within the capabilities of arquebusiers, but equipping in volume remained difficult. Gunmaking required tools and skillsets for blacksmithing, carpentry, and chemistry. Europe had few saltpeter sources, and imported saltpeter was expensive (Crosby 2010, 121). These prerequisites demanded regime-level resources for high-volume production.

However, gunsmithing diffused to local blacksmiths. Soldiers returned with gunmaking skills and deserted with weapons in hand. Firearms became a mercenary specialty. Diffusion drove technical innovations. Historian Bruce Holsinger (2015) writes: "One of the notable characteris-tics of the culture of [European] gun-making in this period was its decen-tralization, as local artisans in cities and towns slowly perfected their craft through a long process of trial and error that led to numerous tech-nological advances." Khan (2006) observes that scale production of cross-bows and siege engines may have given Europe an advantage in making firearms at "remarkably low cost" (52–54). Guilds guarded their positions in the supply chain, but their divisions of labor were more diverse than in Japan. Traveling artisans sought patronage. Some of the first gun controls were protectionist policies favoring domestic guilds over foreign imports, a dynamic that continues into modern gun politics. Europe was condu-cive to technology diffusion. The printing press accelerated this diffusion beyond the imagination of medieval regimes.

Preindustrial artisans made firearms in volume. However, it was difficult to increase output while meeting precise standards. Many preindustrial firearms were outstandingly crafted, but they did not achieve true *mass production* due to the idiosyncrasies of nonstandardized tools and artisanal labor. Preindustrial components weren't interoperable, and good materials were costly. Mining and smelting steadily improved, but it wasn't until the Bessemer process and other nineteenth-century metallurgical advancements that quality gun steel became affordable. Though black powder can be made artisanally, quality varied. Nineteenth-century chemistry enabled mass production of improved propellants. Preindustrial artisans innovated for the first 800 years of gunmaking, but it wasn't enough. Western regimes wanted more guns, not fewer. They wanted guns more capable, reliable, cheaper, and easier to fix. They got exactly what they wanted.

Guns 2.0: Industrialization

> Decidedly the best application of art to industry is when a great many copies are made from an exceedingly good pattern.
> —William Burges (Burges 1865, 1)

European military rationalists devised modern factory production. These principles were adopted by American armorers—the first industrial gunmakers. America's factory gunmaking catalyzed a revolution in manufacture. Decades after the adoption of factory methods, writers still referred to factory manufacture of *any* product as the "American system." However, factory gunmaking originated with the French military. In 1765, General Jean-Baptiste de Gribeauval introduced the Systeme Gribeauval, which tried to make interoperable artillery and firearms (Hounshell 1984, 25–26). The wider tolerances of artillery made it easier to standardize, but Gribeauval never perfected the method on guns. With Gribeauval's support, arsenal inspector Honore Blanc developed interchangeable musket mechanisms. Ambassador Thomas Jefferson met Blanc and quickly wrote to John Jay:

> An improvement is made here in the construction of the musket, which it may be interesting to Congress to know, should they at any time choose to procure any. It consists in the making every part of them so exactly alike that what belongs to one may be used in any other musket in the magazine. . . . Supposing it might be useful to the U.S., I went to the workman. He presented me with the parts of 50 locks taken to pieces and arranged in compartments. I put several together myself taking pieces at hazard as they came to hand, and they fitted in the most perfect manner. The advantages of this, when arms need repair, are evident. (Jefferson and Boyd 1971, 455)

The French Revolution put Blanc out of business before he could perfect his processes. However, French officers in the newly independent United States lobbied for interchangeability. Industrialists Eli Whitney and Simeon North became proponents, and the War Department began demanding interchangeable guns. It ordered 2,000 uniform pistols from North and 15,000 uniform muskets from Whitney. North improved production through standardized prototypes, machine tools, and labor efficiency. In 1808 he wrote, "I find that by confining the workman to one particular limb of the pistol until he has made two thousand, I save at least one quarter of his labor . . . and the work will be as much better as it is quicker made" (Hounshell 1984, 28). In 1813, the War Department ordered 20,000 standardized pistols. North delivered. Whitney was a flamboyant ambassador for interchangeability, but he initially lacked a viable process. In 1801, he randomly assembled musket parts for government officials, but this was a marketing trick. Whitney's initial innovations in the arms business were in accounting and labor efficiency rather than revolutionary improvements to manufacturing processes.

George Washington established the Springfield Armory in 1794. The private industrialists' innovations were soon adopted in the public armories. Rather than requiring contractors to design full production lines, Springfield permitted bids for improvements to processes. For example, after Thomas Blanchard designed a lathe to turn musket barrels, he designed another to mill wooden gunstocks (a previously laborious task). Springfield offered Blanchard "shop space, free use of tools and machinery, water power, and the necessary raw materials." In return, Blanchard granted Springfield licensing to his machinery and processes (Hounshell 1984, 35–39).

At least 150 years earlier, the bustling workshops of Birmingham, England, produced a few thousand muskets annually. By the 1850s, the Harper's Ferry and Springfield armories were making 60,000 muskets per year. Samuel Colt applied these processes to a highly marketable firearm. He had first patented his "revolving gun" in the 1830s. However, his initial attempt at defense contracting was unsuccessful: the guns were too fragile. Colt realized his designs could not be mass-produced artisanally. He collaborated with Eli Whitney Jr. to fabricate with machine tools. Their collaboration produced the standardized, portable, reliable, and affordable revolver. Revolvers became a fixture for militaries, police, and civilian markets around the world.

After struggling to equip its military for the Crimean War, Britain also wanted more guns. In 1854, a parliamentary committee deemed Colt's factory an "almost perfect system" (Hounshell 1984, 19) and recommended adoption of the American factory production model. Germany, France, Belgium, and Austria soon followed. Along with American industrialists like John Browning, some of these European makers pioneered semiautomatics and developed the automatic weapons used by modern infantry. Factory methods increased access to consumer goods. Bicycles, furniture, clocks, guns, tools, and an endless list of products became affordable. Mass-produced goods were cheaper, but centralization had sociopolitical impacts. Among Mohandas Gandhi's anticolonial initiatives was the "home spun" movement encouraging Indians to produce clothing on handlooms. By encouraging local artisanry, Gandhi hoped to demonstrate independence from British imports (Gandhi and Dalton 1996, 15).

Centralized arms production reached its zenith around the world wars. This "oligopoly of production" largely eclipsed artisanal gunmaking. However, partisans exploited the resilience of artisanry, while governments exploited its limitations. Some colonial administrations encouraged subjects to make weapons instead of importing superior guns. Sometimes, local production was suppressed with varying degrees of success. Realpolitik undermined restraint in industrial gunmaking. This shouldn't be surprising. As Sean Watts (2015) argues, "Concerns for the socially and militarily disruptive effects of weapons seems to have motivated as many campaigns for law of war regulation as have concerns for inhumane effects" (616).

The global small arms trade is a status quo arrangement. Powerful industrial states dominated factory gunmaking, but were not existentially threatened by firearm proliferation. Industry diversified through postwar liberalizations. In the 1960s, 69 licensed producers operated in 30 countries. By the 1990s, more than 385 firms operated in 64 countries (Abel 2000, 83). By 2014, more than 1,000 firms operated in more than 100 countries (Jenzen-Jones 2014). The firearms sector is so diverse that regulators can't track the world's *legal* production. As the United Nations (UN) Security Council noted in 2008, "There are no accurate figures for the number of small arms and light weapons currently in circulation globally"(3). Industrialization created an unmanageable supply, but also introduced the possibility of tracking guns through unique markings applied by manufacturers. Markings predated industrialization, but industrial engraving machines could apply sequential serial numbers. Commercial makers introduced serials to track shipments, select units for testing, and recall products. Today, serials enable firearm tracking across legal chains-of-custody. Recordkeeping based on serials has become "an essential prerequisite for limiting the illicit proliferation of small arms and light weapons" (Paoli 2010, 1).

The first major U.S. legislation to regulate the commercial firearms industry, the Federal Firearms Act of 1938, imposed no serial number requirements. Licensed manufacturers and importers were required to serialize firearms for the first time in 1958, but shotguns and .22 caliber guns were exempt ("Identification of Firearms"). Serialization of all commercial firearms was not required by American federal law until the 1968 Gun Control Act, which also outlawed defacement. However, many American manufacturers used serials before they were legally mandated.

International agreements like the International Tracing Instrument (ITI) impose similar standards, though some signatories don't enforce them. Serial number registries were intended to be a cornerstone of countertrafficking. However, today most civilian firearms are unregistered, and trafficking tactics prevent many illicit guns from being recovered through legal chains-of-custody. Massive supply combines with consumer noncompliance to undermine registration. In 2018, just over a billion firearms circulated globally, with around 85 percent in civilian possession, and 88 percent unregistered (Karp 2018, 3).

Unregistered guns outnumber registered guns in many countries. In Japan, 25–50 percent of guns are unregistered (Karp 2018, 55). In Germany, two-thirds of firearms that are supposed to be registered, aren't. In England and Wales, unregistered guns may outnumber registered guns by nearly 250 percent (Karp 2018, 51). More than half of Canada's guns are unregistered, and Brazil has twice as many unregistered guns as registered ones (*Small Arms Survey 2007* 2007, 56). France has 3 million registered firearms, but up to 20 million unregistered. Unregistered guns outnumber legal guns by 300 percent in Mexico. India's unregistered guns outnumber legal guns by a factor of eight. Jordan has 126,000 registered firearms, and 500,000 unregistered. Sudan has 7,000 registered, but 2.2–3.6 million unregistered. In China, illegal guns outnumber legal guns by nearly a factor of 60 (Karp 2007, 47–55).

International regulations reflect a state-centric image of high-volume brokerage. Yet, rather than a few merchants of death, most guns are trafficked through the ant trade—decentralized networks fueled by modern telecom and shipping technologies. Instead of truckloads and planeloads of guns shipped under fraudulent paperwork, micro-trafficking predominates (Bajekal and Walt 2015). Indeed, a 2016 *Small Arms Survey* review of 159 international trafficking cases from the United States found "no indication that any of the traffickers . . . applied for arms export licenses or attempted to manipulate the licensing system" (Schroeder 2016, 12). Instead, most traffickers "simply bypassed the licensing system entirely" (1).

Mainstream regulations focus on diversion from commercial supplies, but they are less effective at combating off-the-books production or the ant trade. Some agreements target illicit production. The ITI requires marking and recordkeeping for commercial firearms. The UN Arms Trade Treaty (ATT) requires export controls on components, though the definition of components is vague. President Trump withdrew from the ATT in 2019, claiming redundancy with U.S. law and noncompliance by other signatories. The UN Protocol against the Illicit Manufacturing and Trafficking of Firearms, Components, and Ammunition (Palermo Protocol) criminalizes unlicensed gunmaking and mandates traceable markings.

Yet, illicit trafficking remains vexing as ever. When broken into small transactions, trafficking becomes harder to detect. Industrialization enabled modern tracing systems, but also produced so many guns from so many locations that it became difficult to prevent diversion. Traffickers steal guns, acquire gray market guns that are unregistered or lack traceable serials, or employ buyers with clean records to straw purchase commercial firearms to resell illegally. If most guns in a jurisdiction are registered, "accidental" losses and staged "thefts" become appealing. And of course, traffickers build firearms off-the-books.

With centralized production came centralized tracking based on industrial compliance. Yet, industry became so productive and diverse that even strict jurisdictions struggle to stop all leakage to illicit users. To understand the numeric problem, let's assume that all murders in the United States in 2015 were gun murders, and all were committed with *different* guns. This is the maximum number of guns needed for all criminal homicides in America in 2015: 15,696 (Federal Bureau of Investigation 2015). Now, compare the number of guns manufactured and imported that year, minus exports: 14,152,976 (U.S. Department of Justice BATFE 2017). Only 0.11 percent of new guns were needed for all U.S. homicides. However, the average age of a crime gun is 11 years (U.S. Bureau of Alcohol, Tobacco, Firearms and Explosives 2015). Many crime guns come from preexisting stock. In America, that stock is conservatively 357 million. So, around 0.004 percent of America's guns were needed to commit all homicides. America's gun supply is massive, mostly unregistered, and growing by millions annually. To influence social outcomes by tracking this supply is a challenge, to say the least. America is a global outlier on guns, but scale is a problem elsewhere too. Industrialization produced so many guns that only a small proportion need be skimmed from legal supplies to fuel most gun crime. Centuries of industrialization gave us this haystack of needles.

Guns 3.0: Postindustrialization

> Progress means the development of improvements and the machine is the instrument of progress.
>
> —Henry Burghardt (1919, 2)

> I'm absolutely positive that there's my evil twin on the other side of the law somewhere who's turning out machine guns out of an underground shop. And he's probably making more money than I am!–
>
> —Mike Crumling, custom gunsmith and prominent DIYer (Interview 2019)

A combination of technologies promises a new age of decentralized production. Electrification, miniaturization, and digitization have vastly expanded the manufacturing ecosystem. Subtractive processes dominated for millennia: these involve removing material from the workpiece to form the product. Craftspeople use analog tools like lathes, soldering irons, cutting torches, welding equipment, mills, planers, and drill presses. These are widely employed in creative and productive trades. Digital subtractive tools like computer numeric control (CNC) mills save the machinist time and effort, but similar work is often achievable through skilled artisanry. One machinist and software developer (2015) explained, "Digital tools are great for certain precision environments, but a truly skilled machinist can still drill 1,000 identical holes by hand." Improved workshop tools have not garnered media attention like their whizbang counterpart 3D printing. In reality, analog tools were improving skilled crafts long before digital fabrication. Hand tools like calipers, wrenches, mallets, files, and screwdrivers are omnipresent in gunsmithing. Power tools like handheld drills, soldering irons, routers, rotary tools, and welding torches are also useful. All are affordable and practically impossible to restrict.

Mainstays like lathes and drill presses have become considerably cheaper. A benchtop press will serve for smaller-scale tasks like finishing a blank. Low-end versions are $100–$500. Many gunsmiths use multifunction lathes. These can be found for a few hundred to a few thousand dollars. Digital tools offer "complexity for free" (Johnston, Smith, and Irwin 2018, 5), reducing the need for artisanal labor or industrial scaling. However, digital fabrication requires machining, IT, and digital design skills instead. Modern industries employ semifinished cast metals. These are routinely purchased by legitimate manufacturers, gunmakers, smiths, artists, and machinists. Metal stock is cut with plasma cutters or a mill. DIYers can extract gun steel from scrap; 0.84 percent–1.00 percent carbon steels are ideal. Many tool steels are suitable, and can be reforged from drill bits, knives, saw blades, wrenches, garden tools, and crowbars (Benson 2000, 50–56). Aluminum is softer and lighter, but useful for some components.

The open source revolution doesn't just make better retail tools available. It also enables DIY toolmaking. Open source engineers develop machine tools that users build themselves. MultiMachines are homemade machining tools capable of commercial precision. Built from discarded engine blocks and other cheap components, they perform tasks like automotive, aviation, and agricultural equipment repair and are used to make water pumps, drilling rigs, and irrigation systems as well as in toolmaking, fabrication, and education. Open source hardware and software architectures like *Arduino* enable DIY design and construction of electronics. Open source architectures are improved by international developer communities. In fact, open source hardware is envisioned as a driver of global innovation and sustainable development. Homebuilt CNC routers, mills, laser cutters, plasma tables, 3D printers, and other digital tools are available as open designs or commercially supplied kits.

The trend is toward democratizing industrial capability. Projects like Open Source Ecology's Global Village Construction Set (GVCS) are most ambitious. The GVCS involves homemade versions of 50 industrial machines needed to recreate modernity from scratch. Researchers have designed 12 machines from their list. The quality and accessibility of tools makes the DIY environment better than ever. Meanwhile, the open hardware movement unleashes global ingenuity by making industrialization a DIY project. The *industrial devolution* is changing our concepts of what can be accomplished outside the factory environment. Compared to rebuilding civilization from discarded engine blocks, making a gun isn't so hard.

Additive Manufacturing and DIY Firearms

The maker movement gives you the power, and I suppose the cockiness to say "I can make whatever I want!"
—Michael Heidrick, Maker and Software Tools Analyst
(Interview 2015)

It's supposed to be automatic but actually you have to press this button.
—John Brunner (1968, 12)

Additive manufacturing is less intuitive. Photopolymerization uses light to solidify liquids. Molten polymer deposition extrudes layers of molten materials to build objects. Granular materials binding fuses particles with lasers. Consumer-grade printers typically involve ABS or PLA plastics. These plastics are ill suited to the pressures generated by firearm cartridges. Consequently, most guns made with consumer-grade printers are low-performance. However, some plastic receivers (like Defense Distributed's printable AR-15) can fire several hundred rounds before failure.

Materials remain a barrier for printable guns. Clever gunhackers have focused on low-pressure designs, or "hybrid" designs combining plastics with metal components. Granular materials binding processes like direct laser metal sintering enable precision metal printing. Texas-based company Solid Concepts pioneered this process in gunmaking, printing an excellent replica of the Colt 1911 and another semiautomatic pistol. The 1911 is proven to 4000+ rounds. Because 3D printers fabricate in high-resolution layers, some commercial gunmakers print internally intricate items like sound suppressors. However, industrial metal printers are large, require advanced skill, require commercial-grade electrical hookups, and are prohibitively expensive for most DIYers and small businesses. For now, these barriers undermine metal printing for DIY gunmaking.

However, the industry is moving toward mass-marketable metal printing. Michigan Tech researchers released designs for a printer that fabricates in steel. It can be built for less than $2,000. Several companies have announced plans for low-cost metal printers. Thus far, most attempts have been delayed. As of this writing, inexpensive metal printers may prove useful for firearm experimentation. However, constructing them requires technical skill, and they must be operated carefully due to fire hazard. Their product is more porous than billet steel, and not ideal for firearms. A major threshold will be crossed when affordable printers can create metal parts with similar quality as CNC or traditional machining, but widespread accessibility may take decades.

Digital toolmakers have expanded to fiberglass, Kevlar, silicone, and carbon fiber. Carbon fiber is increasingly used by commercial gunmakers. Polyether ether ketone can be combined with metal undercoatings to strengthen plastic parts. Though digital gunhackers have developed clever work-arounds to their material limitations, most printable guns remain mediocre. In contrast, traditional machining and digital CNC can produce commercial quality firearms. Most people could improvise a crude gun if desperate. However, making an industry-quality gun from scratch still requires considerable skill regardless of method. In interviews with several gunsmiths, industrial designers, and makers, respondents universally agreed that digital tools are decreasing the labor requirements for standardized results, while becoming increasingly affordable and user friendly. Nevertheless, all respondents *also* agreed that significant skill is required to design and build a *good* firearm.

Even with code in hand, calibrating the machine and processing, finishing, assembling, and testing the components can be challenging tasks for a novice. Industrial design Professor John Wanberg (Interview 2016) argued that good design remains paramount regardless of method:

> International craft manufacturers have very specialized skills. It would take me a lot of time and brainpower to design and make a gun from scratch. . . . If you have manuals that document stuff that's already been done, that's considerably easier than working from scratch. Manuals would be a considerable benefit to a DIY gunmaker.

The balance of skills increasingly encompasses digital design, 3D printing, and CNC machining in addition to traditional analog machining and craft. Makers who are proficient in all of these areas can produce virtually any firearm, while intermediate proficiency in some of these skills can also enable quality design and gunmaking, though not full mastery of all possible designs and build processes. Most efforts to combat digital firearms have involved deplatforming of digital fabrication files. Meanwhile, *digital capture* generates designs based on imagery or dimensional data (Lipson and Kurman 2013). Indeed, one of Defense Distributed's wider objectives is to harness scanning equipment and skilled coders to develop fabrication files for many public domain firearms. Even without digital capture, a dizzying selection of gun schematics, patents, photos, and dimensional drawings are available. Some of these sources are not precise enough to directly translate to fabrication code, but a skilled designer can emulate them.

Digital tools are a major development for gunmaking and smithing. Midwestern gunsmith Tim Staber (2016) told me, "Digital tools will be huge, and we've only just scratched the surface. There will be a lot more use of digital tools in the future." Conversely, some makers believe digital tools are overhyped. One maker claimed that digital tools "aren't important at all for a real skilled gunsmith" (Machinist and software developer 2015). Both responses have elements of truth: some master gunmakers market traditional artisanry. Meanwhile, commercial makers widely incorporate digital fabrication to prototype, customize, and repair. Except for simple designs in cheap plastics, or straightforward milling of partially finished components, we are still a long way from push-button gunmaking. However, digitization provides expanding capabilities. The downscaling of digital fabrication is of particular interest to gunsmiths. A gunsmith may primarily work with traditional tools, but can build certain components with CNC, or 3D-print custom jigs and gauges. Crossovers between traditional subtractive, digital subtractive, and digital additive methods will eventually blur the distinctions between conventional, digital, and 3D-printed guns.

Just as industrial gunmakers were among the early adopters of factory methods, postindustrial gunmakers have been early adopters of digital fabrication. The neoartisanal moment is arriving, but true democratization requires several tipping points to be reached: digital fabrication must become so user friendly that a novice can produce complex objects on demand. Consumer-grade printers must offer better materials. Digital gun designs must be accessible, or the software and fabrication tools must be highly approachable. None of these developments is immediately forthcoming, and some governments have already imposed regulations meant to chill the diffusion of digital gun designs. Nevertheless, if technologic trends are any indicator, prospects for DIY gunmaking will improve.

The more approachable the manufacture of an object becomes, the harder it becomes to control its supply. When feudal Japan controlled artisanal guns, it relied on force monopoly, authoritarian methods, controls on slow-moving information flows, regulations on skilled labor, and international trade barriers. That's a tall order for liberal governance in an exponentially more complex and interconnected world. It's also regularly flouted by DIYers around the globe. These makers operate legally and illegally. They leverage the internet where it's open and where it's closed. They're difficult to combat even in countries with strict controls. The neoartisanal moment is arriving. What does it look like?

CHAPTER THREE

The Global Gun: How DIY Small Arms Are Manufactured and Used around the World

The future is already here—it's just not very evenly distributed.
—William Gibson, "The Science in Science Fiction"
(National Public Radio 2018)

The global gun is a Bulgarian Cold War AK-47. It's an 80% AR-15. It's a knockoff Colt 1911 disassembled and shipped in several parcels and a nicely faked Makarov with false markings. It's a 3D-printed derringer, a submachine gun (SMG) improvised from a .PDF file, a starter pistol converted to fire live cartridges, and a single-shot rimfire embedded in a Maglite. The global gun is purchased, stolen, smuggled, left over from conflicts and never registered. Increasingly, the global gun is *made* by those who want it. What kinds of guns are people making in our postindustrial world?

The Local Is Global: Overview of DIY Production

In some respects, a devolution in modern gunmaking may only reflect a postindustrial reboot of the artisanal model. Before factory methods, all firearms were artisanal. Industrialization led to consolidation as artisanry subsumed into centralized factory environments and economies of scale. This pushed artisanal gumaking to the margins, but never eliminated it. Artisanal gunmaking is resilient: it benefits from technology, but skilled makers can operate with simple tools in austere environments. As postindustrialization evolves, industrial production continues while an increasingly sophisticated neoartisanal model evolves alongside it.

For decades, DIY gun research focused on *craft* guns: an umbrella term for homemade guns usually associated with developing nations. Craft firearms have often (and accurately) been described as crude. Writing for *Small Arms Survey*, Peter Batchelor (2003) described craft production meeting the demands of "geographically isolated, economically impoverished, or legally prohibited buyers" (10). Craft weapons were long associated with disadvantage, violence, and insecurity. However, the demarcation between crude craft guns and higher-quality expedient, knockoff, and counterfeit guns is lessening as improved tools and techniques circulate.

Historically, much independent gunmaking has been legitimate. For centuries, master artisans have crafted remarkably fine firearms for discerning clients. These guns are exceptionally rare in crime. Quality *counterfeit* guns superficially resemble commercial models, though examination quickly reveals internal differences. Some counterfeits include false markings to increase marketability or confound investigators. In wealthier countries, rogue machinists and criminal rings produce small batches of counterfeit guns. In the developing world, mountains of counterfeit guns have been produced by illegal factories operating in enclaves of corruption and state weakness. *Knockoffs* emulate commercial products, but usually display poorer craftsmanship and inferior materials. Nevertheless, many knockoffs function well if the maker is reasonably skilled. They're an inexpensive substitute in many markets.

Unlicensed gunmaking is illegal in most countries (with around a dozen countries that don't prohibit or tacitly allow it at scale). It's fair to assume that illegally made guns are more likely to be illegally used. Around the world, homemade guns are desired for many of the reasons people seek conventional guns. Some applications are clearly illegal or unethical, while others are technically illegal, but understandable. How are illicitly made guns being used around the world?

Street Crime

In some developing and middle-income countries, homemade guns are commonly associated with street crime. In Burundi, Cameroon, Ghana, India, and South Africa, homemade crime guns are common. In Colombia, craft makers sell to "petty criminals residing in urban centers" (Aguirre et al. 2006, 8–9). In Malawi, homemade guns are reportedly used in 55 percent of homicides (Mwakasungula and Nungu 2004, 88). In Nicaragua, DIY guns are the "principal gang firearm" (Rodgers and Rocha 2013, 48). Senegal has a thriving trade in "excellent counterfeit" guns, and 80 percent of gun crime in Dakar involves homemade weapons (Howard 2005). In China, more than half the guns recovered in some large seizures were illicitly made, and homemade firearms are periodically implicated in crime (Guo 2006).

In the United Kingdom, DIY guns have been used in street crime, the murder of a police officer, and the 2016 assassination of a member of parliament. DIY products may have constituted up to 80 percent of crime guns seized by UK police between 2011 and 2012 (Hays and Jenzen-Jones 2018, 47). In Indonesia, one source states that "98% of robberies" are with homemade guns (Jakarta Post 2013). In Papua New Guinea, Tanzania, and Thailand, street criminals are known to use DIY guns. In one high-profile Thai case, a robber killed a British tourist with a homemade gun. Homemade guns are encountered among criminals and poachers in Malaysia and Brunei as well. Street gangs carry homemade guns in Guatemala, though homemade products appear to be on the decline as offenders acquire more commercial guns. In California, gang-connected traffickers have adopted 80% gunmaking. Even in Canada, some DIY guns have been discovered among street gangs and drug dealers.

Adoption of homemade weapons by street-level traffickers and criminals seems to reflect common themes. When illicit consumers face high costs for commercial firearms due to poverty or scarcity, or if traffickers face elevated risks of tracing or police intervention, homemade substitutes become increasingly appealing.

Militia Activity

Homemade weapons are frequently associated with militias. Militias produce weapons in independent factories or purchase from cottage industries. Craft production is longstanding in small wars and insurgencies. DIY weapons have been implicated in tribal, ethno-nationalist, insurgent, and narco-militia activities. However, some militia activities may be considered defensive.

Burundian militias have long used homemade "mugabore" long guns. In the Central African Republic, Christian and Muslim militias have battled with homemade weapons. In 2006, Colombia's FARC "ratcheted up production of submachine guns," as well as light weapons like "mortars, mortar grenades, and hand grenades" (Aguirre et al. 2006, 8–9). In Pakistan, the strong local gunmaking industry supplies various buyers, including the Taliban. The bustling cottage industry in the city of Danao, Philippines, began in the early 1900s, but was kick-started into the modern era by guerilla war against Japanese occupying forces. In the Solomon Islands Conflict of the 1990s–2000s, militias used DIY firearms, though many of these weapons were eventually surrendered (Alpers, Muggah, and Twyford 2004). In Kenya, the Mungiki militia reportedly used DIY guns in massacres. Burmese militias have also relied on DIY: the Mong Thai army produced light weapons until it capitulated in 1996, and the Karen National Liberation Army made their own light weapons. More recently, homemade rifles have been seized from "renegade" groups in Kokang, and militias have reportedly used craft guns against the Rohingya minority. DIY guns are fixtures in Papuan tribal clashes, and South Africa's Inkatha Freedom Party used homemade shotguns and pipe bombs from the 1980s up to 2000. Some of these might have been provided by the South African police covert unit (Gould et al. 2004).

Given the circumstances and motivation of asymmetric combatants, it isn't surprising that armed groups produce weapons in-house. Combatants prefer industry-made weapons, but may lack resources to acquire them in bulk, or their trafficking networks may be interrupted. Under these conditions, armed groups have readily adopted DIY manufacture.

Self-Defense

Self-defense with homemade weapons frequently coincides with corruption and lack of state-provided security. Communities and self-defense groups from Southeast Asia to sub-Saharan Africa have made guns for subsistence hunting or protection against hostile militias. In some cases, cottage gunmakers supply arms to police and security personnel. Some sources cite the difficulty or cost of legal access as a driver of civilian demand for homemade defensive arms.

In Burundi, most guns are homemade. Suffering from poverty and crime, many Burundians acknowledge the negative impacts of unregulated guns, but also express support for defensive firearms (Avendano 2011). In the Central African Republic, self-defense groups have wielded DIY guns for protection from warring militias. In India, many homemade guns are bought for self-defense. Similarly in Malawi, homemade guns are frequently purchased for protection (Mwakasungula and Nungu 2004). Nepali civilians seek homemade firearms due to the "expense and difficulty" of acquiring licensed guns (Karp 2013, 2–3). Pakistani and Filipino craft producers commonly supply civilians, and sometimes they even supply police. In China, a civilian gun culture grows in spite of restrictions, and civilians buy homemade guns for defense. In Mexico, laws are restrictive and permits can be cost-prohibitive. Civilians buy both commercial and homemade guns, and regulations are openly flouted.

In Indonesia, police sometimes purchase artisanal guns in order to illegally resell state-issued sidearms (International Crisis Group 2010). In the

Democratic Republic of Congo, civilians used homemade shotguns for defense against the Lord's Resistance Army. In Papua New Guinea, homemade guns are common defensive arms, outnumbering commercial guns in the southern highlands (Alpers 2005, 117–18). In the Solomon Islands, partial disarmament has been achieved. However, the militias' homemade guns were also used for controlling crocodiles, which have killed more civilians since disarmament (ABC Radio Australia 2008). In Guatemala, 10 percent of weapons encountered by police between 2001 and 2005 were artisanal ("Illegal Firearm Manufacturing and Trafficking" 2006). However, artisanal weapons appear to have declined as commercial arms popularize (United Nations Office on Drugs and Crime 2012). Some Mauritanian citizens acquire homemade guns for self-defense. There are many more examples; when perceptions of insecurity become urgent, otherwise law-abiding citizens are incentivized to make or buy defensive weapons irrespective of law.

Illegal Export

Illicit gunmakers traffic internationally. Traffickers smuggle homemade weapons and tools between India and Bangladesh, and most civilian guns in Nepal are illegally made in India (Paudel 2014, 1–2; Karp 2013, 2–3). In the United States, Mexican drug traffickers have been caught smuggling components, producing "80%" guns, and building components. Cottage gunmaking is longstanding in Pakistan, the Philippines, Indonesia, India, Ecuador, Colombia, Ghana and other parts of West Africa, South America, and Southeast Asia. These industries export to surrounding countries. Receiver blanks, full DIY builds, and CNC tools have been trafficked from the United States to Mexico. DIY guns and components have been exported from the United States and Mexico to Central America and Colombia. Filipino makers have trafficked high-quality craft weapons to Indonesia, Japan, Taiwan, Mexico, Australia, and the Americas.

Some European nations have been a source of deactivated guns that can be reactivated. Italy does not appear to have a strong homemade weapons base, though shortened shotguns called "Lupare" have traditionally been associated with organized crime. Italy once exported enough convertible starter pistols to the United Kingdom and that these conversions constituted between 18 and 40 percent of firearms seized by London's Metropolitan Police some years (Harrison 2009). Smuggling of components, tools, or convertible items is a nontrivial share of global gun trafficking. Like other gun trafficking activity, most DIY trafficking probably goes undetected.

Organized Crime

Organized crime produces weapons in many parts of the world. Their products are sometimes sophisticated, owing to the motivation, resources, and expertise available. Extended capacities, suppressors, modifications, machine guns, counterfeits, and knockoffs have all been produced by organized crime. In Australia, many zip guns and SMGs at varying levels of quality have been seized from drug traffickers and outlaw motorcycle clubs. In Colombia, gangs and narco-traffickers have used homemade guns and light weapons. Filipino traffickers export homemade weapons and skills to foreign crime syndicates (Lal 2007). In the United Kingdom, criminal rings hire illegal armorers. In Mexico, narco-traffickers receive homemade firearms and components from the United States, but also make them locally. In one notable case, cartel associates in Jalisco made hundreds of AR-15s with CNC tools. Illegal gunsmiths in Mexico make knockoffs and build suppressors for contract killers. In Guatemala, organized crime acquires commercial guns, but local gangs use homemade variants. In Kenya, blacksmiths supply guns to drug traffickers. Burmese drug smugglers have been caught with homemade guns. In Canada, traffickers have built expedient and CNC firearms. Japanese Yakuza import DIY guns from the Philippines or import Filipino gunmakers to share skills, and more recently have reportedly built digital guns.

Hunting/Poaching

Hunters and poachers in many countries have long utilized homemade and craft-built firearms. In Central Africa, poachers use craft shotguns and suppressors. Poachers with craft weapons are typically local, and less likely to be financed by international rings (Carlson, Wright, and Donges 2015). Some countries have longstanding histories of local gunmaking for legitimate hunting. Communities where hunters and poachers use homemade weapons tend to be poorer and rural, or in jurisdictions where access to commercial firearms is limited for legal or economic reasons. One exception is China, where privately owned firearms are generally illegal, yet hunting and poaching have popularized as pastimes for the wealthy. Generally, craft hunting arms are described as unsophisticated.

In the Central African Republic, homemade hunting rifles are a longstanding product. In Malawi, DIY rifles are used for poaching and protecting crops from pest animals (Mwakasungula and Nungu 2004, 88). Hunting rifles are produced in Indonesia (Batchelor 2001, 46). In Kenya, poachers use homemade suppressors to avoid game wardens (Carlson,

Wright, and Donges 2015). In Cambodia, Laos, Thailand, and Malaysia, homemade hunting rifles are a longstanding tradition. Papuan hunters commonly use DIY guns. In Tanzania, police have arrested foreign poachers with locally made rifles and gunmaking tools, and in Zambia, where hunting guns are routinely produced, poachers have been arrested with DIY firearms (Mtonga and Mthembu-Salter 2004).

Hobbyists/Collectors

Collectors have illegally produced and modified firearms in many countries—typically involving restricted types (which are defined differently across jurisdictions). In America, much innovation has been legal, while elsewhere it may be strictly forbidden. American hobbyists frequently build, modify, and customize firearms legally, but a minority of hobbyists do produce illegal builds. Collectors (and sometimes farmers and ranchers) from Malaysia, Russia, the United Kingdom, Japan, Canada, Australia, and many other countries have been caught with illegally made or modified guns. These demographics are less prone to involvement in other types of crime, so incidences are likely to be underreported.

Assassinations and Political Violence

Homemade weapons have been implicated in a few assassination attempts. Despite concerns about plastic weapons defeating security screening, no cases thus far appear to involve less-detectable weapons in unconventional materials. In 2004, a political assassination was attempted in Taiwan, and in 2013 an assassination was carried out in the Central African Republic. A British member of parliament was assassinated in 2016 by a right-wing extremist with a homemade handgun.

In a few countries, homemade guns are associated with election violence or shows-of-force. In India and the Philippines, partisans purchase craft guns before elections. Homemade firearms were associated with protests and election violence in post–Arab Spring Egypt. Reactivated guns were reportedly used in the November 2015 Paris Attacks. The 2019 Halle synagogue attacker (Germany) used an expedient SMG. The 2015 San Bernardino attackers used illegally purchased and modified commercial guns. In 1990s Japan, the Aum Shinrikyo doomsday cult (which carried out a deadly sarin gas attack on the Tokyo subway) tried (but failed) to make AK-47s. They might have been more successful if their operation had been *less* ambitious: Aum tried to establish robotic assembly lines rather than employing simpler methods.

Table 3.1 DIY Production Models

	Artisanal/Craft		
Tools and Methods	**Typical Environment**	**Associated With**	**Example Products**
Hand tools	Locales that	Street crime/gangs	Single-shot handguns/long guns
Power tools	• Are less developed	Self-defense	Smoothbores
Skilled labor	• Have lower technology access	Hunting and poaching	Black powder/improvised munitions
Improvised/scrap materials		Local commerce	Zip guns/Pipe guns
Uses commercial components when available	• Have corruption	Disadvantaged combatants	Crude revolvers, multibarrel, and converted firearms
	• Have poverty		Expedient submachine guns and pistols, break-action or revolving shotguns
	• Have insecurity		Improvised suppressors (poaching)
			Passable knockoffs and counterfeits (skilled craft)
			High-quality artisanal guns produced for legal collectors

	Transitional/Semi-industrial		
Tools and Methods	**Typical Environment**	**Associated With**	**Example Products**
Electrified shop tools/machine tools	Locales that	Street crime	Expedient submachine guns and machine pistols
Hand tools	• Are less developed and middle income	Self-defense	Knockoffs/counterfeits emulating commercial products
Skilled and semiskilled labor	• Have corruption	Political violence	False markings/serial numbers
		Local commerce and transnational trafficking	

Tools and Methods	Typical Environment	Associated With	Example Products
Homemade and commercial precursors Emulation of commercial products Adopt popular DIY designs Empowered by digital media May pose as legitimate industry in weakly governed locales	• Have insecurity • Have police cooperation/non-enforcement	Component trade Higher-output cottage industries Equipping of combatants Combatant in-house production	DIY rifling DIY accessories, suppressors, standard/high-capacity magazines

Neoartisanal

Tools and Methods	Typical Environment	Associated With	Example Products
Hand tools/power tools Electrified shop tools/machine tools Greater access and use of commercial components Digital design processes (AutoCAD, etc.) Digital fabrication (CNC/3D-Printing) Empowered by digital media Innovative designs, tools, and materials	Developed nations Restrictive enclaves Smuggling to restrictive enclaves	Hobbyists/collectors Political provocateurs Registry civil resisters Organized crime Gun trafficking Component trade Sophisticated combatants Isolated terrorists, extremists, and active shooters	Frame/receiver builds CNC firearms Hybrid designs (plastic-metal/commercial-homemade) 3D-printed plastic single-shot pistols and repeating revolvers Standard/high-capacity magazines DIY rifling Wide range of DIY modifications, defacement techniques, and accessorizations of commercial firearms

It's no shock that weapons are produced in locales suffering violence, poverty, insecurity, corruption, and poor policing. Yet, DIY guns also challenge weapons control in wealthy, well-policed, and strictly regulated jurisdictions. Illegal gunmaking manifests differently depending on local policing and culture, economic incentives, tool access, types and intensities of demand, levels of corruption, and probably many other variables. However, the underlying motives are usually straightforward: inaccessibility of commercial firearms due to scarcity, poverty, or state countertrafficking efforts.

Three production models (see table 3.1) can be loosely described. *Artisanal* methods predominate in the developing world. Generally, these producers are locally oriented, use simple tools and materials, and produce firearms along a spectrum of quality from comically crude to exceptionally well crafted. A *transitional*, or *semi-industrial*, model predominates in some middle and higher-income states, and is associated with semicovert cottage industries. Some of these players manufacture considerable volumes of counterfeit and knockoff guns, traffic transnationally, and exploit police corruption. The neoartisanal model is primarily adopted by hobbyists, innovators, and small trafficking rings in wealthier locales. This model incorporates increasingly advanced digital fabrication methods alongside traditional techniques and is responsible for considerable innovation and political controversy.

Guerrilla Gunsmithing: Expedient DIY Firearms

The guerilla gunsmithing subculture is geared toward expedient firearms built from accessible materials like tubing, pipes, and sheet metal, with minimal laminating, machining, or welding required. Crude zip guns are built from simple precursors like center punches, pipes, or staple guns. Some variants use rubber bands or springs to move a firing pin (which is often just a nail). *Slam-fire* variants are even simpler, requiring no trigger mechanism.

Zip guns are typically single-shot, unreliable, and frequently unsafe. They pose security challenges when crafted well enough to qualify as a *crypto-gun*, such as a pen gun, flashlight gun, keychain gun, or cellphone gun. Crypto-guns are detectable, but may superficially pass for innocuous items. Pen guns may cost less than $5 to build and require little skill. Some expedient guns were developed for guerillas and intelligence agencies. Perhaps the most famous designer was the ingenious CIA-connected boutique gunmaker Paris Theodore, who developed innovative concealable firearms, accessories, and tactics that inspire mainstream gunmakers today. More recently, commercial maker Ideal Conceal announced plans for a multishot Derringer that looks like a smartphone.

An interesting subset of gunsmithing literature emerged in the 1960s and 1970s. Its authors consider gunmaking a *natural right* and necessary check on state repression. Guerilla gunsmithing manuals are generally of an inoffensive anarcho-libertarian character—most don't advocate violence, but some are explicitly antistate. Expedient gunsmithing authors feel a moral obligation to spread gunmaking methods, emphasizing firearm access under repressive regimes. For example, Ragnar Benson's (2000) *Guerilla Gunsmithing* wryly includes revolutionary messaging with otherwise conventional gunsmithing tips:

> There's no question that elemental sulfur and some low-melting-point bismuth compounds . . . give accurate, machinist-grade readings. But you as a guerilla gunsmith ain't going to have these materials to work with. What you will have is paraffin, which is good enough for government work . . . or at least good enough to put together guns and ammunition with which to work on the government. (72)

Other titles include Gerard Metral's "Do-It-Yourself Submachine Gun" captioned "It's Homemade, 9mm, Lightweight, Durable—and It'll Never Be on Any Import Ban Lists!" Philip Luty's "Expedient Homemade Firearms," Bill Holmes's "Home Workshop Guns for Defense and Resistance," or Professor Parabellum's expedient series. Most of these expedient designs require moderate skill and basic workshop tools. Some designs emulate low-tech military firearms. For example, some emulate the World War II–era Sten Gun, a minimalist SMG meant to be cheaply manufactured for infantry and antifascist guerillas. DIY versions are made from sheet metal and pipes and require minimal machining and a few hours of semiskilled labor. The Sten was ugly and not very reliable but cost only $10 per unit ($150 today). Antifascist guerillas built the Sten in bike shops and auto garages. Later, it was produced at kibbutzim to equip Jewish paramilitaries, and widely copied by insurgents and cash-strapped militaries.

Numerous expedient designs were commissioned by governments to be easily reproduced. DIY Sten .PDFs circulate online. The Carlo SMG has become popular in the West Bank. This design emulates the Swedish Carl Gustav M45. DIY versions are made in auto shops and home workshops and purchased illegally for 10–20 percent the price of a smuggled M16.

One of the more famous expedient designers was UK citizen and British gun rights advocate Philip Luty, who optimized his designs so that:

> All items used in construction were standard hardware products which would not arouse suspicions when purchased or left lying around . . . [and] it would fire a commercially available cartridge and could be clandestinely manufactured without the need for expensive machine tools. . . . More importantly, at least as far as I was concerned, it succeeded in giving the British anti-gun lobby something to think about, which was the whole motivation of the project in the first place. (Gardner 2011)

Luty faced weapons charges for actually producing his designs rather than leaving the matter as purely academic. Now deceased, his approachable designs live on. Dozens of online tutorials depict Luty production, and police have encountered Luty derivatives in Australia, Brazil (where homemade SMGs are notoriously popular), Canada, Russia, Indonesia, and elsewhere. When produced by traffickers, expedient designs often include capabilities that are unavailable in legal commerce. Police around the world have seized expedient guns with illegal magazine capacities, integral or peripheral suppressors, and full-auto capabilities.

While 3D-printed guns receive more media attention, the Open Source Revolution had equally significant impacts on expedient gunmaking. This style of production is far from new, but the affordability of tools and materials, clandestine nature of production, decent capabilities of some designs, and ease of accessing guerilla gunsmithing information have all combined to quietly reboot the guerilla gunsmithing subculture.

Receiver and Component Builds

Most firearms are built around the *frame* or *receiver*. In some jurisdictions, only the frame is regulated. Secondary components like barrels, slides, stocks, and unfinished frame blanks, may be loosely regulated or unregulated. In many countries only the frame is serialized and entered into tracing records. Secondary components may be unserialized or serialized but untracked. Many countries require permits for some secondary components. However, it's difficult to control the full range of commercial components, and impossible to control all nongun parts that can be used for gunmaking.

Modular builds are assembled from all-commercial components. Depending on regulations and the maker's interest in compliance, modularity enables firearms to be configured in different calibers, dimensions, and forensic profiles. Modularity is rarely exploited by criminals, but can be leveraged to change a gun's forensics, disassemble components for smuggling, or customize guns for perceived lethality. Criminal applications notwithstanding, modularity is embraced more frequently by legal shooters who convert practice firearms to lower-cost calibers, or customize guns for sporting. Some hobbyists simply enjoy mastering platforms like the AR-15 in its many possible configurations.

Frame, receiver, or *80% builds* combine partially finished frame blanks with commercial secondary components. DIYers complete the frames and assemble with commercial secondary parts. American aficionados have long enjoyed constructing firearms from kits. Frame builds are satisfying yet approachable with modest skill. Finishing work can be completed with digital fabricators or analog routers, mills, drill presses, or hand tools. Retailers provide jigs and tutorials while enthusiasts trade tips online. Though they've long been legal in America, build kits have become popular since the sunset of the federal assault weapons ban in September 2004. Since then, the AR-15 became America's most popular rifle. Its modular design is well suited to DIY finishing and customization. AR lower receivers are designed to bear relatively low pressures, and can be fabricated in steel, aluminum, or reinforced plastics. Glock handgun builds have also popularized, as Glocks were among the first handguns designed around easily worked polymer frames. Yet, a provocative subtext underlies this enjoyable hobby: in America, most 80% builds are unserialized, can't be traced, aren't recorded in registries, and can't be identified for confiscation. Some enthusiasts derive as much satisfaction from undermining hypothetical restrictions as they derive from the project itself.

Not all frame builds are to skirt regulation. Hobbyists and sportspeople enjoy the challenge and variety of customizations available through frame, hybrid, and full-DIY builds. Price and engineering are also factors: build kits are less expensive than retail equivalents. Receiver builds are among the most accessible DIY projects. As compared to their overall popularity, only a small proportion of frame builds have been associated with crime. However, crimes involving 80% builds do occur, and they've been criticized as a growing source of ghost guns for traffickers, gangs, and active shooters. DIY gunmaking celebrity Cody Wilson responded to media hype by marketing a user-friendly CNC machine called the Ghost Gunner (and its successors the Ghost Gunners II and III). These desktop CNC machines are optimized to complete AR, Glock, 1911, and other blanks. They come preloaded with software and can also engrave. The Ghost Gunner I sold out quickly on release.

All 80% builds are notable for their popularity among legal consumers, the quality that can be achieved, their subtext of uncontrollability, and their increasing use by traffickers and criminals. The last decade has seen 80% builds popularize in the United States, where most 80% gunmaking is undertaken by hobbyists. Nevertheless, 80% builds have quickly gained prominence in gun control debate, as trafficking and shooting cases inevitably rise with their wider popularization.

Digital Fabrication: CNC, 3D-Printable, and Hybrid Guns

Many people who've gazed upon Defense Distributed's 3D-printed plastic Liberator .380 handgun, have asked themselves how this crude object could kickstart a crisis for liberal governance of cyberspace. Does this clunky plastic gun *really* portend a dark future of disruptive technology and technocratic clampdown? This . . . *shitty plastic popgun*?

Nobody should be faulted for such thoughts. The Liberator is unformidable. Like its World War II namesake, it was only a platform for broader tactics. The original Liberator was a single-shot handgun meant to be used by resistance fighters to assassinate Nazis and steal *their* weapons. The digital reboot was similarly incrementalist. Any commercial firearm handily outperforms the Liberator. Yet, by carving a legal niche for printable guns, Defense Distributed became a dominant early adopter of open source digital gunmaking. It also emerged as an important player in the effort to establish digital firearms data as a protected form of speech under the First Amendment.

Depending on equipment, the plastic Liberator can require more than a dozen hours to print, and additional time to chemically treat the parts, finish with hand tools, and assemble. The result is a clumsy single-shot plastic handgun that requires the barrel to be unscrewed and the spent cartridge removed with a tool. The frame is proven to 10+ shots with barrel replacements, and disposability may hold some criminal appeal because the plastic can be melted. Assuming metal-cased ammunition can be smuggled with it (and that its maker chooses not to add the legally required metal plate), its plastic design can defeat metal detectors. Overall, the Liberator is highly impractical.

Opinions vary as to whether plastic builds like the Liberator pose authentic security concerns. One machinist and information security specialist argued, "The scary part is that it does increase access, and people can sell them, so if 3D-printing becomes 'magic' and anybody can spend less than $1,000 and download and print a gun, that's why the public is concerned" (Interview 2015). Others were skeptical of the effort necessary to make a plastic weapon inferior to accessible commercial guns. One DIYer said, "I think the Liberator gave people a wake-up call that somebody could actually do this, but I own weapons and I have the machines to make them, and I've never had the desire to do it. I could sell you a Liberator for $5 and you'd buy it. I own a printer and I would buy it just to avoid the hassle of printing it!" (Machinist and software developer 2015).

The Liberator is undoubtedly the most famous digital firearm. However, Defense Distributed's products also include printable magazines, plastic AR-15 receivers proven to hundreds of rounds, the *Ghost Gunners*, and several open source metal designs in digital fabrication formats. All are superior to the Liberator. The Liberator also doesn't compare to superior products subsequently developed by an international gunhacking subculture. This subculture has developed increasingly sophisticated products made with 3D-printing, digital CNC, traditional workshop techniques, and expedient methods. Several single-shot plastic designs have circulated since the Liberator. None are much more capable, but most are better engineered. Several styles of plastic revolvers and derringers have been proven. Most are chambered in .22 rimfire, a low-power round. Many plastic designs include metal barrel or chamber inserts to handle repeat fire. These designs are increasingly refined, but due to limitations in printable plastics, the products are mostly small-caliber revolvers inferior to conventional versions. Yet, digital gunhackers have always set their sights higher, improving their designs with decreasing reliance on regulated supply chains.

Multimaterial *hybrid guns* are filling this niche. Hybrid guns initially focused on digitally fabricated frames or receivers. Early iterations included digitally fabricated receiver builds of Ruger Charger pistols, AR-15s, and other products that were essentially 80% builds without retail receiver blanks. By fabricating receivers, gunhackers demonstrated that homemade guns can't be stopped through regulation on receiver blanks alone. Gunhackers have displayed impressive innovation in their search for truly untraceable guns. A famous early variant was the Shuty 9mm semiautomatic pistol (named in honor of Philip Luty). The Shuty's frame is printed plastic, with a conventional bolt, fire controls, barrel, and magazines. The improved Shuty MP-1 needs fewer fabrication steps and functions well, though the plastic frame begins melting after rapid fire. The Shuty's designer "Derwood," an American carpenter, posted tutorials about his creations, inspiring further experimentation. Defense Distributed also claimed to design a partly printable machine gun costing $150 in materials. As of this writing, they haven't published it.

For several years, Cody Wilson led Defense Distributed as a provocative global spokesperson for digital firearms. His 2018 arrest on an unrelated sex offense undermined the organization's profile and community support. However, Defense Distributed continued under the management of Paloma Heindorff, who maintained its legal challenges against injunctions that interrupted online publication of their digital gun files and oversaw development of the Ghost Gunner III and other products in Wilson's absence.[1] As of this writing, Wilson himself continues to be involved in the Ghost Gunner's development and the administration of the online firearm file sharing repository DEFCAD, the terms of his plea deal not prohibiting such activity. In that regard, Defense Distributed was stalled in its mission to publish digital firearm code, but the results of its litigation may yet hold major implications for defining the scope of firearms data that U.S. law will permit on the internet.

Even the attempt by 20 state governments to muzzle Defense Distributed has not prevented continued dissemination of files it already published. Nor has it prevented further innovation by a wider subculture of digital gunhackers. Among the most notorious is a decentralized gunhacking collective calling themselves Deterrence Dispensed in a tongue-in-cheek tribute to Defense Distributed. Adroitly migrating between encrypted chat rooms, public forums, and peer-to-peer platforms, "Ivan-TheTroll," "Jeffrod," "JStark," "Incarbonite" and other innovators have developed increasingly practical components that are built without a paper trail. These include printable Glock magazines and frames, a TEC-9 frame that accepts Glock magazines, Vz.61 receivers, suppressor baffles, and other products.

Since rifled barrels are comparatively hard to build from scratch, many DIYers rely on commercial barrels. Dependence on commercial barrels has been an obstacle to full-cycle home production. DIYers are stepping up to the task, providing tutorials on home barrel-making and rifling. Mark Serbu is a commercial producer of .50 caliber rifles and other distinctive firearms. Serbu and other gunmakers have hosted online tutorials on home rifling techniques. Some show the construction of rifling tools, while others show straightforward rifling procedures using rifling buttons: devices pushed through a barrel to cut rifling grooves. Since rifling is a seemingly daunting task, I asked Serbu to put the challenge in context:

> **Tallman:** Generally, is a quality rifled barrel harder to make than a typical frame or receiver?

> **Serbu:** Well, yes and no. I've put out two rifling videos now, and once you have the rifling button and you've got a hole that's the right size, you can beat the rifling button through a hole with a hammer and punch if needed. So, it can be really easy when you have the tools. And now, you can get the rifling button from China delivered for like $20, which is insane.

Tallman: How hard is it to *make* the rifling button and do it on a home press?

Serbu: Not hard. I've actually been meaning to do a video. I'll get to it one of these days. I'll show people how to make a rifling button. It's actually $3 worth of material, a Dremel tool, and a torch.

This method is simple for any semiskilled machinist. However, Deterrence Dispensed has moved home rifling into new territory with *electrochemical machining* (ECM). With ECM, materials are removed from metals by a negatively charged anode in a conductive fluid. This involves boring a metal bar, 3D-printing a mandrel with embedded copper wire, and electro-machining the barrel in a bucket of saltwater. The setup costs less than $100 if the maker has a 3D-printer. This may be the gunhacking community's most innovative move yet, enabling a knowledgeable builder to fabricate quality barrels.

Deterrence Dispensed is integrating its techniques into hybrid designs. The group's FGC-9 (F—k Gun Control 9mm) is a carbine based on the Shuty. It requires a 3D-printer, steel tubing and bar stock, a few other simple items, and AR fire controls that the group plans to make 3D-printable. The semiauto is accurate, accepts conventional and printed Glock magazines, and its upper accommodates optics. Unlike many printable guns, the FGC-9 even *looks* pretty good. Since Cody Wilson's much-trumpeted arrest, mainstream media has largely ignored these developments. Newer generations of digital gunhackers have been less publicly provocative and less focused on litigation. Instead, they are *doing* what Defense Distributed challenged courts for the *right to do*. In that regard, Wilson's vision continues to inspire gunhackers around the world, irrespective of his own legal troubles or the litigation that continues to challenge the organization he founded.

DIY Conversions, Reactivations, and Accessories

DIY methods also apply to other components. 3D-printed fire controls, grips, stocks, and other parts have been installed on commercial rifles. Digital fabrication of obscure components is beneficial for legitimate gunsmiths and restorers. DIY methods also apply to *reactivated* guns. Deactivated firearms are altered to prevent functionality. They're purchased as props, collector pieces, or museum pieces. It's possible to reactivate some deactivated guns, but this requires skilled work, machining tools, and (ideally) replacement components. Depending on jurisdiction, deactivation may require installing a dummy bolt, welding the action, filing or removing firing pins, installing barrel blocks, or other techniques. Deactivations have become more standardized: the European Union (EU) now maintains strict deactivation rules. However, requirements are not harmonized in practice across the EU, where reactivations became an issue after terrorists and drug traffickers embraced reactivated guns.

Strict deactivations may include unsightly welds and no movable parts. Consequently, less-thorough deactivations fetch higher prices and are more common in Eastern Europe, where they can be a source of illicit firearms. The Vz.58 rifles used in the Charlie Hebdo attack and some of the AKM rifles used in the Paris attacks of November 13, 2015, were reportedly reactivated guns from Eastern Europe. Firearms can also be *converted* from nonfirearms. Methods include converting a replica, prop, pneumatic gun, starter pistol, flare gun, or other *alarm gun*. In the United Kingdom, hundreds of converted starter pistols have been seized, and some have been implicated in gangland shootings. Reactivated or converted guns might sound like a far-fetched source of crime guns to American readers, but in countries where illegal guns are comparatively scarce, reactivations and conversions can be a significant illicit source. Depending on jurisdiction, some antiques are exempt from deactivation. In America, antiques are sometimes stolen, but their use in crime is practically nil. Yet, in more weapons-scarce environments like the United Kingdom, criminals have restored antiques for actual use, and even custom-manufactured rare ammunition for them.

Other methods illegally modify conventional guns. Shortened barrels are probably the most common illegal modification. Conversion of semi-automatic firearms to fully automatic can be undertaken but is generally illegal. Some component kits (like the "Glock conversion switch") make it easier to convert certain guns to full-auto. These kits are tightly regulated even in America. However, for many firearm designs, parts allowing for full-auto fire (like drop-in auto-sears) are remarkably simple. Functional auto-sears can be made from items as simple as a small metal bar or wire hanger. Converting a receiver to proper full-auto without a parts kit can be more difficult than some casual "modders" (modification enthusiasts) assume. It's often easier to make an expedient SMG from scratch, though the conversion of some semiauto receivers to full-auto is a trivial task for skilled machinists.

Sound suppressors are subject to a range of regulatory frameworks. U.S. federal law places them under enhanced regulation, with some states permitting and other states prohibiting them. They're prohibited in some countries, regulated in others, and unrestricted (even *required*) in others. However, unlicensed suppressor manufacture is illegal almost everywhere. Nevertheless, suppressors can be made from sheet metals, tubing, or household items like automotive oil filters. A range of actors from organized traffickers to dangerous criminals to harmless (but legally deviant) enthusiasts experiment with homemade suppressors. In some countries, expedient suppressors are frequently seized by police. Online videos and tutorials show DIY fabrication. Suppressors are also addressed by the guerilla gunsmithing canon, including Philip Luty's *Expedient Homemade Silencer* and Bill Holmes's *Home Workshop Silencer* handbooks.

Jurisdictions subject magazines to differing regulatory regimes. This can incentivize illegal fabrication. Magazines can be fabricated with simple tools and materials, but digital fabrication undermines the hope of fully controlling magazine supply. Among the first items embraced by digital gunhackers were 30-round AR magazines. Defense Distributed published code for a 30-round magazine called the "Cuomo," a takeoff on the 2013 NY SAFE Act signed by Governor Andrew Cuomo (which banned 10+ round magazines). Defense Distributed designed other magazines and Deterrence Dispensed has constructed printable Glock magazines among other items. Semiskilled machinists make magazines from sheet metal. Many expedient guns accept easily replicated commercial magazines. For example, the Luty and Holmes SMGs accept Sten magazines (which are themselves easy to make). Counterfeit guns often accept the authentic version's magazines.

As with other DIY methods, the incentives behind illegal conversions, reactivations, and accessorizations seem to reflect some balance of scarcity and illegal incentives. *Small Arms Survey's* Benjamin King (2015) described illegal conversions meeting demand generated by legal restrictions, low access, or high cost, of conventional firearms. Most governments prohibit off-books conversions, reactivations, or manufacture of certain accessories. However, when traffickers see sufficient opportunity, or criminals (and even average citizens in some cases) sense an urgent need, the creative eye will find our material ecosystem well stocked with ingredients that can be converted to functional guns and accessories.

DIY Ammunition

Some commentators argue that ammunition control could have a greater impact on illegal firearms use than gun control itself. In an interview shortly after the 2015 Paris attacks, one faculty respondent from the University of Illinois's Program in Arms Control & Domestic and International Security summarized this perspective:

> If anything would promise the reduction of violence, it wouldn't be controlling the sale of guns, it would be control of ammunition. As much as I

favor and appreciate gun control legislation, it's basically a lost cause. If you can get fully automatic AK-47s in France with their strict gun laws, guns aren't going away. . . . The only way to control use of guns in the United States is to control ammunition. (Interview 2015)

In some respects, ammunition control is plausible. Guns require machining and carpentry, while ammunition requires machining and chemistry, a higher technical bar. Ammunition must also be *replaced*. However, the scale and diversity of commercial ammunition makes for inventory tracking challenges. Globally, over 12 *billion* rounds are sold annually. With the exception of combatants, most gun criminals and even active shooters don't require a great supply. Practiced legitimate users (like police, security professionals, hunters, sport shooters, and well-trained concealed carriers) easily use thousands of rounds per year. Yet, most gun crimes involve only a few shots. Active shootings differ in ammunition consumption, but rarely involve quantities overly suspicious to stockpile. Researchers Philip Cook, Jens Ludwig, Sudhir Venkatesh, and Anthony Braga (2007) described illicit ammunition as a "durable good," since most criminals rarely shoot their guns (F597). Commercial ammunition is nearly as durable as guns themselves—functioning after several decades in storage.

Ammunition restrictions may increase illicit pricing (Cook et al. 2007, F597; F612). However, it's difficult to prevent traffickers from diverting the small volumes needed by criminals. Homemade ammunition adds additional complication. Industrial cartridge cases involve simple materials but moderately complex fabrication processes. Skilled machinists can emulate commercial fabrication, but it's laborious. Nevertheless, print and digital media, and a variety of open source patents provide information on fabricating primer cups and cartridge cases, as well as DIY dies and tooling. Craft makers in developing nations have produced cases with relatively simple (but laborious) methods. Due to labor and tooling requirements, most homemade ammunition involves commercial cases. However, the sheer supply of recyclable commercial ammunition suggests that serious controls on homemade ammunition must target *primers* and *propellants*. These chemical compounds are harder to emulate. Safely producing modern propellants requires industrial laboratories and storage facilities, a lesson hard won by deadly explosions at guncotton factories in the nineteenth century. Modern powders are optimized for energy efficiency, low-smoke deflagration, stability, and low residue. Most DIYers would be challenged to manufacture modern propellants or primers in their garages. However, DIYers can scrounge materials or devolve to obsolete compounds.

Until the invention of guncotton (nitrocellulose plasticized with nitroglycerin), guns operated almost exclusively on black powder (Bhattacharya 2006, 42). Black powder is dirtier, less powerful, and less reliable, but easier to make. Smokeless powders were a boon for gunmakers: repeating guns were invented in the black powder age, but black powder easily fouled repeating guns. Cleaner and more powerful powders were combined with improved percussion-sensitive primers to make semiautomatic guns practical. Nevertheless, it's possible to load modern cartridges with artisanal gunpowder. Craft producers in the developing world (and a few trafficking rings in restrictive environments) continue to do so. Gunpowder is made from sulfur, charcoal, uric acid (which can be derived from urine), potassium and nitrate (or potassium nitrate). This was a high-tech endeavor in prescientific times. Early powder makers had fewer informational resources, and lacked scientific knowledge of the physical principals they harnessed. Bulk saltpeter supply is geographically rare and was unobtainable in many locales except through foreign trade and regime-level investment. Indeed, preindustrial Europe and Japan contained few saltpeter reserves, but both civilizations mastered the gun through a combination of bulk imports and local production.

Many preindustrial cultures lacked bulk gunpowder supply. This impacted interstate conflict, as Elizabeth I discovered when warring against her largest saltpeter supplier: Spain. Lacking domestic industry, England scrambled to increase imports and local production. Centuries later, colonial powers jockeyed for "guano islands" and other territories made valuable by nitrate deposits essential for fertilizer and propellants. The difficulties of bulk gunpowder supply manifested in some preindustrial gun controls. The "shot heard 'round the world" was fired in defense of guns and gunpowder. The colonials protected gunpowder because they lacked a wartime production base. The pre-Revolution Navigation Acts discouraged local production, and George III prohibited export to the colonies in 1774. Eventually, the rebels established alternate supplies, relying on French allies to provide bulk gunpowder (Dick 2013). Yet, then as now, it's possible to produce gunpowder artisanally.

Modern cartridges and bullets are harder to fabricate than musket shot, but hunters and sport shooters do make ammunition. Skilled machinists can fabricate cartridges, primer cups, and customized bullets, though these practices are rare. More commonly, *reloading* practitioners make, customize, and recycle ammunition using commercial cases, primers, bullets, and propellants. Specialized tools facilitate reloading, but general-use tools also work. Because the costliest component is the reusable case, reloading saves money while enabling shooters to bypass retail shortages. Reloading also facilitates customization, aka "wildcatting." Wildcatters customize for pressures, ballistics, or optimum performance in specific guns.

Regulations differ. In America, reloading is generally legal. In most states, powders can be purchased without permitting, but reloaders must not be prohibited from possessing firearms. The United Kingdom and Germany require certification and permits. In Canada, reloading is legal for gun licensees, but regulations govern safe storage and quantities of powder. Reloading is very rare among American criminals, probably because it's a painstaking process and commercial ammunition is accessible. However, traffickers and armed groups have reloaded. Supply-side ammunition control is more plausible where ammunition is rare, strictly regulated, and hard to smuggle. Yet, between the large supply of commercial ammunition, legal precursor supply chains, and the ease of smuggling small quantities, it's difficult to deny ammunition to motivated traffickers.

The guerilla gunsmithing canon addresses ammunition. Skilled (or reckless) DIYers can extract precursors from commercial products, many of which go unnamed in this volume. Benson's *Guerilla Gunsmithing* and Luty's *Expedient Homemade Ammo* provide instructions. Primer and propellant precursors can be sourced from stump remover, cold packs, strike-anywhere matches, film, nail gun blanks, charcoal, fertilizers, urine, and other household items. Mainstream books provide tips for legal reloaders. If accessing commercial powders is difficult, many publications provide gunpowder formulations. After all, gunpowder is a 1,200-year-old technology. Dozens of tutorials circulate online.

Primers are the "primary" charge in modern cartridges. They're loaded into metal cups and struck by the firing pin. Primers are essential for modern ammunition, but the compounds are difficult to make. Indeed, after industrialization rendered commercial ammunition harder to emulate, mainstream manufacturers tried to control primers, fearing reloading would threaten ammunition sales. Dick Speer, the entrepreneur behind Cascade Cartridge Works (CCI), saw an opportunity. CCI's business "literally exploded" when it marketed primers (Pearce 2016). Decades later, many companies sell primers. DIYers generally rely on commercial primers. Bulk volumes of these percussion-sensitive compounds are produced in industrial labs and stored in fortified facilities. However, precursors can be scavenged, or obsolete formulations made from scratch.

Armstrong's Mixture is composed of red phosphorous and an oxidizer like potassium chlorate. This compound functions as a primer, and is extractible from toy caps, party poppers, strike-anywhere matches, and some fireworks. A few online videos show gunhackers extracting precursors and substitutes from household items. Mercuric compounds predated adoption of potassium chlorate in the nineteenth century, or today's improved lead styphnate and azide mixtures. These older compounds are corrosive but functional. They can be synthesized from mercury, nitric acid, uric acid, ethanol, and other precursors. A smattering of online videos show DIYers testing obsolete compounds in modern guns. Propellant production is even rarer than reloading among criminals. Cook, Ludwig, Venkatesh, and Braga observed some street-level American criminals as laughably ignorant about ammunition. Terrorists with the skills to make propellants would probably focus on bombmaking. However, craft gunmakers do illicitly produce ammunition, usually in locales where imported or smuggled ammunition is costly.

Materials have been a challenge for 3D-printable ammunition. Arms consultant N.R. Jenzen-Jones was among the first to assess additive firearm technologies in 2015, writing: "It is important to note that 3D-printed ammunition does not exist, and that 3D-printed firearms such as the Liberator or Solid Concepts 1911 use conventional ammunition" (64). This remains true, but innovations continue. Some gunhackers developed new styles of ammunition that complement 3D-printing technology. The first style is printable ammunition that can be fired from conventional guns. The second is homemade ammunition optimized for 3D-printed guns.

The first style was initially developed by Jeff Heeszel, brain trust behind Taofledermaus, a small DIY group that hosts popular online videos. Heeszel's "red rocket" printable shotgun slug and other creations are loaded into conventional shells. Early iterations in acrylonitrile butadiene styrene, or ABS plastics, were too light to do much damage. Improved variants included bronzeFill 3D-printer filament, which mixes metal powder into the plastic. Others apply similar techniques to print bullets and load them into conventional shells. Pennsylvania DIYer, machinist, and skilled custom gunsmith Mike Crumling pursued a clever approach: he designed metal cartridges that contain pressures, enabling plastic guns to shoot reliably. Crumling tested 19 rounds in his own plastic gun with no component replacements. While materials have slowed the development of all-plastic repeating guns, this innovative style of ammunition could make 3D-printed firearms more viable. However, Crumling told me that this innovation has been largely ignored by the digital gunhacking culture:

> Nobody was really interested in following that avenue. I think it's because the people who are interested in 3D-printing, they lack skills in traditional

machining. They want to be able to press a button and have basically parts off the shelf . . . and those shells, you need to be able to machine the old-fashioned way. (Interview 2019)

Digital fabrication may open new avenues for DIY ammunition while reducing dependence on traditional skills. Cartridges and bullets can be machined with digital CNC. Inexpensive metal printers, or wider adoption of carbon fiber printers, may eventually make fabricating bullets and cartridges easier. Though far-fetched today, chemical printing could enable many compounds to be synthesized from accessible reagents, enabling DIYers to "print" propellants. By then, guns will become a lesser concern as compared to explosives, designer drugs, and poisons. The timeline for these advances is in decades rather than years. However, if unthrottled chemical synthesizers reach the consumer market, they may enable a self-contained firearms supply chain. In that technologic moment, skilled users could combine 3D-printing, digital CNC, and digital chemical synthesis to produce firearms and ammunition in-house with decreased reliance on traditional skillsets or supply chains.

Under the *Palermo Protocol*, virtually all ammunition components are regulated. However, signatories can regulate ammunition domestically as their governments choose. DIY ammunition may be lightly regulated in one jurisdiction and criminalized in another. Controls on propellants increase the challenge of illegal ammunition making, but they can't eliminate diversion, invalidate chemistry, or reduce the availability of chemistry information. That ammunition manufacture is a rarity among criminals implies that criminal demand rarely outstrips traffickers' ability to divert ammunition from legal supplies. Controlling precursors requires control over an expansive list of consumer products. Ultimately, combating *all* forms of illegal ammunition would require a regression to preindustrial market and information conditions. As explosives investigator Christopher Chenoweth (2016) observed, "once the knowledge is out there, you're kind of hosed."

The informational dilemma isn't peculiar to guns. Supply-side drug control hasn't prevented *clandestine chemists* from synthesizing drugs. Controls on pseudoephedrine-containing methamphetamine precursors hasn't prevented traffickers from "smurfing," or breaking their precursor procurement processes into many small legal transactions that are more difficult to profile and interdict. Insofar as commercial ammunition and *any* reloading remains legal (as is likely in America and many countries), traffickers will gain *some* access to ammunition, primers, and propellants. Ultimately, the most plausible reason that criminals rarely make ammunition is that they don't need to. Perhaps illicit makers would gravitate to ammunition if incentivized. This is not a groundbreaking speculation. As James Jacobs, Director of NYU's Center for Research in Crime and Justice, wrote in 2002: "As long as there is demand for new firearms and ammunition, a black market forms; indeed, there are such black markets in the United States, Western Europe, and Japan. Like drugs, guns and bullets would be manufactured in clandestine shops and imported from abroad" (221).

Anecdotally, the incentives behind illicit ammunition seem to mirror the incentives for illegal gunmaking. In hundreds of source articles reviewed for this book, illegal ammunition production is mentioned almost exclusively among artisanal makers in developing states (where imported ammunition is costly), among militias, or among organized crime in restrictive states. It seems that in most locales, traffickers simply don't *need* to make ammunition.

Fundamentally, the message of the global gun is this: some combination of desperation, deviance, insecurity, ingenuity, and profit will motivate human beings to acquire weapons irrespective of law. Humans make extraordinary efforts to acquire firearms, and the global material ecosystem provides tools and materials. The products aren't always legal, pretty, or safe. Yet, to those who are building and buying them around the world, they're better than nothing.

Note

1. After several years during which it was impossible to keep Cody Wilson out of the press, Paloma Heindorff and Defense Distributed declined multiple interview requests for this book. Perhaps this is understandable. Wilson's provocative philosophy brought tremendous media coverage alongside greater scrutiny and backlash than any DIY gunmaker had ever experienced.

CHAPTER FOUR

The Substitution Effect: Would Criminals and Terrorists Make Their Own Guns?

Only a few [criminal] groups would be interested in them. Felons, and terrorists, or domestic terrorist groups. Maybe someone who wants a firearm for protection but can't get it legally, or wants a specific weapon type, but that's a relatively small number.
—Montella Smith, criminologist and violent crimes detective
(ret.) (Interview 2016)

Real criminals aren't going to get involved in this. Some loony tune is going to do some mass shooting.
—William Vizzard, criminologist and BATFE supervisor
(ret.) (Interview 2016)

How could DIY change the game for trafficking, terrorism, or active shootings? To explore this, we should consider the particular appeals that DIY gunmaking could hold for traffickers and terrorists. Problematically, many bad actors get conventional guns through theft, legal purchase, straw purchase, and smuggling. Professional traffickers employ networks to do so. A profile of criminal gunmaking needs to identify why bad actors would choose to *substitute* homemade products.

By that logic, the situation may not change much for sophisticated illicit groups that frequently acquire commercial firearms (and sometimes procure weapons unavailable in legal commerce). If trusted contacts can steal, smuggle, or purchase adequate weapons without raising red flags, there's limited incentive to build inhouse. We do know that terrorists like guns. Though other modalities like vehicular attacks, explosives, sabotage, arson, and weapons of mass destruction (WMD) have potential to generate greater casualties, terrorist firearm use is entirely rational. The

Table 4.1 Firearm Involvement in Global Terrorist Incidents (Lethal)

Period	1970–1980	1981–1990	1991–2000	2001–2010	2011–2017	Total
Incidents	12,576	32,385	26,689	28,052	81,989	181,691
Involving Firearms	4,235	13,162	9,961	9,364	27,007	63,729
Percentage Involving Firearms	33.7	40.6	37.3	33.4	33.0	35.1

Method: Global Terrorism Database searches for all lethal terrorism incidents (including "ambiguous" cases) and all lethal incidents involving firearms (nonexclusive of other weapons).

Table 4.2 Success Rates by Weapon Type

Weapon Type	Attacks: 1970–2018	Successful Attacks: 1970–2018	Success Rate
Nuclear	0	0	0
Radiologic	13	1	07.69%
Biological	37	16	43.24%
Fake Weapons	69	50	72.46%
Chemical	401	314	78.30%
Vehicle (Nonexplosive)	231	198	85.71%
Explosives	97,820	84,300	86.18%
Other	313	270	86.26%
Unknown	17,582	15,456	87.90%
Firearms	67,501	62,233	92.20%
Melee	5,629	5,190	92.20%
Incendiaries	14,654	13,899	94.85%
Sabotage	237	229	96.62%
Explosives (United States only)	1,435	1,101	76.72%
Firearms (United States only)	448	396	88.40%

*Method: Global Terrorism Database searches for all attacks (including lethal, nonlethal, and "ambiguous" cases) involving weapon type, and identical searches excluding attacks GTD characterizes as "unsuccessful."

University of Maryland's Global Terrorism Database (GTD) indicates 33–40 percent of lethal attacks between 1970 and 2017 involved firearms (see tables 4.1 and 4.2). Why are firearms so popular? The simplest explanation is that guns are accessible, flexible, and effective.

Many factors contribute to firearm popularity. Firstly, and most obviously, they're accessible. Terrorists desire military-grade *light weapons* like mortars, grenades, and explosives, but these are harder to access or build. However, light weapons are accessible compared to heavier systems: *Small Arms Survey* describes light weapons as "widely produced and readily available." They are commercially manufactured in more than 50 countries, and the primary reason they aren't manufactured in more countries isn't technical barriers, but rather "the fact that the markets are so open that their needs are easily met through commercial transactions" (Berman and Leff 2008, 12). However, the light weapons supply chain is narrower than the market for firearms, and light weapon inventories are more restricted. Almost all light weapons are sold to military and police services, and they are issued to fewer personnel than firearms. Nevertheless, militias, terrorists, drug traffickers, and even outlaw motorcycle clubs and street gangs have procured them.

The chaos and policing vacuums created by armed conflict, state failure, paramilitarization, corruption, and endemic illicit trade, each facilitate the disappearance of military weapons. Military weapons are occasionally purloined even in well-policed jurisdictions. The complexity of trafficking networks can make recovery difficult. For example, Australian authorities are still looking for antiarmor missiles diverted by an ordnance officer who passed them to the Rebels Motorcycle Club, who sold them to a broker for crime boss Adnan Darwiche, who sold some to Mohamed Ali Elomar, leader of the terrorist "Sydney Cell" busted in 2005. As of this writing, some of the rockets are still in the wild.

Light weapons are practically nonexistent in routine crime, but many armed groups have made their own for use in armed conflict, insurgencies, and major engagements with each other. Examples abound. Holding huge quantities of looted explosives, Iraqi insurgents enjoyed "almost limitless" improvised explosive device (IED) manufacturing (Berman and Leff 2008, 14). Hamas has improved its thousands of DIY rockets, which are made in workshops despite commercial munition embargoes. Daesh and Kurdish militias made antimaterial rifles, improvised fighting vehicles, bomb-laden drones, and other weapons. Syria's Jaish al-Islam used clever "sand casting" techniques to make mortar ammunition "broadly on par with industrially produced models" (Hays and Jenzen-Jones 2018, 39–40). The Moro Islamic Liberation Front emulated rocket-propelled grenade launchers, among other items (Berman and Leff 2008, 15). The Revolutionary Armed Forces of Colombia (FARC) made mortars, grenades, and other light weapons, and received guns from artisanal producers. The Provisional Irish Republican Army (IRA) made mortars, IEDs, and rockets. Members of a Provisional IRA splinter group were caught teaching FARC how to make weapons.

Many cottage arms industries began by equipping terrorists, insurgents, or paramilitaries, then continued production into peacetime. The Viet Cong made Colt 1911 knockoffs and other firearms and light weapons. In the 1980s, Indian communists opened clandestine factories in Bihar, already a gunmaking hotspot. Today, Bihar's gunmakers serve criminals and average citizens alike. Pakistan's unlicensed industry serves combatants and citizens. The Mindanao region of the Philippines is known for quality craft weapons: this industry supplied guerillas combating Japanese occupation, and later served the Moro Islamic Liberation Front, police, and civilians. In Indonesia, a cottage industry around the gunmaking enclave of Cipacing served militias during the Sulawesi and Aceh rebellions. In peacetime, this business continued to serve civilians and even police (International Crisis Group 2010).

Clandestine networks and semicovert cottage industries can produce in volume, but their role in transnational illicit trade is overshadowed by conventional trafficking. Nevertheless, DIY has become a significant source in many countries. In well-policed jurisdictions, a combination of tool and material accessibility, tighter surveillance, and strict weapons enforcement may incentivize terrorists toward clandestine gunmaking. The global security environment has become less favorable toward paramilitary-style logistical infrastructures. Smaller-scale, decentralized, and unpredictable attacks by sympathizers and lone wolves are more likely to fly under the radar. Counterterrorism expert Marc Sageman (2008) called this decentralization *leaderless jihad*, while security researcher Laura Quadarella Sanfelice (2017) argued that we are entering an era of decentralized and opportunistic *DIY terrorism*. In a world of increased surveillance and direct action against terrorist infrastructures, extremist groups slowly plot major attacks while inspiring decentralized campaigns by radicalized sympathizers.

Interest in homemade guns should be more pronounced on this lower rung of the mass-violence ladder. Combatants often regard DIY as a secondary alternative to commercial products. Arms researcher N.R. Jenzen-Jones has been studying combatant adoptions of DIY weapons. He told me "combatants are forthright about their preference for traditionally manufactured firearms over DIY products," and "when we interview people who use these [DIY] firearms, they'd much rather have conventional firearms" (Interview 2018). Lacking logistical networks, isolated attackers face challenges in accessing military-grade weapons. However, their lack of connections often enables them to purchase or construct weapons on a smaller scale without raising red flags.

Guns fit well with the DIY terrorism paradigm: they are relatively inexpensive and comparatively easy to steal, buy, or build. Most guns are unregistered and civilian-owned. The history, culture, and legitimate uses of guns render the politics of gun control more complex than the politics of military arms control. Simple weapons and tactics are more likely to be successful, and guns lie at a coefficient of simplicity, accessibility, and effectiveness. They're more common than explosives, can be tested more discreetly, and involve a shorter learning curve. Experienced shooters understand that it's hard to shoot well, but easy to shoot badly. Police, security professionals, sportspeople, firearm trainers, and motivated concealed carriers spend years developing the skills to prevail against competent adversaries. In contrast, an active shooting against undefended soft targets may be carried out "successfully" by a novice, provided the novice doesn't expect to escape. It's generally easier to build a gun than a reliable IED. It's also easier to practice with guns without raising red flags or blowing oneself up. As an explosives investigator in Colorado Springs told me, "Generally speaking, you can get on them [bombmakers] when they test something, or they get hurt, or there's a call in" (Chenoweth 2016). Gunmaking information circulates more widely than bombmaking manuals. In America, gunsmithing information is constitutionally protected speech about a longstanding practice.

The lower-rungs of mass violence are also populated by seemingly apolitical mass killers. Some do make bombs, but they're often unreliable. The FBI's 2013 study of U.S. active shootings between 2000 and 2013 found several cases involving explosives, but these had not killed anyone. The Columbine shooters might have produced over 200 casualties if their IEDs had worked, prompting political scientist Harry Wilson to remark, "If the Columbine attackers had been better bomb makers, we wouldn't be talking about the Columbine *shooting*, they would have just blown up the school!" (Interview 2019). Indeed, many Americans are unaware that the country's deadliest school attack, the Bath School Disaster, occurred in 1927, and the attacker primarily used explosives.

Unsophisticated terrorists have used bombs ineffectively. The 2002 airline "shoe bomber" was subdued by passengers. The 2009 airline "underpants bomber" injured himself and was subdued by passengers. The 2010 Times Square bomb fizzled. The 2013 Boston Marathon attackers built IEDs from a notorious article in al-Qaeda's *Inspire* magazine titled "How to Make a Bomb in the Kitchen of Your Mom." Those bombs killed three and wounded hundreds. Yet, the coordinated pair could have killed more people with guns. Firearms are also flexible. Explosives are indiscriminate and single-use, while guns lend themselves to a wider tactical spectrum. Daveed Gartenstein-Ross and Daniel Trombly (2012) examined terrorist use of firearms and found that accessibility, reliability, and tactical flexibility make guns persistently appealing. In a study of solo terrorism in the United States, Mark Hamm and Ramon Spaaij (2017) found that attackers have increasingly targeted police and have gravitated toward "a staggering range of high-velocity firearms" (2). Guns can support coordinated assaults, ambushes, active shootings, robberies, assassinations, hostage takings, and repelling counterforce. They are also portable and comparatively easy to smuggle.

Yet as damaging as firearms can be in the wrong hands, the ease of stealing, smuggling, or buying commercial guns renders DIY only one option among many. Almost anybody can make a zip gun, but these have little appeal to an attacker bent on significant casualties. With the exception of frame builds, it remains difficult for a novice to make guns that rival the capability of commercial firearms. Frame or "80%" builds approach commercial quality with relatively low-skilled work. However, their reliance on commercial parts creates some opportunities for tracking and interdiction by law enforcement, and the relatively high cost of commercial components may compare unfavorably if an armed organization is able to produce quality weapons from scratch. DIY gunmaking or modifications from scratch appear to have greatest appeal among a few narrower criminal demographics: those who can't get a gun through other channels, those who desire particularly clandestine procurement, those who want features that can't be accessed otherwise, and those located where semi-industrial operations can be setup with little fear of police action.

Printed guns, crypto-guns, and crude zip guns can be made discreetly, but are poor options for serious engagements. Military and commercial firearms are preferable, but not everyone on the lowest rungs of the mass-violence ladder can get them illicitly (or are willing to try). Gun-sourcing is starkly different for those with contacts. In the United States and other countries plagued by routine gun crime, loose networks trade weapons at street level. A 2019 Bureau of Justice Statistics survey found only 7 percent of gun offenders acquired *any* firearm from a licensed dealer under their own name, and only 1.3 percent of offenders used a gun they'd legally obtained from a dealer (Alper and Glaze 2019).

In contrast, solo attackers and isolated extremists may lack the trusted contacts, wherewithal, or risk-tolerance to illicitly purchase or steal guns. Others have bought retail despite being disqualified, with background check errors allowing the purchases. These cases notwithstanding, most active shooters can acquire legally. A 2018 Department of Justice study found most active shooters didn't have significant criminal records or adverse psychiatric adjudications, and most purchased their guns legally (Silver, Simons, and Craun 2018).

The degree to which apolitical active shooters resemble ideologically motivated terrorists is still unclear. For years, counterterrorism literature indicated that suicide terrorists are rational and ideologically motivated and don't disproportionately suffer from mental disorders (Post et al. 2009; Pape 2006). However, some research suggests that solo terrorists and active shooters share comparatively high rates of mental health challenges (Lankford 2013). Criminologist Grant Duwe (2007) conservatively estimated that up to 28 percent of 1,186 American mass killers suffered mental illness (105). Debate continues between rational choice and psychopathologic interpretations, alongside concerns about stigmatizing those suffering mental illness, the majority of whom are nonviolent.

Regardless, there is evidence of media-driven *contagion effects*. One study found that media coverage of active shootings elevated risk of subsequent shootings for 4–10 days, accounting for 55 percent of shootings in their sample (Jetter and Walker 2018). Another found elevated risk for 13 days, and that each shooting generated 0.22–0.30 *new* shootings (Towers et al. 2015). In an American Psychological Association paper, Jennifer Johnston and Andrew Joy (2016) concluded, "Even conservatively, if the calculations of contagion modelers are correct, we should see at least a one-third reduction in shootings if the contagion is removed" (29). These intersections of media, murder, and mental health are more complex than most gun control *or* counterterrorism strategies account for.

In America, most gun homicides are by street-level offenders who acquire conventional guns through theft, informal borrowing, or illegal transactions. For example, 79 percent of offenders in Pittsburgh, and more than 90 percent in Chicago, acquired their weapons illegally (Fabio et al. 2016; Cook, Parker, and Pollack 2015). These offenders largely bypass registration, licensing, or background checks. Meanwhile, many active attackers suffer mental health problems, and are influenced by media contagion, but don't raise sufficient red flags to be denied legal purchases. In America, increasing passage of red flag laws will be an important test establishing whether homicides, suicides, or active shootings can be reduced by broadening the circumstances under which firearms are seized from potentially dangerous individuals.

However, these laws will also impact some low-risk people. Some civil libertarians and mental health advocates worry red flag laws will be used to prosecute interpersonal grievances, stigmatize the mentally ill, or normalize weapons confiscation from low-risk citizens. Similar trade-offs complicate seemingly commonsense measures like denying purchases to those on terror watchlists. Gartenstein-Ross and Trombly (2012) examined dozens of terrorist firearm cases in the United States. They found most attackers capable of passing background checks or acquiring firearms illicitly, and that secret watchlisting to deny a constitutional right could introduce due process and counterintelligence complications. The underlying concept of secret watchlisting has faced challenges as well. In 2019's *Elhady v. Kable*, the Federal Eastern District Court of Virginia ruled the national Terrorist Screening Database unconstitutional since it watchlisted citizens without notifying them or providing an opportunity to challenge the evidence.

Even where laws are strict, some attackers will purchase legally, while some prohibited attackers find work-arounds. Assuming sufficient demand, supply controls may displace some weapon seekers to less-regulated or illicit access points. This surely doesn't mean jurisdictions should give up point-of-sale gun regulation. However, the regulatory worldview must acknowledge that some portion of bad actors will bypass these systems with illegally made and trafficked weapons and that illicit actors can often do so in spite of commercial controls. Adaptive adversaries can game statutory regulations. It's difficult to deny procurement through predictable rules and universal procedures, yet predictable rules and universal procedures are elements of due process. The justifications for denying a right (or even a valued *privilege*) must typically be disclosed and scrutinized on appeal.

When convenient, adversaries exploit the rights other citizens enjoy. Yet, when restrictive laws and tight policing make this difficult some portion of bad actors are deterred, while others bypass legal frameworks entirely. In that sense, it's plausible that supply-side controls would filter the population of illicit buyers to more deviant and desperate demographics, influence their selection of illicit access points, and incentivize their pursuit of certain types of weapons. However, supply-side controls do not intrinsically reduce illegal demand, and terrorist gun procurement is diverse. In the 2008 Mumbai Siege, a transnational terrorist group used military small arms and light weapons. The November 2015 Paris attacks involved organized cells that acquired through straw purchases, illicit transfers, and reactivations. Australia's Lindt Café Siege attacker illegally procured and modified an unregistered gun. The Oslo attacker (and many solo attackers) purchased legally. A handful of active shooters in the United States have used DIY methods to build guns despite disqualifying records, or to customize commercial guns and ammunition in attempts to increase lethality.

To make gun control an effective component of counterterrorism, it's tempting to harness national security and criminal intelligence methods. This may prevent some harms, but also invites questions about surveillance, due process, scope, cost, and efficacy. Surveillance must be thorough to prevent DIY gunmaking, and resources are lacking. By one estimate, monitoring everyone on current watchlists would require up to 40 percent of British police, 62 percent of American police, and 100 percent of French police (Noack 2016). Despite vast increases in electronic intelligence collection, many attackers have succeeded despite being watchlisted or subject to investigation. Ever more data about citizens is collected, and cooperation from citizens and the private sector continues to be a major source of threat intelligence. The problem lies in filtering, analyzing, prioritizing, and sharing a huge volume of intelligence, and in the inability of law enforcement to act preemptively without revealing sensitive methods or violating due process and evidentiary standards.

There are still many ways for an adversary to fall through the cracks. One of the conspirators behind the 2008 Mumbai Siege was a Drug Enforcement Administration informant. Two of his wives provided tips about his involvement in terrorism, including potential targets. The man responsible for the 2011 Oslo attack attracted attention from Norwegian security by suspiciously importing explosive primer. Several conspirators from the 2015 "Brussels Cell" were named in tips, watchlisted, under surveillance, or had active warrants. After the 2015 Paris attacks, an extremist fatally stabbed two French police officers; that attacker was previously imprisoned for terrorism and remained watchlisted. In response, Interior Minister Bernard Cazeneuve authorized police to carry firearms off-duty.

The white supremacist who carried out the 2015 Charleston church shooting had disqualifying records, but these weren't shared in time to prevent his purchase. Similar lapses prevented purchase denials for the 2017 Sutherland Springs church shooter and several other attackers. The 2015 San Bernardino attackers' unencrypted communications revealed connections with the Nusra Front and al-Shabaab, and their purchasing records indicated IED preparation, but none of this was actionable in time to stop them. In 2017, a rampage shooter in northern California was disqualified from owning guns, but built a DIY rifle instead. Neighbors complained of shooting on his property even after he'd lost his right to firearms, but nobody returned to seize his homemade weapons.

The Orlando Pulse attacker was investigated for extremism in 2013 and 2014. He publicly claimed terrorism ties and was even placed on the no-fly list for a time. The FBI interviewed him three times but couldn't take further action. He committed domestic violence and was dismissed from police academy for bad conduct. Clerks at a gun store became suspicious, refusing his requests for ammunition and ballistic armor, and informed the FBI, but no action could be taken. Coworkers at his security job complained that he often made angry, bigoted, and threatening comments. Despite these warning signs, he received an armed guard license and purchased all of his weapons legally.

Australia's Lindt Café attacker had a record that would be comic if not for the tragic results. He probably entered Australia through immigration fraud. He was the subject of 40 tips to the national security hotline. In 2009, he lectured for a global caliphate and taunted the government, saying "your intelligence service is not working properly." He was on Australian Security Intelligence Organisation's terrorism watchlist in 2008–2009 but was subsequently removed. He was involuntarily committed in 2010. He threatened to shoot one of his ex-wives in 2011, claiming he still had an armed guard license (it was revoked). In 2012, he started a hate mail campaign targeting families of Australian soldiers killed in action, resulting in his losing a high court free speech case. A year later, he tried to join an outlaw motorcycle club, but they rejected him as "weird." He was then charged in the killing of another ex-wife but released on bail. In 2014, he was charged with more than 40 counts of sexual assault. Despite this disquieting record, he was not kept in custody and was able to acquire an unregistered sawed-off shotgun for his 2014 attack—an attack that resulted in killing of two hostages and wounding of three.

It's easy to retroactively critique these "intelligence failures," but security services can't be expected to prevent every case, particularly if we want their methods to remain compatible with civil liberties. Despite their disproportionate impacts, mass killings are rare events carried out by a vanishingly small number of offenders. In mass societies (and particularly *liberal* mass societies), there are just too many places to hide: too many tips, too many targets, too many suspicious individuals, and too many innocent ones for law enforcement and security services to prevent every outbreak of mass killing without also laying suspicions on innocent persons.

Lawsuits and political backlash could create additional costs. CUNY law professor Ramzi Kassem counsels people placed on U.S. terrorism watchlists. He argues that the lists include mistaken identities and unreliable assessments, and "since most of those known to be watchlisted are Muslim, it would further single out, stigmatize and scapegoat that vulnerable minority here at home" (Kassem 2016). Some gang watchlists, such as California's "CalGangs" database, have been criticized for overbroad impacts on minority youth based on unreliable intelligence (California State Auditor 2016). Numerous wide-spectrum private databases (which are increasingly integrated with policing systems) have also been criticized as too inaccurate, opaque, or nonstandardized to justify real-world policing consequences.

It's easier to collect this kind of data on compliant populations than committed adversaries. It's also difficult to prevent committed adversaries from acquiring weapons-of-convenience, and firearms remain convenient in much of the world. Uncommitted attackers may be deterred by point-of-sale regulations. However, deterrent value depends on alternatives. If firearms are accessible through theft, illicit trade, or DIY methods, some offenders will take advantage. If alternative channels aren't available, low-commitment offenders might be deterred, but motivated attackers will substitute with different weapons (as mass killings by explosive, arson, blade, and vehicle attest). Northeastern University criminologist James Alan Fox is building a dataset on American mass killings. He maintains that around 22 percent haven't involved firearms at all (Callahan 2019). Somehow removing commercial guns from the terrorism equation would surely prevent some attacks, but some terrorists would just as surely migrate to homemade weapons or other attack methods.

Terrorists and armed groups have certainly exploited DIY gunmaking. Yet, DIY doesn't add a revolutionary element for sophisticated terrorists who already acquire military-grade and commercial weapons. Nor does DIY significantly change the game for the majority of solo attackers who acquire guns legally, nor those savvy enough to get them illegally. The primary terrorism challenge of DIY lies at the lower rungs of the mass-violence ladder: attackers who lack illicit connections, are unable to pass background checks (or seek particular clandestinity), are not skilled at bomb-making, arson, or sabotage, or want custom capabilities. Compared to the population of legal gun owners or even typical gun criminals, these individuals are exceptionally rare. Yet, in mass societies that struggle to maintain complex background check systems, effective mental health services, and police information sharing, some will inevitably get through the net.

Trafficking Appeal

> You can find Kalashnikovs for sale near the train station in Brussels.
> They're available even to very average criminals.
> —Anonymous EU official (Witte and Adam 2015)

> I think it has to get to a point with cost-benefit. The time, money,
> and effort have to be less than it would take for me to go to Bobo's
> house and buy a pistol for $40. And then I think the interest in DIY
> will skyrocket.
> —Chief of Detectives, Midwestern U.S. City (Interview 2015)

Many DIY guns approach commercial quality, but inferior quality and
lower performance can also undermine marketability. Commercial guns
have achieved impressive quality: well-maintained firearms can fire tens
or hundreds of thousands of rounds before needing serious repair. Criminologist and former BATFE supervisor William Vizzard described the
difficulties of controlling such a durable product: "The average firearm
has the service life of a hammer" (Interview 2016). Crude homemade
guns don't approach this reliability. In the Central African Republic,
homemade shotguns are jokingly called *yerenga*, which means "doesn't
last" (Berman and Lombard 2008, 65).

Almost anyone can make a zip gun, but these hold little appeal if better
options are available. Criminals gravitate toward weapons with higher
capability and greater prestige (U.S. Bureau of Justice Statistics and Zawitz
1995; Julius Wachtel, interview by author 2016). This may incentivize
improvements in illicit gunmaking. Organized crime and street gangs have
produced 80% guns and expedient submachine guns, and occasionally
sponsor rogue gunsmiths for higher-quality counterfeits. These are typically less reliable than commercial guns, but may include custom capabilities (like sound suppressors, extended magazines, or fully automatic fire).

Few countries permit automatic firearms in civilian markets. DIY provides alternatives. Semiautomatic receivers can be converted to full-auto
or select-fire. Aftermarket fire control kits can accomplish similar results,
while crude automatic weapons can be made from scratch. Easier options
emulate automatic fire. In America, aftermarket accessories like "bump
stocks" enabled semiautomatic rifles to emulate full-auto, but after they
were used in America's most lethal active shooting, even the NRA assented
to restriction. Before the 2017 mass shooting in Las Vegas, bump stocks
were obscure accessories purchased by collectors, and had never been
associated with mass violence. Afterward, media coverage incentivized

panic buying while disseminating knowledge of an inconvenient fact: it is possible to emulate automatic fire without buying retail accessories. Simple tricks enable a semiautomatic gun to fire more rapidly. Components can be machined for automatic fire, sears can be modified for runaway fire, or an attacker can use rubber bands, anchor to the body, make a bump stock, install a binary trigger, or construct a hand-cranked or motor-driven trigger actuator. While bump stocks flew off the shelves, media attention disseminated knowledge of their easily emulated principles.

Homemade guns fit the DIY terrorism paradigm by enabling less-sophisticated actors to gain capabilities they might not have otherwise. But will DIY guns be widely embraced for trafficking? Incentives may be clearer in this regard. Some theories anticipate that criminals in locales with black market scarcity would be incentivized to develop alternate sources. By this argument, enforcement pressures can sometimes backfire by encouraging more dangerous illicit substitutes. The "Alchian-Allen Effect" asserts that when premia increase on high and low grades of similar products, the higher-grade product will be incentivized (Thornton 2007, 93). This concept exports itself to the "Iron Law of Prohibition," which asserts that prohibition on in-demand products will encourage traffickers to develop and market increasingly potent illicit substitutes.

By this logic, supply-side enforcement may incentivize illicit substitution in the absence of demand reduction. This dynamic was apparent in alcohol prohibition, as traffickers focused on spirits instead of beer. Similar effects raise the social costs of illicit drugs. As Leo Beletsky and Corey Davis (2017) argue, illicit substitution contributed to a massive rise in America's overdose deaths. America's clampdown on commercial painkillers relied on measures like "prescription drug monitoring (PDM)" programs functioning as a supply-side pharmaceutical registry. However, the pharmaceutical clampdown was not accompanied by commensurate expansions to addiction treatment. This provided traffickers a window to substitute their own wares: synthetics that were orders of magnitude more dangerous than the regulated pharmaceuticals they replaced.

This was forecasted. In an article predicting future forms of illicit drug production, legendary drug researcher Alexander Shulgin wrote in 1975: "As these materials [current illicit drugs and precursors] become better defined and their use better controlled, they will be replaced with substitute compounds, which will provide society with new, unknown, and unmanageable substances" (405). Shulgin predicted the transformation to synthetic opioids was "economically inevitable," and as efforts to combat traditional heroin were strengthened, "the drive to create alternative materials that are not opium dependent will grow" (406). Similar illicit adaptations are found in the "Balloon" and "Cockroach" effects, which describe trafficker repositioning, rerouting, and logistical dispersion to circumvent concentrated enforcement.

Consequently, increased enforcement in one location or market sector may displace illicit activity to less-policed locations or sectors, while clampdowns on desirable products incentivize more potent substitutes. The result, according to the RAND Corporation, is that traffickers drove the synthetic opioid crisis "as new a strategic device for dealers seeking to lower costs or skirt drug control laws," as they were well positioned to exploit new and efficient synthesis methods, anonymous e-commerce, detection challenges, and poor regulation in China (Pardo et al. 2019). Similar effects counteract cocaine control. In 2019, a team of scholars modeled the balloon effect, finding connections between interdiction and criminal adaptations to circumvent it (Magliocca et al. 2019).

How might this translate to illegal gunmaking? If the risks of illegally fabricating a semiauto gun are similar to the risks of making a full-auto gun, or if adding accessories like suppressors or extended magazines does not significantly increase risk, illicit makers may gravitate toward items with greater capabilities. After all, when guns are made illegally to be sold illegally to buyers who will use them illegally, there's little reason to be concerned with magazine capacity laws. If tight laws and strong enforcement act as black market price supports, traffickers are incentivized to penetrate restrictive environments to collect the greatest profit. Meanwhile, enforcement is spread thinner by an ever-widening legal and geographic scope.

While gun running differs from drug running in some important respects, incentives (see table 4.3) appear fundamentally similar. DIY guns are sold at various price points depending on market and regulatory environments, design, materials, and fabrication method. Frame builds are more dependent on commercial supply chains, but commercial supply chains are more accessible in the developed world, and the resulting products are better. In many developing and middle-income nations, illicit assembly from commercial components, or full-cycle scratch manufacture, remains economically competitive against imported guns. Developing and middle-income nations tend to suffer more crime, but patterns in colonialism, industrialization, and international political economy resulted in less industrial gunmaking in poorer nations. Consequently, developing countries have fewer guns and fewer licensed makers. This generates a global supply-demand differential. Police ineffectiveness, corruption, crime, poverty, inequality, instability, and insecurity contribute to weapon demand,

Table 4.3 Selected Respondent Comments: "What Would Be the Appeal of DIY Firearms for Criminal Activity, as Compared to Conventional Firearms?"

Julius Wachtel, Criminology Professor/BATFE Special Agent/Supervisor (Ret.)	"Defeats tracking and regulation."
	"Occasionally a hobbyist or friend might misuse them, but the real threat is in domestic and international terrorism, and I do think there's a threat with sophisticated organized crime."
	"DIY weapons can have customized capabilities."
Christopher Chenoweth, Sheriff's Deputy/ Explosives Investigator	"You can make the argument there's less paper trail. Making them would leave less trail, but most criminals aren't getting guns legitimately to begin with."
	"It's more paranoia about being detected."
Montella Smith, Director University Forensics Program/Violent Crimes Detective (Ret.)	"They're better from the perspective of traceability. No background checks for DIY guns runs contrary to the rest of our legal scheme, but how to enforce that I don't know."
Lynn Trella, State Corrections/IA Investigator/ Homicide Detective (Ret.)	"It would make things easier for gangs, because they don't have to go out and do burglaries to get guns. When they do that, they take a risk."
Max Kingery, Chief BATFE Firearms Technology Branch	"The main appeal is untraceability, hands down. Manufacturers are well-regulated in the industry now. They mark everything."
	"DIY also permits shipment of items in plain sight. It cuts the costs and risks down until the point where they are finished or assembled."
William Schroeder, Law Professor/State Organized Crime Prosecutor (Ret.)	"For terrorists and mafia types, it cuts out all the nuisance of the weapon procurement process."
	"Traceability is another reason they'd be preferred."
Greg Moser, Metro Emergency Manager/State Counterterrorism Coordinator (Ret.)	"The main appeal would be to avoid tracing and ballistics, but most criminals are not very concerned with that."
	"Getting plastic weapons through screening could be a concern. Terrorism, but terrorists seem to get weapons anyway."

(continued)

Table 4.3 Selected Respondent Comments: "What Would Be the Appeal of DIY Firearms for Criminal Activity, as Compared to Conventional Firearms?" *(continued)*

Abhishek Narula, Industrial Designer/Artist/Maker	"It lowers the barriers if you can make your own [illegally] without anybody watching you. And I hate people like that because they put a bad spin on the maker movement."
Brett Steele, Professor/Conventional Weapons Specialist/Civil and International Security Institute	"Criminals might want guns with special capabilities, concealment, range, et cetera."
N.R. Jenzen-Jones, International Weapons Researcher/Consultant	"At the moment, assuming the limits on 3D-printed metals remain, the core appeals pertain to infiltrating secured areas."
	"Other potential applications hold implications for forensic investigators, but the persistent myth that smoothbore weapons are totally untraceable is even less true in the case of craft-produced guns and their ammunition."
	"Disposability, the ability to produce weapons on demand."
Professor/Criminology (Australia)	"The obvious is that you can get a gun without passing background checks."
Philip Alpers, Director of Gunpolicy.org (Australia)	"They're appealing in two contexts. One is that there's not enough money or access to guns. In a place like Ghana or Papua New Guinea, the only reason people get craft firearms is because they can't get an industry weapon. It's scarcity of money and resources in developing nations. The opposite in places with a surfeit of money."
	"Australia is on a path of low tolerance. Fewer and fewer households have firearms. As these social changes take effect, I suspect more and more focus on DIY, especially as the technology improves."
Fiona Haines, Criminologist, Member State Firearm Consultative Commission (Ret.) (Australia)	"I'm not convinced of the conventional organized crime appeal. My sense is they have access to weapons."
	"One illicit area that might come up which would be interesting to explore would be people with 3D printers at home downloading a file, printing a weapon, and sticking it in their drawer for self-defense."

but conventional firearm supplies tend to be smaller, and imported firearms costlier, in nations that suffer these conditions.

In developing economies, it is often cheaper to build local knockoffs or counterfeits than to smuggle commercial guns. Some craft-made guns include false markings, making them superficially resemble commercial guns, raising their value. Others are crude but very cheap. In these locales, DIY guns substitute for commercial guns in a straightforward sense: many people in developing nations want guns, but imported guns are difficult, costly, and frequently illegal to access. Local production fills the gap.

Trafficking risk is higher in restrictive, well-resourced, and well-policed jurisdictions. However, better enforcement is also a price support. In this regard, the difference in firearm supply between the United States and other industrialized countries is stark. Law enforcement respondents from an unrestrictive midwestern city told me that black market handguns could be commonly purchased for $50–$100: less than retail for similar items. Sometimes traffickers want to get rid of stolen or "hot" guns that have been used in crimes. This depresses pricing. However, even in the United States, enforcement can apply enough market "friction" to raise illicit prices 200–300 percent above retail. In restrictive Chicago, a 1996–1997 Department of Justice Survey found median illicit pricing at $150, which translates to a 150–300 percent markup on a cheap retail handgun. In 2007, researchers recorded illicit prices in Chicago between $150 and $400, which was consistent with a 2–3× markup for cheap handguns (Cook et al. 2007).

Friction is greatest in restrictive jurisdictions with small firearm supplies. In Australia, an illegal handgun might cost $1,500–$10,000 (AUD). In the United Kingdom, a "hot" gun might go for £150 in 2006, which translates to about $266 today, while new handguns might fetch $1,800–$2,500 in inflation-adjusted American dollars. Assuming retail pricing for a decent handgun in the range of $350, this puts the UK markup at 500–700 percent, and the Australian markup at 300–2,000 percent. Scarcity may incentivize illegal gunmaking in restrictive jurisdictions. Craft gunmakers in the developing world produce guns cheaply, operating semiopenly while relying on inexpensive labor and police ineffectiveness or corruption. In contrast, illicit makers in wealthier and well-policed jurisdictions must operate clandestinely, cannot overcome friction by trafficking openly, and must make better products to compete with commercial guns.

Adoptions of costlier machine tools or more sophisticated digital tools makes more sense in wealthier and middle-income nations where better tools are accessible, better products are needed, and enforcement drives up illicit pricing. Digital CNC gunmaking from scratch often requires thousands in tool costs, access to design files (or the skills to generate them), and considerable labor time for fabrication and finishing. 3D-printing from scratch has lower barriers to entry, with many home printers available for $500–$2,500, but the products are much inferior. Unit cost can be as low as $5–$20 for plastic guns, but cannot decrease further. Printed guns may then be viable for trafficking, but their appeal is greater where illegal guns are costly and superior options are limited.

Without improvements to the materials available in consumer-grade printers, this dynamic should keep plastic guns a niche product in firearm-soaked markets like the United States, with the exception of tightly regulated enclaves where illicit guns are particularly expensive. This is not to say printable guns couldn't be appealing to those few Americans with no other source, or those who want to try circumventing security screening. However, a crude plastic gun has little to recommend it in the United States. In restrictive, well-policed, and geographically isolated locales with smaller illicit weapons stocks, it's possible to sell these mediocre weapons at greater profit.

There is anecdotal evidence that this may be occurring. Australian police have encountered trafficking of 3D-printed guns and other homemade weapons on deep web fora, where printed guns are purchased for $250 (AUD). An Australian trafficker may only need to sell a handful of printed guns to make their money back. Simpler methods can also be profitable. Australian police periodically bust rings of pen gun makers. These reportedly fetch $100+ on the street (Partridge 2014), but can be made from $3 center punches or other cheap materials. The ease of making expedient guns and difficulty of stopping it led retired U.S. marshal and firearms instructor William Presson to exclaim, "I can make a zip gun before freakin' *lunch*, and it's not traceable!" (Interview 2016).

Skilled machining and digital CNC produce better guns. However, the costs are better-justified where illegal guns fetch higher prices. In restrictive markets where illegal guns cost thousands per unit, an illicit gunmaker with trustworthy clients can break even with only a few units sold. In that sense, the market frictions of enforcement also create counteracting incentives for clandestine manufacture and smuggling. Illicit DIY may also widen the trafficking repertoire to address enforcement friction. DIY gunmaking can be decentralized, customized, and moved closer to buyers. This reduces risks associated with theft, diversion, and interdiction-in-transit. Components can be assembled locally, and smuggling components is easier than smuggling guns. Components are more concealable and harder to identify. If unfinished or nonassembled, they might not be illegal. Expanding interdiction to address component trafficking requires more time, technology, training, and cost.

Traffickers have developed component smuggling to a science. In Malaysia's *Sun Daily*, one Malaysian border officer said: "The smugglers are clever, they only bring in certain parts of the weapon and do not smuggle a fully assembled gun in sacks, boxes, or bags," and complained that his border units "do not have any sophisticated equipment to detect parts of a firearm, while a scanning machine took two hours just to screen for prohibited items in a lorry" (*The Sun Daily* 2013). Anonymized deep web markets like *Agora*, *The Armory*, *Sterling Cooperate Services*, *RUVA*, and a revolving door of other anonymized e-commerce platforms have facilitated trafficking through postal services, and through operational security procedures like cutouts and dead drops which emulate the countersurveillance tradecraft employed by intelligence agencies. These services are periodically shut down by police but have always resurfaced.

According to one dealer from *The Armory* who claimed to send 30–70 international orders per month, components are shipped inside power tools, engine blocks, or other items with similar densities to gun steel (Matthews 2014). This decreases probability of detection by scanning machines. Components may be shipped without oils or packing grease to throw off canines and chemical screening. As digital fabrication becomes more accessible, components may be designed as snap-off parts within other objects, challenging detection. As digital fabrication popularizes, traffickers won't need to smuggle physically: they'll only need to transfer information.

Much remains speculative, but we should expect a few relevant trends. DIY guns will be more attractive for adversaries who are isolated from serious illicit networks. Serious armed groups will continue to make weapons, concentrating on items less likely to be acquired through established connections. However, DIY will constitute only one more procurement option for sophisticated actors. Formidable terrorist organizations should prefer homemade weapons primarily where surveillance is tight and better weapons are hard to get, or if a plot revolves around capabilities to be gained through DIY methods.

More often, DIY guns should constitute a weapon-of-convenience for isolated attackers. While many already acquire commercial firearms, homemade guns should be attractive to these offenders because they are discreet, and because some DIY techniques provide capabilities that retail products don't offer. We should expect these lower-rung actors to continue their interest in improvised weapons, accessories, and modifications as regulators try to reduce their access to conventional guns. We should expect extremist propaganda to encourage illicit gunmaking, much as it already encourages bombmaking, arson, and vehicular attacks. In a world of high-quality commercial firearms, DIY guns rarely constitute the first-choice weapon for terrorists or active shooters. However, they will be an alternative for isolated attackers around the world.

Historic and colonial legacies, broad but poorly enforced weapons restrictions, limited local buying power, and comparatively high weapon demand fueled by crime, insecurity, corruption, and subsistence needs have all encouraged cottage gunmaking in the developing world. Many developing nations fail to control guns effectively, but their weapon-seeking populations lack money to get commercial guns in spite of ineffectual laws. These realities encouraged craft gunmaking in developing nations and are responsible for its continued popularity in enclaves of the Global South. If *effective* gun control encourages substitution, we should expect certain manifestations in wealthier nations where gun control is arguably more effective. We should expect traffickers to focus on DIY where gun controls are tight, policing is well resourced, cross-border smuggling is difficult, comparatively few illegal firearms circulate, organized crime is present to distribute illicitly, and gang crime is present to drive demand. These variables are strong in relatively few countries. Australia, Japan, the United Kingdom, Ireland, Singapore, some Middle Eastern states, and a handful of European countries might fit this description.

If substitution is occurring, traffickers in restrictive venues should show increased interest in illicit gunmaking. We may see domestic manifestations even in America. In the United States, manufacturing guns for illicit trade should be less profitable on a per-unit basis. However, the legality of personal gunmaking, availability of gunmaking tools and information, and the ease of acquiring components could make trafficking to restrictive U.S. enclaves worthwhile. In that case, we should expect to see proportionally more trafficking of DIY products to (or within) restrictive U.S. jurisdictions like California, Hawaii, Massachusetts, New Jersey, or New York, and attempts to profit from cross-border smuggling by traffickers located in good staging areas.

The well-resourced opportunism of Mexican drug trafficking organizations is another complicating factor. These organizations enjoy a diversity of illicit weapon sources, acquiring firearms (and military weapons) through contacts in numerous countries, theft and straw purchasing networks in the United States, and diversion of state-owned weapons. Numerous anecdotal reports suggest that they've increasingly trafficked

80 percent components across the border and engaged in CNC fabrication within Mexico itself. This is not surprising. Mexico's gun laws are restrictive yet ineffectively enforced, and escalations in drug-related violence likely increased weapon demand in recent years, incentivizing broader procurement.

Popular discussion sometimes refers to a 2009 Government Accountability Office report implying most (even up to 90 percent) of seized Mexican cartel weapons were sourced from the United States. However, intelligence firm Stratfor's analysts found the "90 percent" soundbyte to rely on selective exclusion of many seized weapons that were unlikely to originate in the United States. Stratfor concluded that "almost 90% of the guns seized in Mexico in 2008 were *not* traced back to the United States" (Stratfor 2011). The extent to which Mexican traffickers rely on American weapons versus other channels, or on DIY versus conventional procurement, isn't fully established. Consequently, the degree to which a clampdown on DIY alone would disrupt their operations without serious enforcement against a broader array of longstanding trafficking options, remains in question. Nevertheless, an opportunistic embrace of DIY as a supplement to preexisting channels would reflect the adaptive logic of these ruthless organizations.

There are numerous anecdotal indicators that terrorists and traffickers would substitute with homemade weapons under certain conditions. Future research must measure the effect's intensity in response to various tactical, sociocultural, economic, regulatory, and enforcement factors. The idea that traffickers would substitute with DIY guns wherever illicit firearms are costly is intuitive enough to sound obvious. Most respondents and much of the academic literature on craft guns basically endorse the concept that DIY would be embraced as a substitute for illicit commercial guns.

However, while practically everyone endorses some market logic behind substitution, it may not reflect a straightforward rational-choice framework (see Table 4.4). Illicit consumers may gravitate to DIY in response to scarcity, but illicit weapons procurement may also depend on other socioeconomic, cultural, or political variables that don't reflect pure supply and demand. For example, most respondents assumed that DIY guns would play a comparatively minor role in American crime, owing to America's large commercial gun supply. This reflects an assumption that the ease of acquiring illicit guns would suppress criminal demand for DIY. However, some respondents believed that America's less-restrictive environment would result in a *greater* role for illegal DIY simply because

Table 4.4 Selected Respondent Comments: "Do You Think There Would Be a Plausible Connection between the Availability of Commercial Firearms and the Amount of Illegal DIY Activity?"

Greg Moser, State Counterterrorism Coordinator (Ret.)	"Stricter regulations would lead to a popularization of DIY."
Harry L. Wilson, Political Scientist (United States)	"I'd agree with that 100%, that there's no necessity for illegal DIY in the US. Other things are available. And if we're talking about mass shootings, we're talking about some sort of semi-auto, typically. I say regardless of what laws we enact, those types of weapons will be readily available for another century."
Robert Spitzer, Political Scientist (United States)	"There's a logic [to substitution], I'd certainly agree it's true. It's important to see if there's DIY activity in France, Australia, etc. . . my guess is there's very little. Here, there's little market pressure to turn to ghost guns unless you're a convicted felon and you want a gun."
Steven Liebel, Director of University Homeland Security Center (United States)	"That's probable. Tighter restrictions would lead to more DIY activities. Not necessarily criminal or violent, but as a backlash to restrictions."
City Chief of Police (Mid-sized City, State of Missouri) (United States)	"A decrease in factory made weapons, or significantly increased regulation could have that impact."
	"If they went back to the old Assault Weapon Ban from the '90s, I think that would probably inspire more DIY."
Montella Smith, Director of University Forensic Science Program/Violent Crimes Detective (Ret.) (United States)	"Depends on the quality and quantity. If DIY firearms were as high quality as industry-made firearms, they could be appealing. But if it's still easy to do straw purchases, that stays competitive."
Joseph Schafer, Director of University Criminology Program (United States)	"Increased regulations on industry weapons might increase demand for craft weapons."
	"With 300 million guns in the US, it will take a long time before DIY guns supersede the appeal of existing guns."

N.R. Jenzen-Jones, International Arms Researcher/Consultant (United Kingdom)	"There's a strong argument that a reduction in conventionally-produced firearms would result in increased demand for other firearms. However, demand for different products is distinct. It doesn't mean they [illicit actors] would necessarily have a reduced appetite for conventional weapons as well."
NSW Criminal Intelligence Analyst (Australia)	"We're looking at a supply and demand situation." "It's just not huge yet because there are still weapons on the illicit market."
Nick O'Brien, Professor University Institute for Policing and Security/Int'l Counterterrorism Liaison Officer, New Scotland Yard Special Branch (Ret.) (Australia)	"I think in Australia it comes back to, that firearms aren't particularly accessible. Getting hold of pistols, you need to be in the know, have access to high-level criminality. And that's probably what will make homemade weapons attractive."
Lecturer, National Security College/Strategic Intelligence Analyst (Ret.) (Australia)	"In Australia, since there's no market, legal or illegal, or at least a very niche market, I suspect DIY won't make much difference." "The market in America, you can talk about a higher magnitude there."
Levi West, Director Terrorism Studies at University Institute for Policing and Security (Australia)	"I think so, at least in the Australian context." "But my understanding is that the maker community here is nascent at best."
Mathew Leighton-Daly, NSW Police Officer (Ret.)/Prosecutor (Australia)	"I think yeah, because it's so heavily regulated. If people need weapons, they're forced to improvise more than they would otherwise."

American criminals like guns, and because it's convenient to make them in America. This view assumes that criminal DIY would reflect cultural factors even if illicit pricing already reflects an oversupply.

The full balance of variables is difficult to pin down and must become an objective for future research. Even the *appearance* of DIY guns could impact their appeal. Hunters, poachers, terrorists, or assassins should prioritize utility over appearance. However, intimidation is relevant for hostage takings, robberies, and self-defense. Yet, many DIY designs are clumsy, or might not be immediately recognized as a gun. In reviewing the "Shuty," journalist Scott Grunewald (2015) wrote "it looks like a brick, and isn't going to be comfortably or surreptitiously tucked into any waistbands without looking like an idiot." Some DIY designs are nonergonomic, ungainly, or just silly looking.

Ultimately, substitution in response to supply-demand pressures would provide a plausible explanation for the continued role of craft guns in the Global South, and for the embrace of illegal gunmaking in parts of the Global North. A few things are apparent. Criminals and terrorists will continue to desire firearms. They are making and trafficking guns around the world. They exploit less-restricted channels, but also traffic in spite of restrictions (and often in exploitation of them). As clandestine production improves, traffickers may scale toward increasingly capable products that are less-accessible through established channels. The strongest incentives should be in jurisdictions with restrictive gun controls, comparative scarcity in illicit guns, and persistent weapon demand, or in areas from which it's easy to smuggle to higher-priced or high-demand markets. Time will tell whether illicit DIY becomes a serious supplement to conventional trafficking. Yet, if the substitution effect takes hold, disruptions may be greatest in jurisdictions that take restrictive gun control for granted.

CHAPTER FIVE

Scanning Darkly: How Weapons Screening Can Detect Ghost Guns (But Fail to Stop Terrorists)

> Does a passive infrared scanner like they used to use or a cube-type holo-scanner like they use these days, the latest thing, see into me—into us—clearly or darkly?
> —Philip K. Dick, "A Scanner Darkly" (2011, 192)

Much of the DIY controversy reflects concern that nontraditional materials will prove undetectable in security screening. This worry dates back to the adoption of polymers in the 1980s, but has been renewed by media reportage on printable guns. It's true that printable plastics, Kevlar, carbon fiber, and other synthetics are undetectable by metal detectors. However, we are not facing the defeat of all weapons screening as we know it.

Some concerns are premature insofar as virtually all ammunition is metal-cased, and all commercial guns contain metal. The 1988 UFA requires all firearms to contain 3.7oz of steel or detectable equivalent, and they must generate identifiable X-ray images. Other countries have similar requirements. Metal screening devices can be calibrated to detect smaller volumes of steel. The vast majority of firearms, metal magazines, and plastic magazines containing metal springs and metal-cased rounds can be detected, hence the need to divest metal objects smaller than guns at airport checkpoints. Lower-detection thresholds delay throughput, increase false alerts, and are not needed to detect most firearms. However, low-detection thresholds are necessary to detect small blades and individual rounds. Fully synthetic ammunition doesn't exist yet. Printable weapons typically require some metal parts, though some parts may be small enough to pass through metal screening.

It has long been possible to use molded resins to build synthetic firearms. However, this is difficult, exceptionally rare, and the products are mediocre at best. American makers comply with the UFA by adding metal inserts to plastic designs. Adversaries might omit the inserts, but this threat may not greatly outstrip the risks posed by other tricks that criminals employ to defeat screening. Synthetic weapons legitimately concern some security professionals. I interviewed several law enforcers and private security professionals with experience in security screening and VIP protection. Respondents were split as to the wider impacts of printable plastic guns, but all agreed that circumvention of security screening poses greater concern than other criminal applications.

The threat has been exaggerated, but it's understandable why plastic guns invite concern. However, some respondents observed that metal pen guns and crypto-guns had already been of interest to security screeners decades before printable guns. Unlike the "undetectable" Glock, crypto-guns are not a myth. Police around the world have encountered guns disguised as pens, flashlights, phones, canes, hammers, and other nondescript objects. A pair of American deputies recounted a decades-old encounter where a defendant smuggled a pen gun through screening and tried to use it in a courtroom—an incident they described laconically as "an interesting day in court" (Interview 2015).

It's possible to smuggle small quantities of ammunition, a compact magazine, or even a compact firearm through security screening within the body or disassembled and artfully concealed. These techniques are used to smuggle contraband into prisons and onto airplanes. Some prisons employ body cavity scanners, but great outcry (and surely, lawsuits) would accompany such measures in civilian spaces. New technologies might change the game by providing widespread, accurate, flexible, and noninvasive open screening. This public-safety paradigm might be reminiscent of dystopian science fiction, but does promise to detect contraband in public spaces. Some body scanning technologies already detect synthetic weapons. Millimeter-wave and backscatter x-ray scanners are deployed to detect bombs, guns, and blades. Unlike metal screening, these advanced imaging technologies (AITs) produce imagery of body surfaces and objects underneath clothing.

Some AITs are *active*: they beam energy at subjects to measure differentials in reflected energy. Others are *passive*: they measure differentials in signatures naturally emanating or reflecting from the body. Passive scanners might be applied to pedestrians on the move, reducing invasiveness and the need for screening lines. Since they can be deployed in open spaces against moving subjects, they are well suited to busy venues.

Because they detect by shape as well as material, AITs can detect synthetic items. Threat recognition software can be calibrated to discern objects smaller than a firearm (and can discriminate between some materials), thereby detecting other types of contraband like drugs, smuggled food or alcohol, or shoplifted items.

Scanners might be mounted to police vehicles or deployed in high-risk areas, enabling dragnet scans of pedestrians, or identification of armed subjects for police contact. Indeed, it has become a security industry holy grail to invent AITs that can reliably detect contraband on groups of moving people rather than relying on subjects to cooperatively queue up and pass through a screening booth. Security companies like Knightscope market sentry robots resembling R2D2: they're equipped with high-definition cameras and can perform thermal detection, license plate recognition, facial recognition, and other whizbang surveillance functions. Knightscope is among a small club of companies trying to mount passive weapon scanners on security-bots.

The technologies are improving. However, even the best AITs involve exploitable limitations. In 2012, libertarian lawyer, security researcher, and "professional troublemaker" Jonathan Corbett (2012) claimed to discover vulnerabilities in Transportation Security Administration (TSA) backscatter devices. In 2014, security researchers (Mowery et al. 2014) tested a similar scanner and found numerous circumvention techniques. They concluded that "while the device performs well against naïve adversaries, fundamental limitations of backscatter imaging allow more clever attackers to defeat it" (370) and that "the system, while well engineered, appears not to have been designed, documented, or deployed with adaptive attack in mind" (379).

State-of-the-industry scanners like Thruvision's TAC devices are increasingly purchased by public transport agencies. In 2018, the Los Angeles County Metro system purchased several for $100,000 each. The TSA facilitated deployments in the San Francisco, New Jersey, New York City, and Washington, DC, transit systems. I contacted a leading AIT manufacturer[1] in hopes of learning more about their high-tech devices. Staff politely welcomed my inquiry until I sent them detailed questions about the limitations of passive screening, at which point they said they were actually quite busy and referred me to their online product sheets. AITs are promising, but their publicly available technical parameters and the practical limitations to their deployments thus far suggest that they are not yet the silver bullet their purchasers desire.

For example, the TAC product sheet lists a number of outstanding capabilities, including detection of "metal, plastic, ceramic, gel, liquid, powder, and paper—hidden in peoples' clothing at distances of 3 to 10 meters." However, the product's recommended environment is limited to an "indoors, dry and preferably air-conditioned location," with "Max 85% RH [relative humidity], non-condensing," and "ambient air temperature less than 28C/82F." It can reliably detect objects as small as 2 × 2 inches on a stationary subject at 15 feet and objects larger than 14 × 10 inches on a walking person at 24 feet. Illustrations depict deployments at entryways and turnstiles, overseen by uniformed guards and police officers with K-9s (Thruvision 2018).

AIT capabilities have been shrouded in secrecy. Manufacturers rarely disclose their full range of capabilities (or vulnerabilities) to the public, and security agencies redact technical information that an adversary might exploit. This is wise, yet the researchers who hacked an AIT in 2014 stated "the secrecy surrounding AITs has sharply limited the ability of policy-makers, experts, and the general public to assess the government's safety and security claims" (Mowery et al. 2014, 381–82). Worse, it's difficult to maintain perfect secrecy. By procuring security screening technologies and probing underlying network infrastructures and applications, security researchers have identified numerous vulnerabilities. Threat intelligence researcher Billy Rios (2015), among others, discovered vulnerabilities in access control devices and threat-screening applications that could theoretically enable a hacker or insider threat to infiltrate secured areas, or alter software so contraband passes undetected. Informed by white hat security researchers, the Department of Homeland Security has mitigated many vulnerabilities. It would be more ominous if a hostile adversary engaged in security research. When the DHS prohibited carry-on electronics on flights from 10 countries, rumors swirled that Islamic State terrorists stole a screening machine to improve their bomb concealment.

For all its faults, secrecy in security screening is a rational approach for maintaining uncertainty about screening capabilities as a deterrent. As a result, however, much criticism of the technology consequently remains speculative. Most AITs can't see into the body, and some only detect objects silhouetted against the body. AITs detect small objects under controlled conditions, but lose accuracy at greater distance or against moving targets. It may be possible to conceal contraband on a side of the body that will not be scanned, or in body cavities. Compact weapons may defeat some scanners at sufficient speed or distance in open spaces. If an attacker's arms (or breasts, abdomen, posterior, genitals, or other anatomical structures) are large enough, contraband might be concealed behind flesh.

These risks are reduced with multiple scanning positions at narrow chokepoints, but this costs more and slows throughput. Hypothetically, even 360-degree scanning might be defeated by certain tactics. Some materials can distort contraband signatures. By shaping materials, it may be possible to spoof some software into misidentifying contraband. Passive scanners don't penetrate limbs, so detection against serious adversaries would require subjects to raise their arms as they're screened in open areas, yet this slows throughput and undermines the benefit of *open* screening. An attacker might be obscured by an innocent crowd or unarmed accomplices. Some of these exploits are impossible in the controlled environment of a screening booth, but scanning in open environments may prove more vulnerable to these tricks.

The most formidable all-plastic guns currently appear to be limited to small-caliber revolvers. Printable plastic guns can be smuggled through metal screening, as Israeli journalists proved in 2013 (Haaretz 2013). If ammunition can be smuggled, an attacker could plausibly pursue limited applications like an assassination. However, current all-plastic weapons are unconducive to a multicasualty attack. AITs are also increasingly capable of detecting weapon-shaped synthetics. As the focus of weapons screening shifts from materials detection to object recognition, circumvention methods may migrate toward innocuously shaped crypto-guns, or concealment methods that obscure a weapon's shape from the scanner's threat recognition software.

Some software replaces imagery of genitals with opaque boxes. This protects privacy, but also ensures that the human operator won't be able to identify contraband if the software doesn't. In airport settings, shoes, electronics, and small items are divested and examined with penetrating X-rays. However, divesting footwear and small items would undermine the speed and noninvasiveness of open screening, while voids in footwear or other nonsilhouetted accessories are difficult to scan on a moving target. Other technologies detect chemical signatures. K-9s and chemical detection machines sniff the air around a subject for floating molecules of explosives, propellants, or chemical taggants added by commercial explosive manufacturers. These techniques can identify ammunition, but screening must be undertaken in a controlled booth. Requiring taggants in 3D-printer filaments would fail as a security measure. Consumer-grade printers use common plastics and DIYers can recycle household plastics to create filament. Malicious users could recycle plastics that don't contain the taggants, while machines calibrated to detect *all* printable plastics would constantly raise false alarms.

Indeed, in a nation of a hundred million gun owners, widespread weapons screening could produce many false alarms. Likewise, in a country with nearly 20 million citizens and almost a million off-duty officers licensed to carry concealed, many violations are unintentional. Most shootings involve handguns, but licensed carriers also tote them. Some venues configure their AITs to alert for bombs and long guns, but exclude handguns. Where carrying firearms is legal, widespread passive screening in bustling areas will entail false alarms and unnecessary lockdowns. To reduce false alarms, scanning can be throttled so only larger weapons produce alerts, but this undermines their value in addressing more common handgun incidents.

It may become possible to screen for unauthorized weapons while permitting legal ones. Licensees might carry tokens with screening signatures indicating a legal weapon. However, the tokens would be attractive for criminals to steal, counterfeit, or hack. In a nation of guns, detecting all possible weapons in public is difficult and expensive. If detection is granular, the costs of false alarms and unnecessary lockdowns must be considered. If detection is throttled to minimize false alarms, real attackers may exploit the gaps. Even high-security facilities struggle to control contraband. American jails and prisons use invasive screening methods, yet weapons, drugs, and cellphones are smuggled (sometimes by staff or other insiders, another vulnerability of security screening). The most sophisticated screening that most citizens experience is at airports, yet audits find TSA's weapon detection rates are around 20 percent (Kerley and Cook 2017). This sounds bad, but it reflects major improvements. In earlier audits, TSA screening failed up to 95 percent of the time (Costello and Johnson 2015).

Eventually, AITs will be more accurate, portable, reliable, and affordable. Will this solve the problems of terrorism, active shootings, and illegal carrying? The answers are not convenient for weapons screening as a panacea for mass violence. The Department of Homeland Security's (2016) commercial facilities *Patron Screening Best Practices Guide* contains rather vague procedures when weapons are discovered. Civilian screeners (who are usually unarmed, lack arrest authorities, and receive little training in disarms or physical control techniques) are instructed to stay calm and polite, observe the subject, not raise concerns with patrons, call a supervisor and/or the nearest police officer, and, if police are unavailable, "escort" the violator to a controlled location until police arrive (29–31). While these procedures keep lines moving sans lawsuits, they provide no effective guidance for unarmed response to an armed adversary.

The difficulty of unarmed response is problematic. In gun-heavy countries like the United States, most violations are unintentional. These low-risk violators are usually cooperative. But what if they aren't? Now, the unarmed screener's tedious job becomes a deadly force encounter. This is the contradiction posed by weapons screening: most violators are cooperative because they don't intend violence, and naïve because they don't artfully conceal their weapons. Low-risk subjects are more likely to be detected, and rarely require armed response. However, if an authentic adversary attacks the screener or rushes the venue, armed response becomes a mandatory countermeasure.

Security screening is often employed as a visible effort to harden soft targets. Yet, for a determined attacker, facilities equipped with unarmed and poorly trained screeners don't become hard targets, they become soft targets with security theatrics at the door. As security expert Mary Lynn Garcia (2013) writes, "security guards are not an effective delay unless they are located in protected positions and are equipped as well as the adversary (i.e. armed adversary and unarmed guards)" (27). Ruthless adversaries can access victims irrespective of screening. Criminologists James Alan Fox and Emma Fridel (2018) identified at least three U.S. school shootings that bypassed weapons screening. In one case, the screener was the first to be shot. In other cases, adversaries targeted victims outside the secured enclave: attacking students on the playground and pulling a fire alarm to attack victims as they evacuated. In a 2017 attack on the Resorts World Casino in Manila, Philippines, the gunman simply walked past the metal detector as an unarmed guard fled. The gunman then started structure fires that killed 36 guests. At a 2019 festival in Gilroy, California, an active shooter bypassed screening by cutting a perimeter fence.

Rather than sneaking weapons into his target venue, the 2016 Orlando Pulse nightclub shooter initiated a shootout with the door screener, an off-duty cop. Tenacious but outgunned, the doorman returned fire but was driven back. The shooter subsequently entered the club and killed dozens. Minutes later, responding officers joined the doorman in driving the shooter to barricade himself in a bathroom. Nevertheless, counterforce saved lives: most victims were killed during the opening ambush, not after the attacker barricaded himself. In 2017, a mentally ill veteran murdered five at the baggage claim in Fort Lauderdale-Hollywood International Airport. Some were shocked that this could happen in the securitized environment of a U.S. airport. Yet, at most airports the check-in desks, baggage claims, and crowds of travelers waiting to undergo screening are located outside the screening area. Numerous airport attacks have occurred outside the secured enclaves. As of this writing, the attacker in America's deadliest modern active shooting, the 2017 Las Vegas Mandalay Bay attack, defeated weapons screening by firing at throngs of concertgoers from an elevated position hundreds of yards beyond the event's security perimeter.

The willingness of adversaries to circumvent or simply blitz through weapons screening has been a source of security industry discussion. After the 2013 Westgate Shopping Mall shooting by al-Shabaab terrorists in Nairobi, former Interpol Secretary General Ronald Noble generated minor controversy when he stated that "societies have to think about how they're going to approach the problem. One is to say we want an armed citizenry; you can see the reason for that. Another is to say the enclaves are so secure that in order to get into the soft target you're going to have to pass through extraordinary security" (Margolin 2013). Problematically, it's difficult for busy venues to maintain the extraordinary security that would keep determined attackers outside the gate. For better or worse, effective response to active attackers still frequently requires the controversial *good guy with a gun*. Six years after the Westgate Shopping Mall attack, al-Shabaab proved Noble's point. Nairobi's upscale DusitD2 hotel contained state-of-the-art security: visitors passed through two checkpoints and an airport-style scanner. Undeterred, in 2019, the terrorists forced their way into the compound with guns and grenades blazing.

Weapons screening is ultimately a supply-side tactic: it attempts to control the supply of weapons entering a secure enclave so only authorized persons will have them. This approach is undeniably appropriate for some venues. However, *effective* screening at a widening scope of locations would translate to costs and legal liabilities many venues can't afford. Worse, the security payoff is not guaranteed. Serious attackers can circumvent screening with tactical adjustments. Unless screening is deployed at all possible entries to all possible target venues, indiscriminate attackers can bypass hard targets and select a limitless number of softer ones.

Even if many venues adopt state-of-the-art weapons screening, some can't afford it or won't desire it. The possibility that AITs would be used to detect other forms of contraband (such as drugs, alcohol, food, electronics, or other nonweapons), or that AITs would collect marketable data by logging noncontraband, suggests privacy questions. Unarmed screeners may deter casual weapon carrying by low-risk subjects, but effective screening against serious adversaries must be performed by well-trained unarmed guards with ballistic protection, or overseen by armed personnel. Consequently, much of the screening employed in public venues is little more than a speed bump for serious attackers. The good news is that most ghost guns can be detected. The bad news is that terrorists and active shooters don't care.

Note

1. Which shall go unnamed for legal reasons.

CHAPTER SIX

Land of the Gun: Politics and Practicalities of DIY Firearms in America

I would say the biggest tool in ATF's arsenal is the traceability of firearms and production records, and you have none of that for DIY.
—Max Kingery, Chief of BATFE Firearms Criminal Technology Branch (Interview 2016)

We're in a country of 300 million guns, and you can buy all the guns you want. How do you influence that market?
—William Vizzard, criminology professor/BATFE program manager (Ret.) (Interview 2016)

America's gun discourse has a tribal vocabulary. Gun rights advocates are simplistically termed "progun" and pejoratively "gun nuts," "ammosexuals," and "gunsplainers." Gun control advocates are simplistically termed "antigun" and pejoratively "gun grabbers." Advocates routinely call their opposition "extremist." To gun control advocates, a 10+ or 15+ round magazine is "high capacity," while gun rights advocates call them "standard," and 30+ round magazines are "extended." Gun control advocates and federal legislation call noise mufflers "silencers." Gun rights advocates call them "suppressors" since they don't actually silence guns as portrayed in movies.

"Assault rifle" is a military term for intermediate-caliber rifles capable of fully automatic fire. Gun control advocates popularized the term "assault weapon" to reference semiautomatic civilian variants with military appearance. Industry and gun rights advocates soften the violent connotation by referring to these firearms as modern sporting rifles (MSRs).

Even the underlying concepts of gun rights, safety, and control are politicized. Softening the nanny state connotation of *control*, some gun control advocacy groups have rebranded themselves as *gun safety* organizations. The NRA retorts that it is America's primary firearm safety training organization, and counterweights its polarizing right-wing rhetoric by branding itself "America's oldest civil rights organization."

The scale of U.S. gun ownership is so great that even many Americans fail to contextualize it. Commentators occasionally suggest Australia's restrictive framework as a policy model, but there are massive differences in scale. Assuming a mid-range estimate of 357 million guns, America has 30 million more guns than people. Enough American guns are stolen to replace Australia's entire stock every 6–13 years. America could send a gun to *every* Australian, and *every* American could still have a gun.

America's per-capita gun ownership is highest in the world. At least 30 percent of adults own at least one gun, and about 40 percent live in households with guns (Parker et al. 2017). This translates to nearly 100 million gun owners, and up to 138 million adults with household access. More Americans have guns in the house than the populations of England, Scotland, Ireland, Australia, Canada, and New Zealand combined. In America, armed citizens outnumber police and military personnel by 33:1. Armed Americans outnumber the world's ten largest militaries combined. Approximately 7.3 percent of Americans (or more than 18.6 million citizens) are licensed to carry firearms, and even more carry in jurisdictions that don't require licensing (Lott 2018). This is larger than the percentage of Australians (6 percent) licensed to *possess* guns at all. There are four times as many adult gun owners in America as *people* in Australia, and Americans with carry permits translate to three-fourths of Australia's population. For better and worse, America is the *land of the gun*.

While many countries have legal gun cultures, the sociopolitical significance of gun culture is arguably greatest in the United States. America's gun culture grew from a mythologized frontier environment, and includes a deep symbology of independence. The first battle of the American Revolution was fought over gunpowder stores that British forces intended to seize. In America (particularly in "red" jurisdictions), one will note the revolutionary-era's Gadsden flag, with its rattlesnake coiled in warning above the slogan *Don't Tread on Me*. Among Second Amendment supporters, one periodically sees the slogan *molon labe*. According to Plutarch, when Spartan king Leonidas and his 300 hoplites faced a superior Persian force, Leonidas replied to the demand that they lay down their arms with a defiant challenge: *molon labe*, or "come and take them." More than 2,000 years later, Texian forces displayed a flag with the slogan "Come and take it" at the Battle of Gonzales. This opening skirmish of the

Texas Revolution was itself fought over the confiscation of a cannon. Some Americans continue to display the slogan (or a Spartan helmet) proudly.

The firearms industry employs more North Americans than General Motors. America's firearm sector includes dozens of major manufacturers, hundreds of specialty producers, and over 100,000 Federal Firearm Licensees (FFLs) authorized to collect, import, export, and sell firearms. Licensed makers produced 8.3 million firearms in 2017 alone (U.S. Department of Justice BATFE 2017). Most of these guns stay in the domestic market, but U.S. producers also serve a global civilian, police, and military market. America is the world's largest exporter of military arms, shipping about 50 percent of all weapons and equipment. For its part, Australia was the world's sixth largest military arms importer as of 2015, with 68 percent of this stock arriving from the United States (Safi and Evershed 2015).

In America, legal gun owners and gun rights advocates are strong lobbying forces. The NRA claims up to 6 million members, while the hardline Gun Owners of America claims 2 million members (with probable membership overlap between them). The American Civil Liberties Union (ACLU) claims 4 million members; it doesn't prioritize gun rights but occasionally challenges gun laws that infringe other rights. The National Shooting Sports Foundation (NSSF) lobbies for industry, and many smaller organizations populate the gun rights space. Likewise, America has numerous gun control advocacy groups, including the Brady Campaign, Everytown for Gun Safety, Giffords Law Center, and many state and local organizations. Many of these have grown in membership and fundraising within the last decade.

In countries with small gun-owning populations, one outrageous shooting or temporary uptick in gun crime can produce political consensus for restrictions despite the protests of legal gun owners. In America, constitutional protections, cultural symbology, a mainstream gun culture, large industry, and strong gun rights advocacy combine to make gun politics work differently. America's unique gun politics is often attributed to the Second Amendment. The Second Amendment does set legal boundaries and political expectations regarding types of controls that can be implemented, but courts have nevertheless ruled that it permits many controls. Much grassroots support for gun rights might be attributed to familiarity. According to a 2017 poll by Pew Research, 48 percent of Americans were raised with guns, 59 percent have friends who own them, and 72 percent have used guns (including a majority of adults who don't own them) (Parker et al. 2017).

The United States is not unique in permitting defensive firearms, but self-defense broadens user bases and renders firearm access a strongly valued right. As Jennifer Carlson (2018) writes in her study of concealed carry, "Against a backdrop of decline, gun carry is both an apology for, and critique of contemporary policing; it is an attempt to recuperate social order while also rejecting the state's monopoly of it" (174). Gun mortality substantially impacts Americans. Pew Research found that up to 44 percent of Americans know someone who's been shot, and 23 percent of Americans or their family members have been threatened with a gun (Parker et al. 2017). Yet, defensive gun use (DGU) is fairly common, and typically requires no shooting. Pew Research also found that 67 percent of gun owners claim protection as their primary reason for ownership (Gramlich and Schaeffer 2019). Estimates range wildly between 55,000 and 80,000 instances of DGU per year, to more than a million per year (Hemenway 1997; Kleck 2018). Even the low estimates have significant sociopolitical implications. Many Americans are negatively impacted by guns, but many can also cite instances when they were glad to have one.

Powerful history and mythology, constitutional protections, a large sporting, hunting, and defensive firearms culture, diverse gun industry, and a sense that firearms are essential to security and personal freedom, combine to make gun rights a sacred value among American proponents. A 2018 *Economist/YouGov* poll found that 79 percent of Americans would not repeal the Second Amendment, and that 74 percent of American gun owners consider the right to own guns "essential for their freedom." Yet, polarization results from differing valuations of gun rights. Another 2017 poll found that gun owners and nongun owners both strongly support other constitutional rights, but only 35 percent of nongun owners agreed that the right to firearms is an essential element of American freedom (Parker et al. 2017).

Researchers are also examining the connections between media coverage and consumer behavior regarding firearms. Some research suggests a disconnect. Communications professor Brian Anse Patrick (2013) found consistent editorializing in favor of gun control had strengthened the NRA and conservative media. Others find that Americans don't unite behind gun control after mass shootings, but instead they deepen their preexisting views (Jang 2019; Yousef 2018). The overall narrative reflects polarization and declining trust in mainstream political, academic, and media institutions. In 1964, 77 percent of Americans trusted government "all or most of the time." This declined to historic lows of 17 percent in 2011 and 2019 (Pew Research Center 2019b). A 2019 poll found that

58 percent of Americans said the media doesn't understand "people like them," but this reflects partisan divides. Among those respondents, 73 percent of Republicans, 63 percent of independents (including majorities of right [80 percent] and left-leaning [51 percent] independents) said the media doesn't understand them, while only 40 percent of Democrats felt misunderstood (Gottfried and Grieco 2019).

It's evident that media coverage encourages politically motivated buying cycles. Harry L. Wilson is Director of the Institute for Policy and Opinion Research at Roanoke College, and author of 2015's *Triumph of the Gun Rights Argument*. Wilson referenced these purchasing runs, saying "if Democrats win the White House and take Congress in 2020, it'll make some gun manufacturers happy" (Interview 2019). Gun rights advocates accuse media of sensationalizing comparatively rare mass shootings. Gun control advocates reply that this focus is appropriate given the costs they generate, and the routine harms of gun mortality that might be reduced by *any* new policies. Yet, in a country with strong connections to guns, elevated public fear can also strengthen support for gun rights. Gun control advocates see mass shootings as a "fertile policy window" for new restrictions. However, researchers have found that panic-buying in the wake of mass-shootings is motivated more by concern over new restrictions than fear of violence (Porfiri et al. 2019).

America's progun politics are powerful, but they have not remained static. The 2012 Sandy Hook Elementary School shooting initiated a period of sustained coverage and political organizing that reinvigorated gun control advocacy. According to Pew Research, the share of Americans who believe laws should be tightened rose from 52 percent in March 2017, to 57 percent in October 2018, to 60 percent in September 2019 (Schaeffer 2019). The role of mass shootings is evident in this shift. Security professionals know that risk perception rarely maps directly to statistical frequency. FBI statistics indicate a 51 percent decline in violent crime between 1993 and 2018, and the Bureau of Justice Statistics suggests a 71 percent decline, yet decades of polling indicates that majorities of Americans consistently believe crime to be rising (Gramlich and Schaeffer 2019). Mass shootings regularly represent less than 1 percent of gun deaths, and the risks of a student being fatally shot at school have declined 300 percent from the 1990s. Northeastern University criminologist James Alan Fox maintains that neither mass killings nor school shootings have risen significantly enough to indicate an "epidemic" (Callahan 2019). Harvard's David Ropeik observed that the probability of a student being killed by a gun in school on any given day is roughly 1 in 614,000,000, "far lower than almost any other mortality risk a kid faces," and that outsized fear of school shootings bypasses the reality that more American youth are shot *outside* of schools than while attending them (Ropeik 2018).

Nevertheless, a series of outrageous shootings have elevated public fears of random gun violence. Mass media reinforces fear while elevating copycat risk. Criminologist Adam Lankford (2018) estimated mass shooters receive media coverage worth $75 million if purchased. This outstrips public interest in the perpetrators as estimated from online search activity, constituting "free advertising" exceeding the attention available to major celebrities. Jason Silva and Emily Greene-Colozzi (2019) found that media rewards "fame-seeking" mass shooters with disproportionate coverage as compared to mass shooters who don't actively seek publicity.

This web of policy, media, and public backlash leads to increased gun acquisition and retrenchment among gun rights advocates. This outcome might be partially attributed to what academics call *media agenda setting*, and what conservatives call *bias*. A 2016 study found that coverage after mass shootings reduces blame on perpetrators and elevates pressure on lawmakers to adopt new controls, concluding that media "often misrepresented the real picture of gun violence by largely focusing on mass shootings and did not discuss key public health approaches for preventing gun violence" (Jashinsky et al. 2016, 1). This dynamic reflects a capture of the psychologic mechanisms behind risk valuation. Political scientist Jeffrey Friedman (2019) found public endorsement of government intervention to be less dependent on probability, and more dependent on value judgments about victims and the appropriate role of government to intervene.

This explains some dynamics in gun politics. Approximately two in three American gun deaths are suicides, with the majority committed by white Americans and seven-eighths committed by men. Street violence is a consistent tax on disadvantaged African American males: African Americans are six times more likely to be murdered, and eight times more likely to commit murder (Braga and Brunson 2015, 5–6). Yet, political pressures to address routine suicides or gang- and drug-related homicides are dwarfed by the focus on mass shootings. People are less supportive of intervention when risks can be attributed to victim agency. Conversely, indiscriminate shootings have psychosocial impacts akin to terrorism, another risk that receives disproportionate coverage. It's never a victim's "choice" to be randomly bombed or shot at the movie theater. With school shootings, moral outrage and victim inculpability are self-evident. Then again, emphasis on rare-but-shocking events may simply distort perceptions of statistical risk. A 2019 poll revealed that 25 percent of Americans believed mass shootings are the primary form of gun death, 33 believed homicides are the primary form, and only 23 percent understood correctly that most gun deaths are suicides (American Public Media 2019a).

Political developments coincided with an unusual weakening of the NRA, and increased funding and participation among gun control advocacy groups. By the 2018 midterms, gun control groups outspent the NRA for the first time in decades. By 2019, the NRA was roiled by allegations of financial misconduct, leading to reputational damage, resignation of several board members, a campaign to unseat CEO Wayne LaPierre, investigations of the organization's finances, and a falling out with its advertising agency Ackerman-McQueen. Long the dominant force in American gun politics, the NRA has been temporarily weakened during the fertile policy window that opened in the wake of the Dayton and El Paso shootings, which occurred on consecutive days in August 2019, precipitating a sustained call for new regulations.

For decades, the sacred aspect of gun rights has motivated more robust fundraising and political participation by gun rights supporters than gun control supporters. This led many to believe that American gun politics would remain stable. However, this stability had been pushed into flux by high-profile incidents, criticism of the NRA's administration, and more sustained gun control advocacy. I asked Harry Wilson whether his thesis on the stability of American gun politics remained accurate. Citing sustained gun control advocacy after the Stoneman Douglas High School shooting, he replied: "Look, I'm a social scientist, so I'm accustomed to being wrong oftentimes. When I wrote that book, I came from the perspective that Sandy Hook was the worst-case scenario, and that even with the Democrats controlling government and there still wasn't significant movement, then maybe nothing would happen on gun control in America" (Interview 2019).

The recent flurry of gun control proposals and migration of Democratic presidential candidates to more hardline gun control positions, would seem to undermine Wilson's thesis that gun rights advocates have largely, and permanently, succeeded. After consecutive mass shootings in El Paso and Dayton in August 2019, Republican lawmakers and President Trump expressed consideration for new regulations, and Senate Majority Leader Mitch McConnell predicted new legislation would pass in the Fall 2019 congressional session. Yet, subsequent impeachment proceedings interrupted the momentum toward bipartisan compromise. Some form of federal "red flag" legislation is probably forthcoming. However, it's unclear whether more embattled proposals like a renewed assault weapon ban, universal background checks, or assault weapon confiscation can be passed unless the Democratic Party sweeps the executive office and both branches of Congress.

These developments reflect a pendulum swing toward some new controls, but may not indicate a permanent weakening of the NRA or a guarantee of cultural shift toward highly restrictive policies. In the months following Democratic candidate Beto O'Rourke's nationally televised exclamation in a September 2019 debate that "Hell yes, we're going to take your AR-15," NRA fundraising sharply increased, and retail gun purchases in 2019 reached a two-decade record. Polls have reflected increasing support for gun rights across most American demographics from 1994 to 2017 (Parker et al. 2017). Legislative and judicial trends favored gun rights for decades. In the 1960s–1970s, national gun control groups focused on restricting handguns (a more evidence-based objective than the current focus on assault weapons). Some gun control groups pursued full handgun prohibition during this period. However, political support for handgun bans waned, and the Supreme Court's 2008 *Heller* decision made handgun bans unconstitutional. Likewise, gun rights advocates successfully challenged restrictions on concealed carry, which was prohibited (no-issue) or restricted (may-issue) in 41 states in 1986, but as of 2019 it was restricted (may-issue) in only 8 states and prohibited in none.

Since the Stoneman Douglas shooting, younger demographics have gained media attention as a vanguard of reinvigorated gun control advocacy. However, some surveys indicate that millennials are not necessarily more supportive of gun control than prior generations (Parker et al. 2017). Younger Americans appear to support concealed carry permitting and oppose assault weapons bans and magazine capacity limits at slightly higher rates than older demographics, while expressing comparative openness to background checks and registration. If these data indicate a cultural shift, it may be a shift away from policies focused on guns, and toward policies perceived to ensure the responsibility of those who own and carry them. The popularization of concealed carry may have contributed to this attitudinal change. In a country that requires no training or federal licensing for gun ownership, concealed carry permits represent the sole form of mandated training and licensing in most states. The concealed carry movement introduced a generation of Americans to the idea that guns could be beneficial in responsible hands, while popularizing the training and vetting of gun owners in exchange for escalated rights (rather than blanket permission or bans on entire classes of firearm irrespective of the quality of owners).

Unlike policies that restrict broad swaths of legal owners or entire categories of legally purchased guns, red flag laws only remove guns from those suspected of posing a danger. Considerable debate revolves around their due process requirements. Due process concerns are not simply obstructionist: red flag laws authorize confiscation of private property, potentially violent confrontations between citizens and police, and lack of prior notice or legal defense. When red flag proposals substantially erode due process protections, they draw wider concern from civil libertarians. For example, the California ACLU opposed AB61, which proposed to expand the state's preexisting red flag laws with "significant potential for civil rights violations" ("Assembly Floor Analysis 2019). Nevertheless, the ACLU and even the NRA have expressed consideration for red flag laws which meet high due process standards.

Consequently, red flag laws haven't generated the opposition among gun owners that blanket bans and confiscatory policies do. A 2018 poll by Washington Post/ABC News found that 85 percent of U.S. adults supported red flag laws, including 81 percent of conservatives ("Washington Post-ABC News Poll" April 8–11, 2018). One might even interpret red flag legislation as a longer-term benefit for gun rights advocacy. Wilson found that gun rights supporters tend to stay mobilized, whereas gun control advocacy strengthens after major incidents but wanes after passage of new laws or during periods between major shootings. In other words, conservatives and gun rights supporters consistently rank gun rights as a high political priority, while support for gun control tends to reflect cyclical backlash to high-profile shootings while only occasionally achieving the political urgency to be placed above other components of the Democratic Party platform. *New York Times* analysis of voter polling by UCLA and the nonprofit Democracy Fund found that Republican voters ranked "don't ban guns" as their second highest political priority. Additionally, while more than 90 percent of surveyed Republican voters agreed in principal with universal background checks, they ranked the importance of universal background checks below more than 20 other issues. Conversely, the highest gun-related priority among Democratic voters was universal background checks, with more than 95 percent in agreement. However, they ranked the importance of universal background checks fifth below several other major Democratic Party positions (Vavreck, Sides, & Tausanovitch 2019).

In this environment, the most likely scenario is passage of federal red flag laws, with uncertain results for universal background checks, bans, or confiscatory proposals. Yet, if red flag laws work well, support for further controls may wane. As the laws are implemented, gun rights advocates can (and will) focus on cases in which police confiscate guns unnecessarily, and their warnings on the dangers of confiscation will be reinforced if seizures turn violent. A contrary trend in recent years has been the passage of laws against "SWAT-ing," in which troublemakers call in fake tips to fool police into dangerous raids on innocent homes, and generalized calls for reduced police paramilitarization. If gun seizures result in shootings and lawsuits, gun rights advocates may undermine support for red flag laws, working through courts and legislatures to demand stricter due process requirements. Gun rights advocates may then gain political and legal ground over any flaws in red flag legislation, while any merits of the legislation may undercut the urgency of additional controls. Insofar as gun rights advocates continue to prevent universal background checks and national registration, and to thwart (for the time-being) the rhetoric of several Democratic presidential candidates who called for assault weapon bans and confiscations, they will have largely repulsed America's most significant push for gun control in decades.

How do these developments influence ghost guns? Red flag laws don't impact the ability to build guns, though they might be used to seize firearms from dangerous people irrespective of whether the guns are commercial or homemade. Red flag laws would have less influence over the ghost gun issue than the more embattled calls for national registration, universal background checks, and assault weapon bans or confiscations. These wider supply-side proposals have been among the most ambitious objectives of gun control organizations for much longer than red flag laws. Likewise, firearm bans (and data infrastructures that would support them) have always stoked stronger concern among gun rights advocates than targeted measures like red flag laws or enhanced penalties for gun crimes. Indeed, a great deal of gun rights advocacy has been devoted to thwarting these potentially confiscatory data infrastructures, many guns have been purchased in fear of them, and considerable creativity has been exercised to undermine them.

Don't Expect Them to Comply: America's Sociolegal Frameworks for Ghost Guns

I do not expect criminals to comply with this law; I do not expect the underworld to be going around giving their fingerprints and getting permits to carry these weapons, but I want them to be in a position, when I find such a person, to convict him because he has not complied.

—Homer Cummings, U.S. attorney general
(National Firearms Act 1934, 21–22)

Man, gunsmiths have the knowledge to make stuff they're not supposed to, and it's their own integrity alone that prevents those things from happening.

—Tim Staber, U.S. gunsmith (Interview 2015)

Historic law plays a role in modern regulation. 2008's landmark *District of Columbia v. Heller* Supreme Court decision derived in large part from historic interpretation. In *Heller*, the Supreme Court relied on legal-historical interpretation to affirm a Second Amendment right to handguns for self-defense. Gun rights proponents felt vindicated, while gun control advocates critiqued the ruling as historically revisionist.[1] Longstanding regulations are more likely to be ruled constitutional. Since federal legislation didn't clearly regulate guns until the National Firearms Act of 1934 (NFA), older laws may prove relevant as DIY regulations are tested in court. Federal regulation developed under the framework of interstate commerce. The NFA regulated machine guns, suppressors, and other items. None of these items were outright prohibited, but the NFA did authorize de facto registration. The 1968 GCA was the most comprehensive federal gun legislation of the twentieth century. It established a multitiered commercial licensing system, broadened the categories of "prohibited persons," required manufacturers to serialize firearms and retailers to maintain sales records, outlawed serial number defacement, and broadened controls on commerce and interstate transfers. However, fearing a confiscatory infrastructure, gun rights advocates prevented national licensing and registration.

The GCA's focus on commerce is obvious: it defines "manufacturer" as "any person engaged in the manufacture of firearms or ammunition for purposes of sale or distribution." It also exempts unfinished frames and finished secondary components from the definition of "firearm." The GCA doesn't regulate private gunmaking except through prohibition on possession by disqualified persons, and outlawing unlicensed commerce. As the ghost gun debate escalated in the 2010s, gun rights advocates argued that federal law has never prohibited personal gunmaking. Defense Distributed's attorney Josh Blackman summarized this point: "For as long as there's been an ATF, people have had the right to make guns for personal use. I really don't see a need to depart from that principle just because a different medium is being used" (Interview 2015). A strengthening subsector of component retailers have also adopted this argument.

Gun rights advocates appear correct insofar as private gunmaking has never been prohibited. A 2013 BATFE posting clarified the framework, stating: "An individual may generally make a firearm for personal use. However, individuals engaged in the business of manufacturing firearms for sale or distribution must be licensed by ATF" (U.S. BATFE 2013). The NFA does prohibit unlicensed production, transfer, or possession of machine guns and silencers, while the Undetectable Firearm Act of 1988 prohibits undetectable guns. Under the NFA and GCA, firearms fall into two broad regulatory categories.

Title I firearms are typical shotguns, rimfire guns, and center-fire handguns and rifles up to .50 caliber. They may be repeating or semiauto, but not full-auto. Title I guns are widely possessed, purchased at retailers with background checks, and transferred privately with and without background checks depending on state law (and the transferor's interest in compliance). Handguns can't be sold privately across state lines, but may be shipped through licensed dealers where the recipient must pass a background check.

Title II items include machine guns (and conversion kits), silencers, explosive devices, short-barreled shotguns and rifles, firearms larger than .50 caliber, and a variety of items in the catch-all category of "any other weapon (AOW)." Notably, the AOW category includes concealable smoothbores, covering many zip guns. Title II items can't be made or transferred without a background check and registration. Some states further restrict Title II items. Under this framework, Title I items can be made without license provided the guns are not meant for transfer, the maker is not prohibited from possession, and state law doesn't prohibit it. Are gun rights advocates correct when they say that personal gunmaking has *always* been legal?

To explore the question, I reviewed a gun law compendium assembled by Mark Frasetto (2013), Senior Counsel for Second Amendment Litigation at Everytown for Gun Safety. This compilation is a valuable resource: SUNY-Cortland political scientist Robert Spitzer (2015) counted 758 unique laws in the compilation, calling it "by far the most comprehensive" collection of pre-1934 gun laws in the United States (39). To see if it contained regulations on personal gunmaking, I ran keyword searches for the terms "Manufacture/Manufact," "Register/Registration," "Gunsmith," and "License."

The results were interesting, but provided little indication of historic restrictions on personal gunmaking. "Gunsmith" returned one entry prohibiting shooting within the town of Vanceburg, Kentucky, except by "watchmen, gunsmiths, and militiamen in discharge of their duty, or unless in defense of life or property" (Frasetto 2013, 50). "Register" and "Registration" returned two laws: a Louisiana law prohibiting firearms at voter registration, (95) and a 1921 Georgia law prohibiting "any dynamite, nitroglycerin, gun cotton [nitrocellulose], or any high explosive . . . without first having registered"(35).

"License" produced 39 returns. As Spitzer observes, numerous historic laws *did* require licensing. However, none in the compilation assembled by Frasetto appeared to require licensing for production. Numerous licensing laws reflected dispossession of Native Americans, slaves, and black freemen. An 1806 Virginia law required every "free negro or mulatto" to hold a license to possess "any firelock of any kind, any military weapon, or any powder or lead" (81). A detestable 1715 colonial Maryland law prohibited any "negro or other slave" from carrying weapons "without license from their said master;" and authorized citizens to capture armed slaves, bring them to a justice of the peace to be whipped, and personally keep the weapons (82–83). In America, it's difficult to differentiate the public safety underpinnings of historic gun laws from their practical applications as tools of racial supremacism and anti-immigrant sentiment. University of Sunderland (United Kingdom) historian Kevin Yuill (2016) details a long history of American gun laws written to sound race-neutral, but enforced exclusively against African Americans.

Handgun licensing regimes were more clearly envisioned as a public safety measure, but regimes like New York's Sullivan Act of 1911 were also rooted in political and ethnic prejudice. This prejudice was aimed at anarcho-leftist agitators, gangsters, and Italian immigrants. The law's namesake, "Big Tim" Sullivan, was said to support the legislation so police cronies could plant weapons on political opponents (Lankevich 2002). However, not all licensing reflected prejudice. Many "license" laws related to hunting. In fact, Frasetto found so many hunting laws that he omitted some for redundancy. Ultimately, there were 11 postindependence "license" laws regulating manufacture, but all appeared applicable to gunpowder and explosives rather than firearms. The keywords "Manufacture/Manufact" produced 29 hits. Most were not applicable, containing the keyword but only regulating carrying. Altogether, these searches of nearly 800 historic gun laws returned only three that clearly regulated production of *firearms* or *ammunition*.

An 1898 Mississippi law taxed but did not prohibit cartridge manufacture (Frasetto 2013, 83). An 1814 Massachusetts law required firearm barrels to be "marked and stamped" (61). This sounds like modern serialization, but the law referred to *proofmarks*: stamps identifying the proofing house that tested the barrel. Today, most European firearms continue to be stamped with proofmarks. American industry doesn't require third-party proofing, but manufacturers do stamp proofmarks (Fjestad 2013, 2403). Proofmarks can help authenticate guns, but were not intended to trace individual weapons. Modern tracing systems are based on serial numbers universally adopted by commercial manufacturers over 150 years later.

Perhaps the most relevant entry was a 1929 Michigan statute prohibiting manufacture, sale, or possession of "any machine gun or firearm which can be fired more than sixteen (16) times without reloading" (Frasetto 2013, 35). This law banned *production* of certain guns. However, like the Second Amendment, its meaning lies in interpretation. If "any machine gun or firearm" is interpreted conjunctively, then the law prohibited automatic weapons. If interpreted disjunctively, the law would also cover semiautomatics above sixteen-round capacity.

Second Amendment scholars spend years debating linguistic minutia that most people would rather not deal with. However, a court's interpretation of linguistic details can have major policy impacts. Current federal law prohibits unlicensed production of machine guns, but since expiration of the 1994 assault weapon ban, semiautomatic rifles and magazines of any capacity are legal to make. Today, several states regulate assault weapons, but Michigan isn't one of them. Additionally, the Michigan law didn't prohibit *all* personal gunmaking, and it wasn't *longstanding*, being superseded two years later by legislation omitting capacity limits and only prohibiting machine guns (Michigan Penal Code 750.224). This would place the 1929 Michigan law alongside similar state laws that propagated in the early twentieth century in reaction to use of machine guns by robbers and rum runners. This legislative trend culminated in the NFA's nationwide machine gun regulation. Current law allows Michiganders to build semiautomatic rifles of any capacity.

The compilation provides considerable evidence for historic regulation of gunpowder and explosives. This makes sense. Bulk gunpowder posed significant risk before modern firefighting, hazmat procedures, and building code. The danger escalated with the invention of more powerful and volatile nitroglycerin. Different search methods might reveal other relevant laws, or perhaps relevant laws existed but weren't included in the compilation. However, University of Denver law professor and gun rights advocate David Kopel (2016) finds "no example of any law requiring that persons with full civil rights request government permission before obtaining a firearm" prior to the twentieth century (340).

Colonial militia law is an interesting supplement. Historically, militias required able-bodied males to equip themselves with firearms suitable for military service and to bring those arms for inspection to ensure readiness. As Fordham University historian Saul Cornell wrote, "In an era that relied on everyday citizens to provide for community and national defense, the idea of a right to keep and bear arms was a given. To provide the best defense, however, the state also had to ensure that the men were trained and that their equipment was in working order" (Cornell and

DeDino 2004, 487). Nevertheless, the role of a "well regulated" militia in supporting modern controls like individual registration of privately held firearms is not totally clear. Cornell points to a 1775–1776 Massachusetts militia law requiring clerks to record an "exact list of his company, and of each man's equipments, respectively" as implying some level of surveillance over individual militia arms (510). That law did provide for the lending (and subsequent recovery) of government-owned arms to militiamen too poor to equip themselves, but it also required the majority of militiamen to equip themselves privately if they had the means. The law did not appear to provide any mechanism for standardized markings or inventory tracking of privately furnished militia weapons, nor does it seem to imply that the militia law would be used to track privately held firearms not intended for militia service.

The circumstances of these early militia frameworks were fundamentally different than the circumstances of modern-day legal gun ownership in America. Rather than a general restriction on gun ownership, militia service obligated it. With some exceptions, the federal Militia Act of 1792 required "each and every free able-bodied white male citizen" to acquire guns suitable for military service. Most preindustrial militia firearms were personally owned and artisanally produced. Standardized serial number tracking systems were technically difficult to implement and could not be reliably enforced within an industry of small-batch artisanal makers. Mustering and inspection requirements generally extended only to service weapons. However, the same *unorganized militia* framework did support some elements of regulation. Militia members were required to be trained and could be penalized for drunkenness or absenteeism, and their guns were inspected for safety and proper function. However, one might also interpret the militia framework as encouraging gun ownership and independent gunmaking. In contemporary terms, it seems that militiamen were allowed to make or purchase any number of untraceable, unserialized, artisanal ghost guns but then had to reveal their gun ownership to the state in order to meet service obligations. In that sense, the militia framework suggests that there were conditions under which gun ownership would not enjoy perfect privacy from the state, but it is not clear whether the framework supported individualized tracking of all private firearms as some modern registration regimes attempt to do.

Likewise, if personal gunmaking was broadly regulated before 1934, it was difficult to find evidence within one of the most detailed compilations of historic gun laws. The assertion that gunsmithing was rare in early America has been critiqued in detail by Clayton Cramer (2018), who reviewed records showing significant levels of private gunsmithing.

Historian Randolph Roth (2002) estimated gun ownership at 40–50 percent during the early nineteenth century. A historic case thus exists for the right to make and own guns, but there is also precedent for licensing guns or gun owners. Complete prohibition of personal gunmaking would surely face tenacious legal challenges, and might indeed be ruled unconstitutional.

Yet tunnel vision on the constitutionality of gunmaking misses an important point: the primary controversy over ghost guns isn't really about *making* guns. It's about *having* guns the government doesn't track and can't easily confiscate. In recent years, legislators or attorneys general in Oregon, Washington, Connecticut, Washington, DC, Pennsylvania, New York, New Jersey, California, and Maryland have proposed or passed some form of DIY gun regulation. Yet, none (of which this author is aware) have imposed outright bans. Federal proposals have also been made. H.R. 1278 or the Ghost Guns are Guns Act of 2018 would reclassify as firearms "any combination of parts designed or intended for use in converting any device into a firearm and from which a firearm may be readily assembled." This would presumably place build kits under commercial background check requirements, but it would not totally prohibit them. H.R. 7115, or the 3D Firearms Prohibition Act of 2018, potentially goes further. It would prohibit advertising or sale of unfinished frames and receivers and require home gunmakers to undergo a background check and apply for serial numbers for every firearm made (presumably without the benefit of commercially purchased receiver blanks).

Can legislation obligate registration and serialization of homemade guns? Much of the above legislation has resulted in legal challenges, but so far, the answer appears to be *yes*. Historic law provides numerous examples of gun licensing and registration. These have generally been ruled constitutional. As Spitzer argues, "In fact, no gun law had been declared unconstitutional as a violation of the 2nd Amendment until what became the *Heller* case came along" (71). This may be true federally, though in the cases of *Nunn v. Georgia* (1846), *In re Brickey* (1902), and *State v. Rosenthal* (1903), the Supreme Courts of Georgia, Idaho, and Vermont did strike gun regulations under the federal Second Amendment or state-level adoptions of it. Regardless, registration and serialization laws don't prohibit gunmaking, but do allow government to impose tracking requirements on guns whether they are commercially manufactured or homemade. However, Kopel (2016) argues that historic registration was practically exclusive to handguns and unimplemented in most jurisdictions. He describes the legal record permitting *de minimis* handgun registration (360).

Ultimately, precedent probably supports registration of homemade guns, yet most U.S. jurisdictions don't require registration of *any* guns. In fact, a federal registry is prohibited under the 1986 Firearm Owner's Protection Act. Currently, only two states and Washington, DC, have universal registration, two states register handguns, and six register assault weapons. Meanwhile, eight states prohibit registries, and the remaining 33 don't prohibit registries but also haven't passed them. Because most American DIYers are low-risk hobbyists, the vast majority could presumably pass background checks, or register and serialize their homemade guns. Why don't gun rights advocates want them to? The answer lies in the tension between regulations that attempt to track all guns, and deep distrust of any data infrastructure that might be useful for future gun confiscations. In jurisdictions with registries, legislators periodically propose confiscation of legally purchased and registered firearms. Meanwhile, a counterintuitive 1968 Supreme Court decision established that felons can't be punished for failing to register illegal guns, as this would constitute self-incrimination (*Haynes v. United States*, 390 U.S. 85 (1968)).

Modern factions accuse each other of defying common sense. For some gun rights advocates, requiring licensing or registration for private gun-making is akin to requiring a license to own a printing press or copier. After all, the Second Amendment is enshrined in the Bill of Rights alongside robust protections for speech, religion, due process, and freedom from unreasonable search and seizure. Indeed, registration for speech or religion would strike most Americans as a constitutional affront. UCLA law professor and libertarian-leaning blogger Eugene Volokh (2009) attributes some of this tension to the differences between anonymous and nonanonymous rights.

Volokh observes that rights may be deanonymized in some cases, and anonymized in others. Most speakers "don't need to register their speech, or submit their typewriters for testing so that their anonymous works can be tracked back to them" (1546). However, some speech is deanonymized: political campaigners must register, and protests might require permits even as they are constitutionally protected. Citizens have rights to marry, vote, or own cars, but the government requires marriage licensing, voter registration, and driver's licensing and vehicle registration (albeit only to authorize operation on public roadways rather than to own the vehicle itself).

In this view, the question is whether a deanonymizing regime imposes unacceptable burdens on the right. For example, the government can't collect the names of women who receive abortions because that would chill exercise of the right, though the government can require clinics to report anonymized information. Since *Heller* declared self-defense a core Second Amendment right, Volokh frames the question as whether a tracking regime imposes unacceptable burdens on legal self-defense with guns. Many gun rights supporters believe that onerous licensing or registration requirements do undermine the Second Amendment, particularly if they are structured to chill legal activity or facilitate general confiscation (which they vehemently believe to be unconstitutional). Gun control advocates argue that registration is a longstanding and constitutional regulatory method. Besides, even if home gunmaking were prohibited, a huge variety of commercial firearms would remain available from retailers. Ergo, even prohibition of home gunmaking wouldn't overburden the Second Amendment. For example, California's microstamping law requires commercial manufacturers to micro-serialize firearms, a program the manufacturers argue is impossible to implement. This regulation prevents introduction of new handgun models in the State of California, but the Ninth Federal Appellate Court ruled the de facto ban on new handguns didn't overburden gun owners because hundreds of nonmicrostamped models remain available (*Pena v. Lindley*, No. 15-15449 D.C. No.2:09-cv-01185-KJM-CKD (2018)).

Despite application of *strict* scrutiny to many cases involving constitutional rights, American courts typically apply the lower standards of *intermediate scrutiny* or *rational basis review* to Second Amendment cases. These lower standards are more favorable toward regulation. Then again, strict scrutiny doesn't guarantee civil libertarian outcomes: the first Supreme Court case to apply strict scrutiny was 1944's notorious *Korematsu v. United States*, which affirmed federal power to detain citizens without evidence during wartime. The Supreme Court overruled *Korematsu* in 2018's *Trump v. Hawaii*.

Ultimately, personal gunmaking regulation is an approaching battle yet-unfought, though historic law does support regulation on propellants. It's already illegal for "prohibited persons" to buy or possess ammunition. However, according to the Federal Ninth Circuit Court of Appeals, the Second Amendment doesn't permit total prohibition of ammunition (*Jackson v. City of San Francisco*, 746 F.3d 953 [9th Cir. 2014]). This guarantees that commercial ammunition will remain available—and that some will inevitably leak to illicit users irrespective of how tightly it is regulated. Homemade ammunition is rare in American crime, and the availability of commercial ammunition ensures that restrictions on reloading would bring marginal anticrime benefits unless combined with nationwide controls on commercial ammunition. Nationwide ammunition background checks are proposed in the form of H.R.1705/S.1924 and might be ruled constitutional insofar as they stop short of a ban. Yet in America, nationwide ammunition restrictions could prove more politically troublesome than regulating homemade guns in the first place.

Politics, Privacy, and Trust: Disobedience and the Politico-Material Ecosystem

> That's one of the more fortunate things. The truly passionate people are not criminals. They'll never do anything wrong with their guns, but there are people who will.
> —Chief of Detectives, Midwestern City (Interview 2015)

By the logic of Second Amendment absolutism, the second gun I built is *not your business*. It complied with federal, state, and local law. Insofar as it was legal, some gun rights advocates believe I shouldn't need to say more. This illustrates the tension between DIYers who believe firearm acquisition should be kept private absent clear indicators of illegality, and regulation proponents who believe it reasonable for everyone to surrender gun privacy to assist authorities in identifying traffickers and removing guns from risky people. This tension illustrates an oft-ignored aspect of the home gunmaking movement: ultimately, the fight over DIY isn't about guns. It's about *data*.

Lack of paper trail is more a feature than loophole for consumers who fear the confiscatory potential of gun tracking infrastructures. This argument sounds less *fringe* if we consider registration compliance. For decades, New York City's regime has been among the strictest in America. In 1993, there were 58,000 licensed firearms in the Big Apple, yet the Department of Justice estimated around 2 *million* illegal guns in the city (U.S. Department of Justice n.d.). Journalist J.D. Tuccille (2013) recounts that in the 1970s, Illinois passed mandatory handgun registration, with compliance potentially reaching 25 percent, and California's 1990 assault weapon registration reached around 3 percent. After Sandy Hook, Connecticut passed mandatory registration of assault weapons and 10+ round magazines. Two weeks after the registration deadline, compliance may have reached approximately 13 percent for the rifles, and 1.5 percent for magazines (Gordon 2011; McQuaid 2014). New York's SAFE Act of 2013 enacted similar requirements, but rural police agencies were accused of nonenforcement and compliance reached around 4–5 percent (Edelman 2015).

Without credible protections against confiscation, a nontrivial portion of American gun owners will not comply with mandatory registration. Without forced registration at retail (or retention of background check records) it is difficult to hold anyone responsible for not surrendering guns. When New Zealand implemented buybacks of unregistered semi-automatics in the wake of the Christchurch Mosque shootings, for example, Gun Control NZ co-founder Philippa Yasbeck admitted: "These weapons are unlikely to be confiscated by police because they don't know of their existence" (Stoakes 2019).

Pro-gun commentators increasingly frame ghost gunmaking and registry noncompliance as legitimate forms of nonviolent civil resistance. Anyone who participates long enough in American gun culture will hear jokes about boating "accidents," "burglaries," and other alibis to explain the loss of guns their owners *meant* to surrender. Buyback refuseniks might purchase waterproof containers like the MTM "Survivor" Burial Can, which preserves guns and ammunition if their owner decides the safest storage is underground. Ground-penetrating radar can detect underground caches, but techniques unmentioned here can make detection more difficult. DIYers can fashion similar devices from plumbing pipes, as occurred in New South Wales Australia after its Labour Government passed registration and confiscation of semiautomatic rifles in 1988. This legislation reportedly prompted a run on plumbing pipes at hardware stores. This registry was scrapped and many confiscated rifles returned to their owners after election of the new Liberal Government (Kopel 1992, 225).

Gun control supporters sometimes criticize noncompliance sentiments as *insurrectionist*. Yet, a less pleasant strand of insurrectionism orbits the absolutist Second Amendment discourse. These hypotheticals are distasteful to moderates and ignored by confiscation advocates. Some commentators fail to comprehend the difficulties accompanying broad gun confiscation in America. Assuming 350 million guns, if general prohibition resulted in one fatal encounter per 10,000 recovered, this would translate to 35,000 deaths. If limited to America's 17+ million civilian assault weapons/MSRs (not counting a minimum of hundreds of thousands of latent DIY variants), one fatality per 10,000 recoveries translates to 1,700 deaths: more than four times the number of Americans killed by *all* rifles in a typical year.[2]

It's unsettling that this may be an *underestimate* of violence potential. It also doesn't account for police and military nonenforcement,[3] nor billions in enforcement and buyback costs, nor the illicit production and trafficking it could incentivize, nor millions of guns and components that would be purchased before prohibition, nor the possibility of political violence. Gun control supporters occasionally dismiss insurrectionist Second Amendment agitprop, claiming that hotheads armed with small arms, light weapons, and DIY platforms could not resist the United States' high-tech military. Ergo, the insurrectionist justification for gun rights evaporates. Unorganized forces certainly don't last long against the U.S. military in direct force-on-force engagements. Yet, this dismissal is belied by robust Second Amendment support among American military and law enforcers, and by the costs and difficulties of achieving decisive success in several counterinsurgencies since World War II, prosecuted against foreign adversaries who U.S. personnel didn't share cultural frames, constitutional obligations, economic interdependence, or personal connections with.

If 0.1 percent of American gun owners radicalized, the population of solo terrorists and small networks would number around 100,000: about the size of the Taliban and all chapters of al-Qaeda combined. These individuals would be active domestically, difficult to profile, and most would enjoy legal protections as U.S. citizens. Some would have support networks, or would be equipped with ballistic protection, drones, high-tech optics, and other tactically useful consumer technologies. Some would be veterans or experienced in mechanical trades—elevating the possibility of a *gun problem* becoming a *drone, bomb,* and *sabotage* problem. This doesn't account for exploitation of the resulting power vacuum by thousands of armed criminals, some of whom already interface with transnational drug trafficking organizations that smuggle military-grade weapons and engage in narco-terrorism. Policing the drug war already entails substantial risks and social costs, but policing a politicized "gun war" could quickly become unacceptably dangerous and costly. Paramilitarization and retaliatory violence could undermine unified democratic governance. Surveillance and censorship would vastly expand, and the role of media in providing peaceful discursive alternatives might be delegitimized.

In the case of sustained domestic terrorism, securing America's soft targets and vast infrastructures could quickly impose extreme costs. Foreign direct investment would stall. The global balance would be disrupted if U.S. forces were recalled for stabilization. America's authoritarian adversaries would make geopolitical gains, perhaps interfering for their own benefit. The free world would be weakened, while the United States might emerge as a degraded, delegitimized, and less-democratic state even with decisive counterinsurgent victory. In the authentically stupid event of domestic conflict in America, "red" team insurgents may, at unnecessary cost, plausibly force concessions from "blue" team's counterinsurgent metropoles. Minimally, the tactics required to forcefully repress such a movement would transform America to a husk of its virtue, and the social costs of every gun seized would be greater than the costs they generated when legal. The America worth fighting for would no longer exist after fighting over it.

In a more trusting era, these conjectures were beneath the dignity of security analysts. American civil conflict has long been regarded as the province of tin-foil milliners. Yet, as America has devolved to an increasingly polarized and lower-trust society, serious thinkers have broached the subject. In October 2019, 47 percent of Democrats and 45 percent of Republicans described their own party as too extreme, while 76 percent in *both* parties described the *other* party as too extreme. Meanwhile, 75 percent of Democrats and 64 percent of Republicans believed supporters of the other party were "close-minded," while majorities of Republicans characterized Democrats as "unpatriotic (63 percent)" and "immoral (55 percent)." In September 2019, 79 percent of Democrats and 83 percent of Republicans considered themselves "very cold" toward members of the other party (Pew Research Center 2019a). Political scientists Nathan Kalmoe and Lilliana Mason (2019) found 15 percent of Republicans and 20 percent of Democrats agreed the country would improve if opposing partisans "just died." They also found that 9 percent in both parties endorsed political violence as occasionally acceptable, while 18 percent of Democrats and 13 percent of Republicans endorsed partisan violence upon 2020 presidential loss.

When *Foreign Policy* journalist and Senior Councilor for Harvard's *Project on US Civil-Military Relations* Thomas Ricks (2017) surveyed security experts on the likelihood of U.S. civil conflict within 15 years, he claimed an average guess around 35 percent. Writing for *Foreign Policy*, Lt. Col (Ret.) Robert McTague (2017) and former special operator and Foreign Service officer Keith Mines (2017) estimated the chances around 40 percent and 60 percent, respectively. A 2013 Fairleigh Dickinson University poll found 18 percent of Democrats, 27 percent of Independents, and 44 percent of Republicans agreed that "in the next few years, an armed revolution might be necessary in order to protect our liberties" (3). It didn't reinforce America's sense of stability that President Trump shockingly alluded to civil conflict when threatened with impeachment, tweeting in September 2019: "If the Democrats are successful in removing the President from office (which they will never be), it will cause a Civil War like fracture in this nation from which our Country will never heal." Conservative commentators allude to gun confiscation as a flashpoint. Shortly after Democratic presidential candidate Beto O'Rourke's 2019 declaration that he'd confiscate AR-15s, Tucker Carlson warned of "civil war," and Meghan McCain warned of "a lot of violence." *National Review* editor Charles Cooke penned a column titled "Meghan McCain Is Right about

AR-15 Confiscation, and You Know It." One need not believe the most pessimistic assertions to understand that forced disarmament would be to cross America's most dangerous political Rubicon.

Fraternal bloodshed in defense of gun rights (or support of gun control) should strike reasonable readers as madness. Yet, even if remote, the stakes of violent backlash render general confiscation in America so absurd as to boggle the mind that advocates on both sides continue to mobilize supporters by discussing it. Fortunately, American gun owners possess a more ethical and patriotic form of protest. Harvard political scientist Erica Chenoweth (2013) found no sustained nonviolent campaign in the post–World War II era to fail once it gained participation by 3.5 percent of a national population. Under this assumption, if American gun owners truly perceive regulations to be intolerable, they could make their voices heard through nonviolent civil resistance just as they already do through lobbying and electoral politics. If only 12 percent of American gun owners participate in sustained, adaptive, peaceful, and nonsecessionist civil resistance (and if such efforts are not muzzled by the tech sector or spoiled by violent hotheads), they'd likely succeed at any reasonable political goal.

Ultimately, peaceful civil frameworks should be more than sufficient to resolve what is essentially a balance of cultural, constitutional, crime control, and public health issues. America's emergencies are mostly of our own making. Violent crime and student risks of violence have both declined, and domestic terrorism remains a remote risk to most Americans, having declined from its peak activity in the 1970s. The human costs of gun mortality are undeniable, with 30,000–40,000 deaths in typical years. Yet, in callous risk management terms, the problem is not so intractable as to justify the Pandora's Box of political destabilization in a country where 480,000 die from tobacco, 250,000 die from medical errors, 80,000–90,000 die from alcohol, 50,000–70,000 die of drug overdose, and 35,000–40,000 die from car accidents each year. The truth is that life is cheaper in America than in Britain, Australia, or even Canada. A megasociety of 330 million people with greater income inequality than Russia must choose its public policy battles wisely.

Likewise, the prospects of widespread gun confiscation being passed, upheld, implemented, enforced, and effective are so remote that most gun owners might regard it as a joke rather than *casus belli*. Only incrementalist measures can seriously reduce gun ownership in America, and it would take generations of litigation and cultural conflict before these measures could be said to produce unambiguous crime reductions that couldn't have been achieved via less politically toxic methods. Meanwhile, other developments in policing and policy may continue America's long-term crime decline (which concurred with increased firearm sales and loosening of many gun laws), undermining the urgency of supply-side gun regulation as a primary crime control.

Gun control supporters correctly note that courts have upheld many regulations, including registration, licensing, background checks, assault weapon bans, carry restrictions, and transaction controls. That these go unpassed or unimplemented outside of blue state strongholds is less a result of the Second Amendment than of advocacy forces and political cultures that resist these measures in large swaths of the country. As UCLA law professor Adam Winkler observes, 43 state constitutions include rights to firearms. Even a Second Amendment repeal would not eliminate these protections without upholdings of restrictive federal legislation. Some states would then regulate or prohibit unlicensed gunmaking, while others would remain laissez-faire. Even if a restrictive national framework prevailed, some jurisdictions might declare themselves "Second Amendment sanctuaries," leaving enforcement to the under-resourced Feds.

I asked Winkler if this means only national legislation or a Supreme Court ruling could establish uniform policies on homemade guns. He replied, "Yes, and not just on homemade gun issues, but for almost *any* gun issue" (Interview 2019). Ultimately, that describes the strange dynamic of American gun politics. Everyone fears the other side is winning, and everyone can justify their fears given extreme regional policy differences that are rarely clarified by the Supreme Court or Congress. Stricter laws are proposed in blue jurisdictions, while restrictions are repealed in red jurisdictions. The culture wars continue, but the national needle rarely moves to the satisfaction of ideologues on either side. In this zero-sum game, jurisdictions become testing grounds for intemperate proposals. Moderates are marooned, policies are inconsistent, and nobody stays happy for long.

Measuring the Immeasurable: Evidence of Illegal DIY

The days of zip guns are pretty much gone. What we're seeing now, they're [criminals] buying some of the best [commercial] technology available.
—William Presson, security consultant and chief deputy U.S. marshal (ret.) (Interview 2016)

Illegal DIY is not much of an issue, but if it were to be an issue anywhere, it would be an issue in Australia.
—Richard Evans, Australian criminologist (Interview 2016)

There's a gang war in the Bronx. A teenager lays dying in a hallway known as a gang hangout. In the basement, detectives find six homemade guns similar to what killed the victim. Ghost guns are a growing concern in New York, and they're becoming popular among gang members. Policymakers are increasingly concerned. Coincidentally, the murder happened the same day as a conference in Manhattan focused on the ghost gun problem.

The seriousness of the issue is evident from the list of attendees: two state assembly members, a special sessions judge, the King's County assistant district attorney, representatives from the New York State Conservation Council and Associated Sportsmen's Council on Firearms, and the executive director of the NRA himself. The conference recommends a review of applicable laws, and a youth education program on firearm safety. A committee will try to "devise regulations that would eliminate zip guns and indiscriminate use of .22-caliber ammunition without at the same time affecting more responsible users of firearms." This story is extraordinary for two reasons. First, the conference reflected unusual bipartisanship. Second, all of this happened on December 19, 1953 (*New York Times* 1953).

The conference had little effect. Gangs continued building guns. From the 1920s to 1970s, zip guns were periodically blamed for fueling gang violence. Yet, it wasn't new restrictions that suppressed America's twentieth-century zip gun problem. More likely, increased accessibility of illicit commercial handguns deflated the zip gun craze. By the 1970s, zip guns were rare. However, DIY guns and modifications remained a criminal alternative. In 1976, BATFE's Operation CUE (Concentrated Urban Enforcement) found DIY guns and illegal modifications had risen to 17–22 percent of seized firearms in Washington D.C. The report observed this increase in homemade products "to indicate shifts to alternate sources as the enforcement effort is concentrated against the normal concealable handgun by the criminal element" (U.S. Department of Justice BATF 1977). When ATF clamped down on illegal handguns, many offenders substituted with homemade guns or sawed-off shotguns. However, by the 1980s and 1990s, homemade crime guns became a curiosity as offenders gravitated toward commercial pistols. For decades, most police never even saw a homemade gun.

Today, *legal* DIY has unquestionably popularized. Yet, it's impossible to reliably measure it. Scratch-built firearms are virtually untraceable unless encountered by police. Precursors aren't reflected in background checks. In almost all states, sales data for frame blanks and secondary components remains proprietary. One way to estimate *illegal* gunmaking trends would be comparison of police seizures over time. Problematically, this data is loosely standardized and often unreported. The closest analogue is federal eTrace records. However, these may be unrepresentative even for conventional crime guns. Seizure data also suffers an inherent defect: it can't be decoupled from police *action*. If more contraband is seized, does that mean criminals are manufacturing more of it, or does it mean police are putting more effort into finding it? Sometimes, it only indicates improved recordkeeping. How do we compare homemade guns to the overall number of illegal guns in circulation? Fundamentally, we can't.

eTrace introduces another problem: not all traces are for crime guns, and while detectives usually record crime guns in eTrace, they don't always. eTrace may be *less* representative for homemade products. If detectives know that a crime gun is homemade, some may skip recording it in eTrace. Product categories are loosely defined, and it's unclear that detectives would always know how to classify them. If an unserialized AR-15 is seized, would detectives enter it as "rifle," or "receiver?" If a fully automatic receiver is seized, do detectives enter it as "receiver" or "machine gun?" Some categories are catch-alls. One state may report DIY guns in a "receiver" category, while another may report receivers in an umbrella category of "other," which also includes some items that aren't homemade.

Ultimately, the data is inadequate to reliably estimate street-level trends. If the following analysis illustrates anything, it illustrates that agencies must standardize their data collection to reliably interpret "ghost gun" trends. Media and advocacy groups frequently draw wider-ranging conclusions from fragmentary data than knowledgeable police or academics would endorse. BATFE cautions against drawing significant conclusions about crime trends from eTrace. These provisos stated eTrace is the closest approximation to a national dataset on firearm types seized over time. I analyzed eTrace reports to attempt to estimate some loosely plausible trendlines, imperfect as the data and analysis must be. Reviewing all national and state eTrace reports between 2008 and 2018, I counted "receivers" or "any other weapons" since these categories are reasonable proxies for the popularity of homemade products. I also counted "silencers" and "other," since these categories are moderately likely to be homemade. Problematically, some of the items are surely *not* homemade, so I include 20 percent downward adjustments for oversampling. The result is clearly imperfect, but generates a loose proxy for criminal popularity of DIY items.

The data seem to indicate that the proportion of plausibly DIY products increased by around 500 percent over the last decade. However, this increase began from an extremely low baseline, representing only 0.44–0.55 percent of traces even with the possibility of oversampling. If clearly labeled "machine guns" are included, DIY-relevant traces may increase to 0.75–0.94 percent. However, the unadjusted estimate is probably a significant overstatement, as this would assume *all* seized machine guns were DIY, an unlikely scenario.

It's plausible that police have seized substantially more homemade products alongside their wider popularization among legal consumers. Yet, they probably continue to represent a small minority of crime guns. To explore the possibility that criminal DIYers would scale toward restrictive controls on conventional guns, I estimated the percentage of traces occurring in the ten most restrictive states, and the ten states that export the most crime guns to other states (Brady Campaign 2015). These results (see Figures 6.1, 6.2, and 6.3) seem to support the possibility of criminal substitution: DIY-relevant traces were 2.5–3.0 times more numerous in restrictive states, and rose more sharply within those states as well.

Nevertheless, the data collection mysteries of ghost guns currently outwit attempts at reliable analysis. Correlation is not causation, and many variables could distort these estimates or imply different conclusions. Perhaps more restrictive states prioritize DIY gun enforcement, or apply their laws more restrictively on the ground. Generally, restrictive states are more populous, and population or urbanization may play an unaccounted role. To a significant degree, *legitimate* consumers have embraced DIY gunmaking as prophylaxis against prospective bans. Nevertheless, if trace records are rough proxies for criminal interest, this result is consistent with suspicions among police and security professionals that criminals

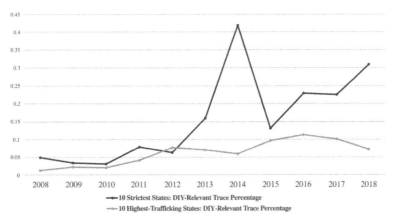

Figure 6.1. DIY-Relevant Traces, United States 2008–2018

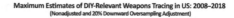

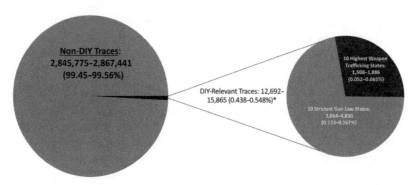

Figure 6.2. Maximum Estimates of DIY-Relevant Traces, United States 2008–2018

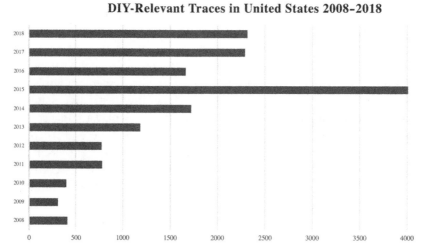

Figure 6.3. Relevant Trace Percentages—"Strict" and "High-Trafficking" States

would substitute illicit "ghost guns" to bypass restrictive commercial regulations.

The most restrictive states tend to embrace supply-side schemes like universal background checks, registries, and assault weapon regulation. The AR-15 is America's most popular DIY build: this firearm was federally banned in the past, most likely to be banned in the future, and is often regulated or banned in restrictive states. Google Trends searches for "80% receiver" between 2004 and 2019 reveal strongest interest in Texas and California. Texas has a large gun culture with little reason to fear state bans, but many Texans might build ARs as prophylaxis against a federal ban. However, search interest was greater in California, where gun rights advocacy is comparatively disempowered and AR-15s are tightly regulated. Additionally, California's gang and organized crime populations may be incentivized toward procurement that bypasses the state's restrictive laws.

Police in California claim significant increases in gunmaking by gangs and cartel associates. Indeed, in 2019 ATF claimed that 30 percent of guns seized in California were unserialized, an unusually high proportion (Stephens 2019). While some are surely defaced commercial firearms (a technique that can render commercial guns as untraceable as homemade guns), clearly some portion of the seizures are DIY builds. In America (and most countries), crime guns are disproportionately handguns; 80 percent Glocks are probably the most popular DIY handgun. Searches for "80% Glock" might better indicate criminal interest (and to some degree, interest among civilians who wish to avoid registration, licensing, or waiting periods). Google Trends searches for "80% Glock" reveal greatest interest in California, Washington, and Texas. Notably, peak interest in Texas reflected less than *half* peak interest in Washington *or* California.[4] Unlike Texas, California registers handguns and assault weapons, while Washington regulates assault weapons and maintains de facto handgun registration. Both states require universal background checks and prohibit private manufacture of unserialized guns. If DIY is an appealing substitute under restrictive supply-side laws, these observations appear supportive.

They also contrast with national eTrace data (which may nevertheless fail to capture, or misclassify, many DIY items). eTrace reports imply very low rates of DIY encounters nationwide. Likewise, anecdotal feedback I received in 2015–2016 from serving and retired BATFE agents and police from less-restrictive states and from Illinois (a restrictive state in close proximity to unrestrictive states), implied lesser criminal interest in DIY gunmaking. Respondents attributed this to the ease of trafficking and stealing commercial guns (see Table 6.1). Indeed, among 19 federal, state, and local law enforcers who primarily worked gun crimes and counter-trafficking in midwestern and mountain states (see Table 6.1), none claimed that DIY constituted more than a small fraction of crime guns they'd encountered.

More recently, the COVID-19 pandemic illustrated America's relationship with firearms as a sociopolitical Rorschach test. As pandemic fears gained urgency, Americans flocked to firearm retailers. Consumers were unsettled not only by the virus but by projections of 30 percent unemployment, economic collapse, and release of (largely nonviolent) inmates as the virus ripped through correctional facilities, reduced policing and first responder capacities, and the potential for increased crime and emergency gun bans in the aftermath. In March 2020, retail background checks rose to 3.7 million, the highest on record. Gun control advocates and law enforcement brass in restrictive cities discouraged the sales run, while leading online retailers (and some brick-and-mortar stores) sold out of defensive firearms and ammunition. Reputedly, many panic buyers were new gun owners in restrictive jurisdictions who became spooked by the newly uncertain security environment. Meanwhile, some states and major cities effectively shut down firearm retailers by excluding them from lists of essential businesses, even if they pledged to follow required public health precautions. Gun rights advocates were reinvigorated by the opening of a new battlefront. Arguing that the Second Amendment should not be curtailed under emergency powers and that the firearms industry is itself essential for equipping the American police and defense sectors, gun rights groups successfully lobbied the Department of Homeland Security to classify the firearms industry as a critical infrastructure sector whose operations should be preserved in a national emergency. Several jurisdictions subsequently backed down from their emergency restrictions on firearm businesses.

Like conventional firearms, homemade guns are also a proxy for economic and sociopolitical uncertainty. Leading online retailers of 80 percent kits also widely sold out. This was driven to some degree by first-time buyers from restrictive jurisdictions that had shuttered (or threatened to shutter) mainstream retailers under emergency powers. Some first-time buyers in restrictive jurisdictions realized that background checks, licensing procedures, and waiting periods would slow their purchases. Likewise, some consumers probably turned to 80 percent guns as a faster and more discreet alternative to attaining legal licensing and undergoing background checks at mainstream retailers, particularly as legal licensing and background checks were subject to slowdowns and freezes in some jurisdictions.

If Google Trends are any indicator, this speculation is plausible. Assuming searches for "how to buy a gun" would proxy for consumer interest in first-time gun purchasing, Google Trends recorded its second highest volume of "how to buy a gun" searches in March 2020. Searches for "80% gun" are a better proxy for interest in gunmaking kits. Strikingly, as of April 2020, Google Trends searches for "80% gun" were projected at their highest level on record.[5] Interestingly, the five states with the most "80% gun" searches were Maryland, California, Washington, Texas, and New York, respectively. Four of these five states are among the most restrictive

Table 6.1   Selected Respondent Comments: "How Prevalent Are DIY Firearms and Products in Crime?" (Interviews conducted 2015–2016)

Director, State Police Training Institute (Illinois)	"Not at all prevalent"
Chief of Detectives (Midsized Missouri city)	"In our experience, not prevalent. Not to say they aren't there, but in our experience it's a very low percentage."
Chief of Police (Midsized Missouri city)	"You can find so many stolen guns that I imagine it'd be harder to find a DIY weapon."
Julius Wachtel, Criminology Professor/ BATFE Special Agent/Supervisor (Ret.)	"It's a very small proportion."
Montella Smith, Director University Forensic Science Institute/Homicide Detective (Ret.)	"Not common."
William Vizzard, Criminology Professor/BATFE Special Agent/ Resident Agent-in-Charge (Ret.)	"It's less than 1%, and I mean *way* less."
William Presson, U.S. Marshal (Ret.)	"They don't come close to mainstream."
Arson and Explosives Investigator/ Court Security Officer (Midsized Illinois City)	"All things being relative, still minimal."

in the country, with regulations against acquiring or building guns without background checks. While 80 percent kits already held appeal among some violent criminals and many nonviolent registration refuseniks, it seems that the COVID-19 crisis laid bare the appeal of the ghost gun's legal gray zone for many average consumers as well.

Does criminal DIY scale toward restrictions? Australia may provide some additional insight. Americans and Australians share similar values, enjoy similar media, and generally expect similar things from their governments. Yet, on guns they're not different countries, they're different planets. Differing historic, constitutional, sociopolitical, economic, and geographic variables create vast differences in gun politics and the conditions behind violence. Consequently, they have major differences in policy framework.

Australia's small industry is import-based, with little domestic manufacture. Its legal gun culture is small, predominantly rural, and based in agriculture and sport. In 1996, a mentally disturbed attacker perpetrated the Port Arthur shooting with a semiauto rifle purchased illegally from a licensed dealer (who neglected to check the validity of the attacker's license). Twelve days later, Australia passed the National Firearms Agreement. The Agreement imposed universal registration, tightened licensing requirements (while eliminating self-defense as a reason for licensing), and initiated nationwide buybacks of most types of semiauto firearms. Unlicensed gunmaking is strictly criminalized, and possession or transfer of digital firearm files is prohibited. Receivers are serialized and require licensing to purchase. As in America, compact pistols are the predominant crime guns. However, compact pistols are virtually banned. For historic and geographic reasons, handguns never extensively popularized in Australia, and handguns have been commonly registered. Today, illegal guns are said to number between 260,000 and 600,000+, but unregistered handguns are estimated at only 10,000–20,000, perhaps around 3–8 percent of total unregistered guns (Phillips, Park, and Lorimer 2007; Bucci 2016).

Debates continue as to the Agreement's role in reducing crime. Australia's violence has always been a fraction of America's. Gun mortality was declining pre-1996, and continued declining afterward. In 2012, the homicide rate was 1.1/100,000, less than a quarter of America's, and has declined further since. Yet, violence varies by temporal, economic, demographic, sociocultural, and other variables that range beyond weapons alone. The same year, Australia's Northern Territory had a homicide rate of 7.0/100,000, 1/3 higher than the U.S. national rate, and about six times higher than gun-toting New Hampshire's.

Chapman, Alpers, Agho, and Jones (2006) credited the Agreement for reductions beyond preexisting trendlines. Leigh and Neill (2010) attributed an 80 percent drop in firearm suicide to the Agreement, but found nonfirearm suicide unaffected, and less-reliable effects on homicide. Reuter and Mouzos (2003) found a 10 percent homicide reduction might be attributed to the Agreement, but "the buyback alone was an implausible candidate for reducing crime rates because the targeted gun type was not much used in homicides, or, presumably, other types of violent crime" (141). They found the buybacks would've decreased homicide by 5 percent. Baker and McPhedran (2007) credited the Agreement for decreased firearm suicide, but no significant effect on homicide. Some research is inconclusive on suicide or homicide (Lee and Suardi 2010; Klieve, Barnes, and Leo 2008; McPhedran 2016).

Regardless, Australia is a safe country, and its strict framework is popular. Many Australians derive an element of national pride from the perception that their approach has been vindicated over American gun-liberalism. As University of Melbourne security lecturer and American expat David Malet said, "Australia on gun control is like Canada on health care" (Interview 2016). Popular discourse credits the Agreement's most controversial initiative: mandatory buybacks of semiautomatic guns. However, supply reduction was only one component. Popular discussion bypasses an important fact: Australia has more guns today than before the buybacks. Household gun ownership declined from 25 to 6 percent since 1988 (Alpers, Rossetti, and Picard 2019), and about a million firearms were surrendered. However, they were replaced by new imports of legal types (Alpers 2016).

No active shooting to rival Port Arthur reoccurred, and they continue to be exceptionally rare. However, an active shooting occurred in 2019, and several post-1996 shootings might have qualified if more of the wounded had died. Several arson and knife massacres have occurred; arson killings nearly doubled in two decades (Scott 2015). However, with the exception of the Port Arthur spike in gun homicides, firearm mortality clearly declined the decade prior and decades following the Agreement. The remaining debate is not whether gun deaths declined, but how much credit the Agreement should take for it.

Every legal gun in Australia is now registered, and every unregistered gun is illegal. However, 90 percent of Australia's homicide guns are unregistered (Chan and Payne 2017). Six percent of handgun offenses are by licensees, and only 8 percent of crime handguns are registered (Bricknell 2008). Comprehensive licensing, registration, and databasing are credited with further declines in violence and suicide among licensees. However, the tracking systems don't capture most crime guns or gun criminals. As former NSW cop, prosecutor, and counterterrorism financial investigator Mathew Leighton-Daly (2016) observed, "One might argue that the system is very good for regulating those who obey the law, but it'd be much easier to go buy a gun out of a van than to get it lawfully. The system creates even more of a black hole for people who don't comply with the law" (Interview 2016). Some estimates of illegal firearms in Australia range between 260,000 and 6 million (McPhedran 2016).

The intensity of smuggled imports is unknown, but the criminal popularity of historically scarce restricted handguns suggests that traffickers have been smuggling, defacing, reactivating, and building them. In 2012, the Australian Institute of Criminology found seized crime guns (between 2002 and 2011) were "disproportionately skewed towards restricted firearm categories" (Bricknell and Australian Institute of Criminology 2012, 35). Theft and DIY methods may play a prominent role. Nine percent of long guns were sawn-off, and 19.7 percent of seized guns had defaced serials (36). About 10 percent of handguns were confirmed to be illegally made (xi). Half the nonrestricted handguns, and 31 percent of restricted handguns, were stolen. Overall, 70 percent of seized crime guns weren't traced.

Restricted types are the rarest, yet seizures of them have increased. *The New Daily* observed, "The fourfold rise in handgun-related charges in NSW in the past decade points to the existence of a big illegal market for concealable firearms that seems to have been underestimated in the past" (Lekakis 2015). *The Advertiser* stated: "Police admit they cannot eradicate a black market that is peddling illegal guns to criminals." A SAPOL Assistant Commissioner said: "We have seized automatic firearms . . . rifles, semi-automatics, fully automatic weapons, shotguns, cut-down firearms. There are a lot out there and, as quickly as we take them out, (criminals) are sourcing other illegal firearms" (Robertson 2011). In the last decade, dozens of media articles have referred to seizures of homemade submachine guns, silencers, pen guns, and component builds. Some articles include police spokespersons claiming at least 10 percent of illicit firearms in their jurisdictions are homemade. Reports suggest some adoption of printable guns among criminals and rogue enthusiasts. As Cody Wilson asserted in 2015, "Plenty of people all over Oz have printed them throughout Australia and the police have no idea where they are" (Farago 2015).

The 2012 AIC data suggests that scarcer, more-restricted, and more criminally appealing items were less likely to be traceable (see Table 6.2). "Gray market" weapons are primarily long guns that weren't surrendered in the buybacks. Nonrestricted weapons were more often stolen (probably because more are circulating). Handguns and restricted types were more likely illegally made, falsely deactivated, or illegally reactivated. The report states, "data on the source of illicit handguns was largely incomplete" (Bricknell and Australian Institute of Criminology 2012, 47). If only successful traces are considered, the role of transnational smuggling appears modest, but it's difficult to explain the proportion of untraceable handguns without speculating about smuggling and illegal gunmaking. Two types of DIY activity (domestic manufacture and reactivation) outnumbered thefts for restricted handguns, and this doesn't account for 60 percent of restricted handguns whose origins couldn't be attributed. Some portion of that untraced stock may have been smuggled or built from smuggled components. Around 20 percent of all seized guns were defaced, making them difficult or impossible to trace.

Is it plausible that traffickers could smuggle enough weapons and components to account for so many untraceable crime guns? At this stage,

Table 6.2 Types, Origins, and Traceability of Seized Guns (Australia AIC 2012)

	Nonrestricted Long Gun	Restricted Long Gun	Nonrestricted Handgun	Restricted Handgun
Percentage Untraced	12.6%	11.7%	49.6%	60.8%
Origin: Traced Weapons Only				
Gray Market	86.1%	92.3	N/A	N/A
Theft/Loss	11.8%	4.3%	50.0%	31.4%
Domestic Manufacture	N/A	1.5%	11.6%	8.2%
False Deactivation/ DIY Reactivation	N/A	N/A	21.0%	39.2%
Failure to Notify Receipt	N/A	N/A	N/A	5.2%
False Export	N/A	N/A	N/A	3.6%
Illegal Import	N/A	N/A	N/A	3.6%
Other*	2.1%	1.9%	17.4%	8.8%

*Depending on category, "other" may include deactivations/reactivations, unregistered transfer, illegal import, false theft/loss, "diversion by spare frame," false export, false disposal, or serial number transfer. AIC report does not disaggregate origins when classified as "other."

Data from: Bricknell, Samantha, and Australian Institute of Criminology. 2012. "Firearm Trafficking and Serious and Organised Crime Gangs." Research and Public Policy Series No. 116. Canberra: Australian Institute of Criminology.

answers are speculative. Australia enjoys the island advantage: it is geographically isolated, tracks legal guns tightly, and has negligible licensed manufacture. Respondents in Australia were split. GunPolicy.org director Philip Alpers was skeptical: "There's no interdiction agency that can point to a serious illegal importation of firearms since the 1980s" (Interview 2016). Criminologist Ian Warren offered a different perspective: "Of the container ships that enter Australia, only a small number are searched thoroughly. You can imagine a certain proportion of illegal firearms getting in anyway" (Interview 2016). Former cop and counterterrorism investigator Leighton-Daly said "Obviously, some is coming in on containers, and diversion from the military" (Interview 2016).

Australia's customs, border, and transit systems should be comparatively easy to secure. However, Australia is a global trade hub, and its bustling economy relies heavily on imports. It's costly to secure these systems without impacting legal commerce. As of 2011, Australian Border Force and Customs X-rayed 4.6 percent of inbound maritime containers, and inspected 0.6 percent (Australian Government 2011). In 2012, less than 1 percent of outbound containers were inspected. Anecdotally, Australian trafficking rings have been caught shipping hundreds of handguns through parcel services. About 25 percent of incoming mail is inspected, but the National Audit Office estimated that "only 13% of prohibited imports arriving in international mail were seized in 2012–2013" (Australian National Audit Office 2014). In 2014, Customs announced plans to increase air cargo inspections to 6 percent (Snow 2014). Australian criminologist, transnational crime, and dark web researcher Roderic Broadhurst observed "Basically what's been happening here is many more seizures of weapons or weapon parts in the post. One in every five or six gets caught" (Interview 2016). In 2014–2015, the Border Force reportedly seized 1,800 illegal guns and 4,000 replicas, air guns, and firearm components (*Herald Sun* 2016). If Broadhurst's ratio holds, this implies thousands of weapons may still get through.

Australia is undoubtedly less violent than America. It always had far fewer guns, and its restrictive framework surely increases the difficulty of getting them illicitly. Yet, even Australia's famously strict and reputedly successful gun tracking systems are challenged to stop motivated traffickers. It seems that if criminal demand persists, illicit makers and traffickers will deface, smuggle, and build untraceable guns to circumvent even the most comprehensive regulatory systems.

Notes

1. Adam Winkler's *Gunfight: The Battle over the Right to Bear Arms in America* and Brian Doherty's *Gun Control on Trial: Inside the Supreme Court Battle over the 2nd Amendment* describe the historical-interpretive issues in fascinating detail.

2. Calculated as average of rifle homicides 2013–2017, derived from "Murder Victims, by Weapon, 2013–2017, Crime in the United States 2017, Federal Bureau of Investigation Criminal Justice Information Services Division, Expanded Homicide Data Table 8."

3. One activist group, the Oath Keepers, is composed of serving or retired military and first responders who swear they will not conduct warrantless searches, unlawfully detain citizens, confiscate property, or obey orders infringing free speech, assembly, or petition. The first point of their oath is "We will not obey orders to disarm the American people." The group describes itself as peaceful and patriotic and claims to have 30,000 members. The group's numbers have

been questioned, but it has occasionally orchestrated shows-of-force by hundreds of armed protesters. The Southern Poverty Law Center describes the Oath Keepers as "one of the largest radical antigovernment groups in the U.S. today" (https://www.splcenter.org/fighting-hate/extremist-files/group/oath-keepers). However, interest in gun rights is not limited to libertarian, conservative, or right-wing groups. Left-wing organizations like Redneck Revolt/The John Brown Gun Club, the Socialist Rifle Association, LGBTQ+ organizations like the Pink Pistols," elements of Antifa, numerous African American gun rights groups, some black nationalist groups, and some individuals within the mainstream civil rights movement themselves, have exercised gun rights at various points. In a January 2020 gun rights demonstration in Richmond, Virginia, some left-wing groups also demonstrated in favor of gun rights. In that case, despite a state of emergency declared by the governor prior to the protest, and the presence of more than 20,000 protestors (with around half of them armed), only one arrest was made and no violence occurred. America's legal gun culture entails a unique combination of respect for law and law enforcement, alongside an open willingness to forego compliance with laws considered unconstitutional. The popularization of homemade guns can best be understood within this unique cultural framework.

4. Queries included "80% receiver" and "80% Glock" between the years "2004-present," performed 10-28-2019.

5. Google Trends searches conducted April 5, 2020, included "80% gun" and "how to buy a gun."

CHAPTER SEVEN

"You'd Be Better Off Brain-Scanning People": How the Industrial Devolution Complicates Weapons Control

> From an Orwellian perspective, you'd be better off brain scanning
> people for malicious intentions than controlling for 3D-weapons.
> —John Wanberg, industrial design professor (Interview 2016)

Some DIYers purposefully push legal and technical boundaries. This is consistent with the anarcho-libertarian politics of certain DIY subcultures. Indeed, some makers practically *invite* a backlash. By provoking intemperate countermeasures, some DIYers hope to set favorable precedents, or illustrate the inefficacy of traditional gun control in a postindustrial age. Some proposals would likely chill casual consumer gunmaking. However, short of invasive controls on speech and communication, few measures would shut down motivated makers. How does DIY challenge traditional control?

Legal Frameworks

> It really depends on the technology. If it becomes easy to make
> weapons, we'll either have far more intrusive policies, or we'll give
> up on supply-side weapons enforcement.
> —William Schroeder, law professor/organized crime prosecutor
> (ret.) (Interview 2015)

Components? 80% receivers? That's where things get weird. At the street level it's very difficult to differentiate between what's legal and what's illegal. The lawyers can come up with all kinds of regulations, but it's a whole other story when you're on the street trying to enforce these laws.

—Dee Cross, Midwest U.S. police officer and crime scene investigator (Interview 2015)

What's in a name? In gun law, *a lot*. Complex definitions of "firearms" or "components" have encouraged adaptations to skirt the *spirit*, if not *letter* of restrictions. Mark Serbu is a reputable commercial gunmaker specializing in powerful .50 BMG rifles and other distinctive firearms. A mechanical engineer, he began designing guns as a side project in the 1990s. He's also a bit of a joker. When New York passed the SAFE Act in 2013, he joined a few commercial makers in refusing to supply New York police unless the same products were relegalized for citizens. He distributed T-shirts depicting the "Soup Nazi" character from *Seinfeld* saying "No guns for you!"[1]

To criticize buybacks, Serbu designed his GB22, a single-shot handgun that users can build and surrender for profit. Gun rights supporters do occasionally make crude guns to surrender at buybacks, sometimes with joke labels like Glock & Wesson. Serbu sells GB22 plans, but he doesn't post them online. This isn't because he fears censorship. Instead, he told me "We print it out in paper because it's too easy to pirate otherwise." I asked Serbu whether anyone actually brings the GB22 to buybacks. He replied, "Well I don't know, but I think they just liked the gun! Whether or not they turn it in to a buyback, they just like the thought of building their own very simple gun, and we've sold the hell out of the plans. We sold over $10,000 worth of the plans within the first year, which is pretty crazy!" (Interview 2019).

When California banned .50 BMG rifles, Serbu redesigned for .510 DTC, an unbanned caliber. The Violence Policy Center's list of crimes involving .50 caliber rifles contains 51 cases; primarily trafficking, illegal possession, or threats. However, the compilation appears to contain only two cases where an American was killed by one, and a couple more where it wasn't clear whether .50 caliber rifles were the murder weapon (Violence Policy Center 2015). The .50 BMG cartridge is among the most powerful on America's civilian market and can inflict serious damage in the hands of an expert. However, thus far .50 caliber rifles have been implicated in few American homicides. Given this backdrop, I asked Serbu's opinion of legislation crafted around superficial design characteristics:

Tallman: So, California put some kind of restriction on 50 BMG, correct?

Serbu: They sure did!

Tallman: So then, for California compliance, you offered some of your stuff in .510 DTC? But that's almost the same ballistics, if I understand correctly.

Serbu: It's *exactly* the same ballistics.

Tallman: What's your perception of this regulatory approach of superficially defining design characteristics that are permitted or not permitted?

Serbu: As someone who likes to solve problems, like most engineers, it's a fun little carnival on the side. From a business standpoint, it's just fucking stupid. Often, the luxury in these cases is that these idiots don't really give a crap. They just want to get some legislation passed so they can say they did something. California didn't even care about the .510 DTC round. Nobody went back to say "we need to ban this too because it's equally bad." It's like, no, none of it was bad at all. The whole point wasn't to stop any problems with gun crime in .50 caliber, it was just about these lobbyists getting a feather in their cap. (Interview 2019)

Serbu isn't alone in designing around restrictions. Federal law restricts armor-piercing handgun ammunition. Bullets in tungsten alloy, brass, bronze, iron alloys, beryllium copper, depleted uranium, or with the jacket constituting more than 25 percent of mass are considered armor piercing. Meanwhile, many rifle cartridges penetrate armor without prohibited materials. These can't be banned without virtually eliminating the ammunition market for hunters and sport shooters. With new manufacturing techniques, handgun ammunition might penetrate armor without using banned materials. An aerospace engineer named Austin Jones is working on just that: 9mm armor-penetrating hollowpoints called the Dagny Dagger (named after the *Atlas Shrugged* protagonist). The round is designed to penetrate level III armor, then expand without over-penetrating. Jones's Atlas Arms intends to market retail, but also promised to publish their crowdsourced CNC code.

Similar gray zones accompanied 80% builds. Under federal law, completed receivers are firearms: they must be serialized, and retail sales require background checks and recordkeeping. Yet, at some point the law must demarcate between a firearm and a piece of metal or plastic in the general shape of one. Frame and receiver *blanks* are sufficiently incomplete to be unregulated. For decades, BATFE drew the line between "blanks" and "receivers" on case-by-case bases. Prudent retailers submit their designs for a letter certifying their blanks are sufficiently unfinished to be sold without background checks. BATFE has occasionally pursued boundary pushers. One California company, ARES Arms, sold about

75,000 AR-15 blanks annually for several years. ARES's manager Dmitri Karras explained their mission: "Our goal was to get as many of these onto the streets as humanly possible. In my opinion, an armed society is a just society, and every time someone builds one of these guns, our society gets a little more justice inside of it" (ABC News 2014).

This is more than trolling: it reflects a practical strategy. The more unregistered AR-15s circulate, the greater the enforcement challenge of a ban. Likewise, more AR-15s in circulation might undermine the constitutionality of bans. In 1939's *United States v. Miller*, the Supreme Court found the Second Amendment protects guns "in common use." This contrasts with the *Heller* decision's acceptance of restrictions on "dangerous and unusual" weapons. Thus far, courts have not considered modern sporting rifles to be common enough for protection. Yet, they are now the most-purchased rifles in America. Some advocates hope to persuade the Supreme Court that they are common enough to render bans unconstitutional.

Regardless, sellers must carefully tread between regulated "firearms" and unregulated components. In 2014, BATFE warned ARES that its polymer blanks were too-easily completed, rendering them "firearms." BATFE demanded ARES' sales records. ARES refused, arguing their blanks were not "firearms." BATFE raided ARES, but prosecutors declined to charge and returned 6,000 blanks that didn't qualify as firearms (which Karras then sold). In 2014, ATF raided Polymer80, a popular marketer of frame blanks, but also declined to press charges.

In 2016's *United States v. Jiminez*, a convicted felon accepted a completed AR-15 lower receiver from an undercover officer. His defense relied on definitional counterarguments: the 1968 GCA defines operable receivers as "firearms," and felons *are* prohibited from possessing firearms. However, Section 479.11 of the Code of Federal Regulations defines a "receiver" as the "part of a firearm which provides housing for the hammer, bolt or breechblock and firing mechanism, and which is usually threaded at its forward position to receive the barrel." Problematically, some guns aren't designed this way. AR lower receivers contain the hammer and firing mechanism, but their unregulated *upper* receivers contain the bolt and receive the barrel. Siding with Jiminez, the court referred to obscure documents dating to the 1970s indicating that the government was initially unsure which AR component should be considered the "receiver." For decades, BATFE treated the lower receiver as the "firearm" based on its internal determinations rather than the federal definition. The court concluded that BATFE's definition was too vague to be enforced against Jiminez. Similar arguments had vindicated ARES—it simply wasn't selling "firearms."

In 2019's *United States v. Roh*, Roh owned a machine shop that sold blanks and offered "build parties" where "members" could learn to complete them. The educational content was laughable: students paid $1,000, then pressed a button on a CNC machine that completed the receivers automatically. Staff assembled the guns and gave them to "members," which included felons. Indeed, the perpetrator of the shooting described in the opening pages of this book had a receipt for components from Roh's company. BATFE warned Roh. His "educational" activities were indistinguishable from unlicensed commerce. Roh continued, and BATFE arrested him.

The unlicensed gun selling charges were valid. However, because BATFE's definition differed from federal law, and its internal process for defining "receivers" didn't comply with the federal rule-making process (which includes a public notice and comment period), prosecutors dropped the manufacturing charges rather than risk a precedent that would undermine illicit manufacturing law. As of this writing, federal ability to enforce illicit manufacturing laws against guns that don't fit the federal definition of "firearms" or "receivers," remains uncertain. Ultimately, if components are to be governed by coherent legal definitions, the definitions must encompass a huge range of designs in order to declare specific thresholds where a "blank" becomes a "receiver" becomes a "firearm." Without specificity, the law is vague and not enforceable. Even with specificity, many designs (and redesigns) could skirt definitions. How can the law pace with material innovation?

"I think how you do it is by not taking the formalistic legal view of the definition. If you get stuck in the reductionist view, you get stuck in the question of 'when is a firearm a firearm?' That's how there are all these loopholes and accessories that come right up to the edge." I was speaking with Nicholas Suplina, Managing Director for Law and Policy at *Everytown*. As a prosecutor, Suplina actually pursued one of New York's ghost gun trafficking cases in 2015. He argues for a less rigid approach toward defining firearms, and a broader approach toward defining *nudge-wink* firearm activity. "Where we are right now, a lot of it is because we've taken these formalistic definitions. It's arbitrary. When we're talking about unfinished lowers on the internet, they're not hiding what it is. They're selling full kits to make a functional firearm . . . It's in the marketing that the intent of the object is revealed" (Interview 2019).

The conversation was intelligent and civil. Suplina mounted thoughtful defenses of universal background checks, expressed respect toward legitimate hobbyists, and never veered toward confiscatory language. However, we never fully settled the definitional problem. Without specific definitions, couldn't prosecutions be stalled by challenges that the item wasn't actually a "gun" part? Would vendors learn what terms to avoid in their advertising? Cannabis was illegal for decades, but head shops openly sold bongs labeled "for tobacco use only," and hydroponics stores knew they were supporting illegal growers. These retailers never mentioned "cannabis," and customers knew if they mentioned marijuana they'd be shown the door. Yet, anyone who wanted a bong could get one. Policing gray market items is hard enough, but how much harder will it be to police gray market *speech*? Linguistic limitations are surely frustrating to those who support regulation of DIY, but I feared that rejecting specificity would risk the worst of both worlds: broad abilities to criminalize physical items, but ineffectiveness against clever gray marketeers who know what *not* to say.

For now, the ability of manufacturers to redesign components (or offer them at lower levels of completion) introduces complications. The pace of engineering is faster than the pace of legislative reaction, particularly with gun rights proponents holding regulations to standards of coherence, procedure, and constitutionality. Most component sellers are more scrupulous than Roh. "Build parties" are now regulated and have mostly disappeared. Usually, hobbyists buy kits and learn to finish guns themselves. Sales numbers are proprietary. Given the number of 80% retailers and the popularization of frame builds, it's plausible that a *minimum* of 100,000–200,000+ blanks have been sold annually for a decade. This supplements 16+ million civilian-owned and mostly unregistered modern sporting rifles sold retail. Many kits are never built, and it's impossible to know how many are completed. Kits are typically 10–40 percent cheaper than finished guns. Even unfinished kits hold some appeal. If AR-15s are banned, most kits will go unrecovered. The buyer may enjoy knowing he *could* build one if desired.

While many hobbyists are primarily interested in the craft, rather than avoiding the generation of background check records, the rapid and widespread popularization of 80% builds reflects distrust of government among many enthusiasts who perceive instability in their rights. *KT Ordnance* produced blanks for decades. "I was one of three guys making them in 1999," said proprietor Richard Celata. "Now there's lots of competition. My business really started to grow after 9/11. Before 9/11 it was hobbyists; after, it changed to 'I don't want them to know'" (Baum 2013). September 11 combined with domestic politics to popularize modularity. Mainstream gunmakers (particularly those specializing in Armalite Rifles) increased production during post-9/11 securitization and military interventions. Some commercial makers may have reduced waste by marketing surplus components toward the DIY market (Vizzard, Interview 2016). By 2016, BATFE Firearms Technology Criminal Branch Chief Max Kingery told me "[Legal] Receivers increased tremendously in the last eight years or so," and "As far as numbers, I would guess that anybody who wants to do it is already doing it" (Interview 2016).

Insofar as manufacturers unloaded surplus, they were capitalizing on longstanding trends in politically driven purchasing. Savvy manufacturers exploit these cycles, but they're also disruptive. As journalist Jon Stokes (2016) observes, unpredictable booms are not ideal for an industry that makes durable products. The booms focus on controversial items, but are followed by shortages, overruns, and reduced demand for other products. Stokes writes these boom-bust cycles are "good for stock traders who like to bet on big moves in gun company share prices, but they make it very difficult for gun companies themselves to forecast demand and adjust production capacity accordingly."

America's assault weapon laws have historically focused on characteristics with little bearing on capability. Secondary features like telescoping stocks, bayonet lugs, pistol grips, barrel shrouds, or flash suppressors may render a rifle illegal even as they make little functional difference. When 1994's now-expired federal assault weapons ban was drafted, manufacturers gained exceptions for popular rifles with identical capabilities. Arguably, assertions of the ban's effectiveness are undermined by the fact that the "ban" didn't prohibit rifles that were functionally identical insofar as no mass shooters used bayonets. Today, only seven states maintain assault weapon bans, two subject them to enhanced regulation, and the remaining 43 have no assault weapon regulation.

California adopted stringent assault weapon laws, but this encouraged an entire commercial subsector devoted to engineering around the restrictions. California required semiautomatic rifles to include magazine releases that are inconvenient to operate by hand, slowing the reloading process. Commercial gunmakers designed compliant *bullet buttons* that quickly released magazines with simple items like a loose round. In 2016, legislators required reloading to entail "disassembly" and opening the action. Makers redesigned to enable the actions to easily open to release the magazine, creating technically legal variants that could again be reloaded quickly.

Some accessories enable semi-auto guns to emulate automatic fire. The results are neither as accurate, reliable, nor rapid firing as a proper machine gun, but depending on design, have been legal because they didn't modify the firearm's *action*. Rather, bump stocks and *binary triggers* assist a human in manipulating the trigger faster, or by firing as the trigger resets. Bump stocks are now banned, but binary triggers remain legal in some states (and unlike bump stocks do have legitimate uses among competition shooters). Rarely, DIYers have experimented with pneumatic machine guns. Since they don't use chemical propellants, most jurisdictions regulate pneumatics loosely. Nevertheless, some are clearly deadly. Irrespective of legal options to emulate automatic fire, many *illegal* methods accomplish the same. Some of these methods are incredibly simple, such as rigging certain firearms with a rubber band or shoelace to enable bump fire. Some states prohibit 10+ or 15+ round magazines. Some sellers straddle gray zones with magazine kits that theoretically aren't prohibited until assembled. Suppressors are subject to enhanced regulation under the NFA, but gutsy suppliers have marketed *solvent trap* suppressors assembled by the purchaser ostensibly to catch solvents during gun cleaning. BATFE has warned or arrested solvent trap sellers whose activities it considered to be a transparent end-run of firearms law.

Complex definitions of design characteristics can be difficult for police to identify, and often require more prosecutorial resourcing to charge. Unfinished or disassembled components may exploit jurisdictional differentials. As of this writing, all Title I components except receivers are unregulated until assembled. Some jurisdictions are trying to expand regulations. In 2019, California's AB879 passed restrictions on "precursors," requiring unfinished receivers to be sold through licensed dealers. It also establishes a blank registry and criminalizes importation and transfers except through authorized dealers.

In 2019, New York State Attorney General Letitia James sent warnings to 80% retailers, demanding suspension of sales on the basis that they facilitate construction of assault weapons. The notices demanded preservation of customer data, requiring retention not only of active and archived data, but also "deleted data (still recoverable through the use of computer forensics)." Likewise, in 2019 Pennsylvania Attorney General Josh Shapiro issued an interpretation of state law expanding the definition of "firearm" to include unfinished receivers on the basis that they are "designed" to fire a projectile and may be "readily converted" to do so, even if they are not capable of functioning as a firearm as-is (Shapiro 2019). All such changes have invited lawsuits. The NRA's Institute for Legislative Action described the Pennsylvania rule change as "absurd," arguing that "Shapiro's 'theory' of treating nonfunctioning blocks of polymer, steel, or aluminum as 'firearms' is the equivalent of calling a pile of aluminum tubes a bicycle" (NRA-ILA 2019).

Engineering adaptations illustrate the challenge of supply-side control in a world of flexible design and fabrication. Gunmakers are ultimately engineers, and engineers are motivated by the challenge of designing around constraints. Sometimes, commercial makers *benefit* from new sales or barriers to competition generated by design restrictions. Indeed, accusations that the NRA agitates against gun confiscation in the interests of industry rather than its membership are arguably undermined by the profits confiscation could generate. In a large-scale gun ban, the government would pay the buyback costs, millions of guns would be purchased prior to the ban, and many prohibited guns would be replaced with new purchases that technically comply (as in Australia). Regardless, as lawmakers argue legal semantics, traffickers continue transporting components to restrictive markets, and DIYers adopt increasingly sophisticated techniques to make guns from scratch irrespective of any legal redefinitions.

Regulating Materials

This comes down to computers, code, and digital fabricators. All of these are general purpose technologies. You have to target the application, not the technology.
—Adam Thierer, Mercatus Center at George Mason University
(Interview 2018)

They can't figure out what to do, meanwhile Rockler sells a machine for $3,200 that prints, mills, has a laser cutter, fits on a bedside table and runs on 110-volt single phase power!
—Anonymous "maker" (Interview 2015)

Skilled machinists can build any gun component, and no legislation can prevent all DIY gunmaking. As legislators consider 80% builds worthy of new restrictions, we are seeing broader component regulations. In America, there are only two realistic options: extending background checks and serialization to blanks, or extending them to commercial barrels. Rifled barrels are generally harder to make than frames. Requiring background checks and serialization for barrels or blanks would be a way of applying commercial controls to 80% builds.

These measures wouldn't stop motivated illicit gunmakers (as evidenced by illegal manufacturing in jurisdictions that already restrict all components), but might chill DIY by unskilled criminals. However, compliance costs and legal opposition are nontrivial in America. Anything less than *comprehensive* component restrictions might only incentivize legal redesigns and illicit trafficking. If illegal makers improve their frames and barrels, supply-side controls must expand to more components, inviting a complex system that defines and tracks all gun parts. Meanwhile, DIYers already build guns that don't require commercial components.

In America, restrictions on unfinished components could invite a *race to the bottom*. If a component is regulated at "80%" completion, what about 75 percent? Each step down makes fabrication harder for a novice. Yet, at some point courts must determine that an object is not a "firearm," lest they endorse restrictions on any vaguely gunlike item. Stricter definitions may create markets for components sufficiently unfinished for exemption. DIY would become more challenging, but an ecosystem of retailers and enthusiasts would share tips. DIYers might embrace even simpler methods. As custom gunsmith and skilled DIYer Mike Crumling observed:

> If they're going to start regulating those things more heavily, like the 80% parts, it's gonna be the like the same situation with California where you have somebody making rules, and somebody else making stuff that gets around the rules. Somewhere I have some plans for AR lowers that are literally just flat steel bolted together. Don't get me wrong, they're ugly, but functional. So, you know, a few steel plates with a couple holes in them? I mean, that's even *less* work than an 80% lower now. (Interview 2019)

Controls on materials are harder to imagine in a world that runs on plastic and metal stock. Extruders recycle household plastics into printer filament. Users can build or purchase the extruders. Plastic firearms don't require much filament or produce much waste. Only high-volume printing could be profiled based on plastic consumption. Controls on metals are virtually impossible. Industrious DIYers can reforge scrap, a technique employed by craft gunmakers in the developing world. As Crumling points out, "Every car would have to be plastic. You can take steel out of cars and make gun parts. In fact, a lot of material I get is scrap steel from cars, motors, it's good steel" (Interview 2019). Controlling DIY through regulations on components and materials will carry trade-offs. It would probably achieve some success against casual makers, but limited success against traffickers. Meanwhile, an ecosystem of clever makers will challenge any technical or legal constraint they consider an infringement on their rights or livelihoods.

Second Amendment Meets the First: Regulating Data

> The debate is over. The guns are downloadable. The files are in the public domain. You cannot take them back. You can adjust your politics to this reality.
> —Cody Wilson, Defense Distributed (CBS News 2018)

> Cody wasn't wrong. He was just really early, which is another kind of wrong.
> —Jon Stokes, technology and firearms journalist (Interview 2018)

After developing the first digital firearm fabrication files, Defense Distributed promptly posted them online. Founder Cody Wilson alternately stoked and mocked the media hysteria. Arguing that his code was First Amendment–protected speech about a Second Amendment–protected activity, he dared the government to stop him. The Obama administration scrambled for a solution. Wilson soon received a takedown order from the State Department, asserting that posting the files constituted an illegal munitions export under the International Trade in Arms Regulation (ITAR). This allowed a takedown without forcing the government to argue the files were illegal. Under ITAR, it's only illegal to "export" the files by posting them online where foreigners can see them. Defense Distributed hadn't broken firearms law. The government didn't assert that personal gunmaking was illegal, nor did it prohibit Americans from creating or sharing the files *offline*.

The argument wasn't unprecedented. An earlier series of cases resulted in dissemination of encryption technology that became the cybersecurity backbone of the civilian internet. "Strong" encryption began as a restricted military "munition." The "crypto-wars" began in the 1960s as industry desired encryption to protect banking. The National Bureau of Standards (now NIST) set standards for sensitive but unclassified systems. Civilian need for strong encryption accelerated with e-commerce. By the 1990s, lawsuits petitioned for looser regulation. In *Junger v. Daley*, computer scientist Peter Junger challenged export controls preventing him from teaching foreign students or publishing cryptography education materials. In *Bernstein v. United States*, Daniel Bernstein challenged restrictions on his "Snuffle" encryption system. In both cases, courts concluded that code was First Amendment–protected speech. Phil Zimmermann, developer of PGP encryption, was investigated after his algorithm reached the internet. Zimmermann challenged export control by publishing the code in a book through MIT Press. This was based on the assumption that books enjoy greater protection. Prosecutors didn't pursue charges.

Encryption diffused. The Clinton administration reclassified civilian encryption to the Department of Commerce's "Commerce Control List (CCL)." This prohibits export to specific adversaries like rogue states and terrorists, but regulates exports less stringently. Encryption algorithms are now widely published, including open source code that can't be eliminated. Other speech is unprotected, but digital guns fall awkwardly into this framework. Under *Brandenburg v. Ohio* and other rulings, inflammatory speech can be restrained, but only if directed to incite (and actually likely to incite) imminent lawless action. However, if gunmaking is legal, it's difficult to argue that gunmaking media should be illegal unless packaged with violent exhortations. An exception under *Giboney v. Empire Storage and Ice Co.* restrains speech integral to criminal conduct. This exception targets materials supportive of criminal activity, and has been applied to child exploitation imagery, crime solicitations, bomb-making manuals, and doctor recommendations for medical marijuana.

Giboney might be applied to manuals for illegal bombs or drugs. However, if gunmaking is legal, it's harder to argue firearm code is integral to crime. Just as the "Feinstein Amendment" to the 1998 National Defense Authorization Bill only targets bombmaking information in furtherance of violence, attacking digital firearm files wouldn't eliminate public domain information that can be used to develop them. The Feinstein Amendment doesn't eliminate patents or educational materials from which an intelligent person could construct a bomb. The legality of guns suggests that restrictions on firearm files would require exceptions for industry and educational purposes.

The Invention Secrecy Act of 1951 and the Atomic Energy Act of 1956 allow the government to censor patents on national security-sensitive technologies. Consequently, some technologies are *born secret* if dissemination threatens national security. Secrecy orders are issued on patent application, yet most DIYers don't apply for patents. Public domain materials are not classified, and born secrecy is meant to prevent nonpublic technologies from circulating. However, firearms are a legacy technology that exist in every country. Thus far, born secrecy is usually rescinded when the same information enters public domain. The first major challenge was 1979's *United States of America v. Progressive, Inc., Erwin Knoll, Samuel Day, Jr., and Howard Morland*, in which *The Progressive* magazine published descriptions of hydrogen bomb design. The government argued for suppression, but dropped the matter when similar information was published abroad.

Defense Distributed hopes to leverage these arguments. Conventional gunmaking media is already public. If code is speech and guns are legal, why shouldn't firearm code be publishable? This bypasses an important counterargument. Clearly, the code isn't actually a gun: it's converted to a gun by a combination of digital tools and skilled and semiskilled labor. However, the files are also a machine language directing the tool to operate. Skilled machinists appreciate the nuances of digital fabrication code, and machine instructions are essential for education about digital fabrication and growth of the industry. However, the code's superposition between expressive speech and machine language may be relevant for future argument. On one hand, machine language doesn't seem like traditional speech. Yet, the language of code is applied to expressive purposes— just ask video game programmers. Neither position is pristine. If the government prevails, authorities may gain broad powers to censor software code, thereby extending greater regulatory oversight not only into software, networks, and online platforms but also into the functionality of networked "smart" devices. These powers might impact a broader spectrum of technology and online speech whenever the government asserts a security need. If Defense Distributed prevails, freedom of information and a wide spectrum of digital innovations will be protected, but supply-side weapons regulation will be undermined toward ends we cannot know.

Defense Distributed complied with the takedown order (while continuing to deliver the files domestically), and submitted export applications. Receiving no response, they filed suit in *Defense Distributed, Second Amendment Foundation, Inc. v. United States Department of State*. Defense Distributed was represented by prominent gun rights attorneys and supported by amicus briefs from the Electronic Frontier Foundation, Cato Institute, Congressman Thomas Massie, and 14 supporting congress members. Much of the civil liberties concern extended beyond gun rights and into the government's assertion that American speech can be censored from the internet under export law. The NRA has offered guarded support to Defense Distributed's arguments without explicitly supporting its case. Its low-key response has generated speculation: perhaps mainstream advocacy groups would see digital fabrication and the DIY movement as a threat to commercial industry.

However, the NRA has made also made statements favorable to legal DIY. In 2013, the NRA Institute for Legislative Action opposed expansions of the UFA (though supporting the Act as-is) on the basis that it would preclude development of emerging firearm technologies. In 2015, the NRA-ILA urged members to submit public comments on the ITAR revision, arguing that the State Department's interpretation was "as much an affront to the 1st Amendment as it is to the 2nd," and "gunsmiths, manufacturers, reloaders, and do-it-yourselfers could all find themselves muzzled under the rule and unable to distribute or obtain the information they rely on to conduct these activities" (NRA-ILA 2015). If the NRA is concerned about DIY's potential to undercut mainstream industry, it doesn't seem worried enough to accept precedents establishing new frontiers in gun control, nor has it been willing to oppose a legal space which many grassroots supporters wish to keep.

Years of litigation followed. The Western District of Texas and Fifth Circuit denied Defense Distributed's preliminary injunction without hearing the First Amendment claim. By January 2018, the Supreme Court denied *certiorari* and remanded the case for hearing on the merits. Yet, to widespread surprise, the Trump administration settled before the merits were heard. The settlement exempted code for Title I firearms from the State Department's more export-restrictive "US Munitions List (USML)" and placed it on the Commerce Department's less-restrictive CCL. Defense Distributed appeared victorious. As media concern rose to fever pitch, Defense Distributed re-released the files for several days before receiving new takedown orders. The new orders derived from emergency injunctions filed by 20 states, challenging the legality of the settlement. In November 2019, a judge from the Western District of Washington ruled that the Trump administration's settlement didn't follow the full rule-making procedure and was therefore "arbitrary and capricious," rendering open posting of the files illegal yet again.

Meanwhile, New Jersey passed SB2465, which prohibits unlicensed gunmaking and transfer of digital firearm files to anyone who isn't a licensed manufacturer. Defense Distributed sued, arguing New Jersey's restrictions are unconstitutional. In December 2019 the Trump administration followed the full rule-making procedure to again propose regulating Title I firearm designs under the Commerce Department, making firearm designs and components "exportable" again through online posting.

Still without naming Defense Distributed, the NRA's Institute for Legislative Action staked its strongest public position yet: welcoming the peel-back of ITAR, which it described as burdening legitimate gunsmiths and firearm businesses. Jason Ouimet, Executive Director of the NRA-ILA wrote that, under the ITAR restriction, "Any business hoping to manufacture the most basic component of an item on the USML was forced to register with the State Department and pay a $2,250 annual fee. These regulatory burdens soon fell upon every small business making firearm components." Regarding fabrication data, Ouimet argued, "As the USML's scope extended beyond physical items and onto 'technical data' about items, the government began to regulate blueprints, diagrams, and service manuals. . . . Before too long—and unconcerned by the Constitutional implications—the State Department was threatening to flex ITAR jurisdiction over everyone who dared to 'publish' a parts diagram or handloading formula online" (Ouimet 2020).

Finally, to muted outrage in the midst of the COVID-19 crisis, Wilson relaunched his online firearm file sharing repository DEFCAD under a different model meant to minimize liability. This time, DEFCAD membership would be paid and invite only, subject to policies insulating the platform from illegal user activities, and access would be theoretically contingent on platform approval after IP-based verification that the user's device is located in the United States. Dozens of established DIY firearm innovators soon joined as partners, and as of this writing the platform claims nearly 17,000 users. After several years of skirmishing, the battle lines over firearms data have become clearer. Both sides continue their lawfare campaigns for and against the legal sharing of firearm data. DIYers continue leveraging technology to push the limits of firearm innovation, while legislators push the capacities of law in cyclical attempts to stop them. Yet, as of this writing neither faction has achieved decisive legal victory.

Can't Stop the Signal? Controlling Firearms Information

To prevent distribution of data they don't like? I think that's kind of a fool's game. If you clamp down on free traffic of data it puts a real drag on your economy and lots of industries. Some countries are trying it. You can only allow authorized things to be transmitted, but at that point you start worrying about steganographic techniques. It's always going to be a problem. In an open society where you don't clamp down on everything, you really have no way. People will use encryption, and you can't really stop them.–
—Jonathan Poritz, computer science professor/cryptographer
(Interview 2019)

100,000 downloads? That's bullshit, I know 20 guys in town with that file!
—Anonymous machinist and software developer, commenting on reports that the "Liberator" code was downloaded 100,000 times before takedown (Interview 2015)

Gunmaking information takes many forms. Gunsmithing books and magazines, schematics, patents, photography, and manuals are available in print and digital formats. A growing number of countries and jurisdictions criminalize expedient gun manuals or digital firearm files. In America, prohibiting conventional gunsmithing literature is surely unconstitutional. Restricting educational material about digital fabrication is an economic drag and probably unconstitutional. Consequently, it's impossible to restrict the informational building blocks behind digital guns. For skilled makers, the distinction between "information," "data," and "file" is more legal contrivance than functional reality. Defense Distributed attorney Josh Blackman alluded to this, arguing that restrictions on digital firearm files are "totally attacking the medium, not the content" (Interview 2015).

Print can be physically traded or digitized. Fabrication files are strings of script. Script can be posted online, transferred through peer-to-peer communications or physical storage devices, scanned with optical character recognition, or manually transcribed. Without specialized software, most police can't identify script for illegal products. If encrypted, the code may be unintelligible. If obscured by steganography, it may go undetected. Legal media transactions might be surveilled. For example, customer information from libraries and retailers could be tracked. Even data from publicly accessible Xerox machines and documents from home printers can be tracked, but knowledgeable adversaries can use handheld scanners, cameras, editing techniques, and other methods to digitize materials or disseminate print without leaving breadcrumbs.

Additionally, library dragnets are unconstitutional. In *Stanley v. Georgia*, the Supreme Court recognized the "right to receive information and ideas." In *Griswold v. Connecticut*, the Court recognized rights to "receive," "read," and "teach" information. Anonymous speech is protected by *Talley v. California*, and *Anonymous Online Speakers v. United States District Court for the District of Nevada*, among others. *Lovell v. City of Griffin* states that the First Amendment protects the right to publish ideas without permission. *Tattered Cover v. City of Thornton* recognized that the constitution protects anonymous book procurement, and permits targeted warrants but requires a compelling need and circumscriptions to counterweight the chilling effect of state access.

The USA PATRIOT Act of 2001 carved out some exceptions, including "Section 215," which allowed access to library and bookseller records for counterterrorism and counterespionage. Even the broadest iterations of the PATRIOT Act stipulated these powers can't be applied to constitutionally protected activities. The American Library Association's "Library Bill of Rights" includes protections for public access to information, and obligations to maximize user privacy. Libraries and booksellers challenged

Section 215, playing key roles in reforming provisions that authorized warrantless access to citizens' reading materials.

Even if firearm files are censored, new ones will be generated. Digital fabrication files are based on object dimensions coded into file formats like .stl, AMF, or PLY by widely accessible CAD/CAM software. Converting dimensions to digital formats is a basic industry task. Restricting digital gun files might reduce access among the unskilled, but the capabilities to generate new files are integrating into mainstream economies and workplace skillsets. As industrial design professor John Wanberg observed, "One of the first things a student needs to do is reverse engineer similar products. Any of my students could sit down with a gun manual and code a design file. It seems outlandish to regulate the files when the same information is available in print" (Interview 2016).

Open source subcultures have also made efforts to preserve controversial information—sometimes in backlash to perceived state overreach. One anonymous respondent from the maker community asked sarcastically, "How many people even *wanted* to 3D-print a gun before they started talking about banning it?" (Interview 2015). Another machinist and information security specialist said matter-of-factly, "If you tell me I can't do something, that's going to make me want to do it" (Interview 2015). Anonymized peer-to-peer services facilitate dissemination. As mainstream social media pushes gunmaking data to more obscure platforms, the data becomes more prone to contamination with malware. An Australian criminal intelligence specialist suggested exploiting this ghettoization of firearms data by salting the files: "You can perhaps modify designs mid-stream to ensure it won't work, or it backfires." However, this pushes policing norms even in Australia, where firearm code is illegal, encryption backdoors are mandated, and censorship is constitutional. After a moment, the thoughtful intelligence specialist added, "But that might be taking it pretty far" (Interview 2016). At any rate, knowledgeable makers can examine code for errors.

Defense Distributed's code recirculates, and the company physically disseminates the files to thousands of users. Others have posted digital firearm files without receiving takedown orders. Without broad prohibition and invasive enforcement, no ruling can eliminate the data. Controlling flash drives, print media, and digitized documents would require a broad security regime entailing legal challenges and little probability of success. The legality of the data offline guarantees continued dissemination.

As Michigan State professor Ann Larabee (2015) observed in her fascinating history of improvised weapon manuals, users digitized and reposted bombmaking and narcotics manuals from notorious publishers like *Paladin* and *Loompanics*. Some of these reposters alluded to the "Feinstein Amendment" as an abridgement of speech and motivator behind their repostings. However, unlike popular bombmaking or crime manuals (which include outdated or incorrect information), firearms information is regularly generated and improved by knowledgeable users. A vibrant DIY bombmaking subculture doesn't exist: most IEDs are intrinsically illegal, and it's easier to penalize sharing of bombmaking instructions. Conversely, firearms are protected by the Second Amendment. American policing is high-tech, fairly effective, and relatively uncorrupt, but must operate within a political culture that strongly protects civil liberty. Most countries can easily restrict firearms. Many countries can easily restrict speech. Some countries can easily restrict both. The United States of America is none of these countries.

Here, at the confluence of security and speech, DIY gunmaking (and its countermeasures) hold greatest disruptive potential. As Larabee writes, "The history of popular weapons manuals reveals that their danger may lie less in their informational content than in their provocation of the emergency state in pursuit of public enemies and its vulnerable hold on its own means of violence" (2015, 190). Since the DIY phenomenon is information-driven, the countermeasures we select to arrest it may hold wider implications for privacy, speech, freedom of information, and cybersecurity writ large.

Charles Duan is a clever guy. As Director for Technology and Innovation at the R Street Institute, he wrote a *Lawfare* column detailing an ingeniously roundabout method to censor digital firearms. It involves another authority that irks civil libertarians: *eminent domain*. Often necessary for public works (and controversial when the *public* purpose involves awarding property to *private* developers), eminent domain allows government to seize property if courts believe it would serve sufficient public need. Since they don't hold copyright, third parties can't subject firearm files to digital rights management (DRM) software. Media companies use DRM to combat unauthorized redistribution. Nevertheless, hackers "jailbreak" DRM, while casual users find circumventions. Duan has a work-around: by creating the file, Wilson gained copyright. So, the government might apply eminent domain. This strategy could bypass Defense Distributed's free speech argument under copyright exceptions. However, the government would be seizing intellectual property while bypassing First Amendment defenses. That could be a slippery slope toward limitless censorship. Judges probably wouldn't allow it. So, the government wouldn't keep the copyright. It would be transferred to a gun control nonprofit which would sue anyone who distributed it.

Duan knows his plan sounds wild. "I'm pretty sure the whole scheme I've come up with shouldn't be possible," he said, "the government probably shouldn't be able to take people's copyrights and give them to others under those circumstances." Duan is up-front about this. His objective wasn't to propose copyright as a realistic gun control. Rather, he wanted to illustrate how copyright law has strengthened beyond normative understandings of free speech. "This is a very, very powerful system of laws. . . . That's why I found the Defense Distributed case interesting, because copyright is this entire system of law that's declared the First Amendment doesn't apply to it, even though everything involved is speech" (Interview 2019).

Duan's plan foreshadows the legal gymnastics necessary to declare widening swaths of digital speech to be censorable. "I actually think the [Defense Distributed] First Amendment challenge will be a big deal, because courts have already ruled that code is speech," he said, "the larger question is that it doesn't matter what you do with the law, people have all sorts of technical methods to get around it. That's why, ultimately, my fear on the trajectory of the technology is what regulation will do for average consumers." This isn't a trivial consideration. Much innovation relies on the legal space to create devices, content, and software that interoperates with preexisting technology or content. New requirements may strengthen big-tech at the expense of upstarts who can't afford to comply with tighter censorship, content moderation, or copyright mandates.

Digital toolmakers don't want to enable crime. Yet, much of digital fabrication's appeal lies in its ability to make whatever a user designs. Rendering digital toolmakers liable for criminal use would be reminiscent of the controversy over Section 230 of the Communications Decency Act of 1996, which insulates online platforms from liability for illegal activity by individual users. Section 230 isn't blanket immunity: platforms can't encourage or tacitly allow criminality. But when users act illegally against the platform's policy, Section 230 protects the platform. Without Section 230, platforms might be criminally charged or sued to bankruptcy for activities they explicitly forbid (and try to prevent) users from undertaking.

Subjecting toolmakers to liability would encourage limiters on digital fabrication machines, but might prove ineffectual. Open source architectures like RepRap or Arduino enable users to make digital fabricators (and other custom electronics) without relying on proprietary platforms.

Gunhackers will make their own machines and jailbreak proprietary machines. Digital fabricators don't need to be networked, and clandestine makers will airgap. A database of approved designs would be unworkable: slowing innovation, generating intellectual property and confidentiality concerns, and failing to reach rogue makers who would continue outside the approval system.

Cloud services and social media platforms use "hash databases" to prevent storage or reposting of prohibited media. However, these systems are essentially supply-side tools, and they suffer some supply-side vulnerabilities. The databases compare signatures of known prohibited content with newly posted content. This prevents reposting of previously flagged content, but extremists and copyright violators try to alter content to avoid these techniques, and hashing does not catch new content unless somebody flags it. Encrypted content transferred between users who don't flag it is harder to stop. More recently, "endpoint filtering" has been proposed as a method to apply hashing within otherwise-encrypted applications. Theoretically, this would enable platforms to maintain encryption while scanning for specifically prohibited files. However, as Erica Portnoy (2019) writes for the Electronic Frontier Foundation, governments could scale out these systems to monitor and censor any information it wished, including legal content. Meanwhile, some platforms will refuse to implement them or shelter outside jurisdictional boundaries, and some users may employ steganographic techniques to randomly alter file signatures, leaving data traffickers with options while typical users are thoroughly surveilled.

Media coverage of the Liberator pistol repeats an estimate that the file was downloaded 100,000 times before takedown 48 hours later. However, the file has clearly diffused beyond 100,000 users, including in jurisdictions that ban it. So long as any form of anonymous speech, and any corner of the tech ecosystem, are untouched by total surveillance, restraint of illicit fabrication will rely on cooperation among platforms and users.

Even mandating encryption backdoors could incentivize circumventions. Steganographic applications like *Disarming Corruptor* "encrypt" digital designs by randomly altering their dimensions. Only a recipient with the key can reverse the alterations. As these techniques improve, prohibited fabrication files may take the form of innocuous objects, and the "contraband" would be accessed by applying seemingly unrelated code that converts the file to the contraband design. By introducing "Network Investigative Techniques" (otherwise known as "malware" if used by cybercriminals) onto user devices and digital infrastructure, it's possible for authorities to access encrypted data in plaintext. However, these methods require secrecy, and some surveillance-based policing entails questionable tactics like "parallel construction," in which police methods are fabricated rather than revealing the true origins of criminal intelligence in court.

Police and intelligence agencies have demonstrated abilities to unmask cybercriminals with these methods. In a high-profile 2014 case, the FBI used NITs to shut down the "Playpen" hidden Tor service for child pornography, and collected user and administrator IP and MAC addresses. This case foreshadowed some of the ethical issues implied by an expanding scope of police hacks. Many NITs are privately developed. Carnegie Mellon's Software Engineering Institute originally developed the hack. When the FBI learned of it, they subpoenaed the private researchers for access. Nation-states enjoy many technical advantages, but their advantages derive in part from their ability to use tactics that are illegal for the private sector.

One trend among public agencies is to hoard "zero-day" exploits: attacks that exploit undetected software and hardware vulnerabilities. However, innocent users pay for this strategy with weakened security against malicious private hackers and nation-state cyberattacks. Hacking tools are occasionally leaked or stolen, providing a bonanza for cybercriminals while rendering innocent users insecure. As revealed by several high-profile leaks, even encrypted and anonymized traffic has been bulk collected by national intelligence agencies, with the potential for traffic analysis or full decryption as new hacking techniques are developed. These methods might enable retroactive surveillance of previously "secure" communications. For example, users who ordered firearm components or other items from online retailers could later be unmasked. While that might sound reasonable to supporters of DIY gun regulation, the same capabilities could be put to sinister use by a malicious regime (particularly if combined with artificial intelligence (AI) to reverse engineer the workings of entire national populations, economies, critical infrastructures, or defense systems).

Problematically, public-private bulk surveillance may prove better for monitoring typical citizens than for targeting savvy data smugglers. Data smuggling doesn't require digitization or association with targetable networks. Forcing mainstream platforms to provide backdoors (or quietly embedding undisclosed backdoors) may fail to stop dissemination among authentic traffickers, while leaving expanding swaths of commerce and consumer "IoT" devices insecure. One-time pads are inconvenient but theoretically secure even against quantum cryptanalysis. This may suffice to transmit data across surveilled networks and national firewalls, at which point criminals can trade data physically. Physical shipments of electronics or print media can hide illicit data. Each shipment must be intercepted, and hidden data discovered, to prevent dissemination. Even repressive regimes like China, Cuba, and North Korea have been unable to halt smuggling of foreign data or digital media into their territories. If quantum computing enables brute-force attacks on public key cryptography, platforms and users may embrace quantum-safe methods.

Courts are still working through the ethics of secret IT surveillance. In the *Playpen* case, investigators dropped most charges rather than reveal the source code of a hacking tool that commandeered web browsers. Without a review of source code, defense attorneys claimed it was not possible to confirm the integrity of evidence, or ensure collection within the bounds of the warrant. Police agencies argue that disclosing hacking methods can reveal sensitive information about investigative capabilities. They are right. When hacking techniques are revealed, administrators quickly patch vulnerabilities. Failure to do so would place innocent users at risk. Some journalists and cybersecurity researchers believe that, in addition to its targets, the Playpen hack compromised hundreds of Tor-Mail users who may not have committed any crimes. Browser company Mozilla protested the FBI's nondisclosure of its hacking technique, as it may have rendered all Firefox users insecure. Researchers estimate that the FBI may have commandeered servers that hosted much of the child exploitation materials running through Tor (Sullum 2016). If true, this implies that police disseminated illegal materials (and allegedly improved their dissemination) in order to catch more users receiving it. Ultimately, only a few hundred of Playpen's 215,000 global users were arrested, and only a handful of American users were convicted.

Many private cybersecurity experts argue against encryption backdoors or other forms of mandated access, asserting that the public safety benefits are not outstripped by the costs of forcing innocent users to operate less securely, and that motivated criminals would communicate nonetheless. Police agencies have argued for mandated (or "exceptional") access to encrypted communications, as widespread adoption of encryption increasingly complicates lawful investigations (National Academies of Sciences 2018, 1–2). Problematically, many cybersecurity professionals have argued that lawful techniques can't selectively target malicious users without undermining the security of e-commerce, IoT devices, mainstream users, dissidents, journalists, repressed groups, and human rights campaigners. The ethical dilemma is significant. In 2019, encrypted messaging service WhatsApp sued two Israeli cyberespionage firms under the Computer Fraud and Abuse Act of 1986 for subverting their users' security. WhatsApp alleged that the Israeli firms enabled foreign intelligence agencies to subvert its systems to target journalists and human rights campaigners. Allegedly, one target was *Washington Post* columnist and Saudi dissident Jamal Khashoggi, who was purportedly spied on with hacking tools developed by the defendants before his assassination by Saudi agents.

Even if their trade-offs are unfavorable, encryption backdoors and (ostensibly) lawful hacking techniques are tame compared to the international competition to subvert technology supply chains. Commercial electronics rely on broad supply chains: software may be developed in numerous countries, hardware made in other countries, assembly completed in other countries, and users located in unrelated countries. At each chokepoint, a nation-state could insert vulnerabilities. That's ostensibly why the United States restricts government agencies from using ZTE or Huawei devices (Chinese), or Kaspersky software (Russian), and why China forbids Kaspersky and Symantec software (American).

Mandated backdoors would probably be announced under law, and potentially detectable even if undisclosed. However, zero-days and supply-chain exploits often go undetected, and undermine confidence in communications, defense, and commerce. Governments and cyberwarfare contractors are competing to render the tech sector insecure in order to spy, set up cyberattacks, and control communications in accordance with their own preferences. Formal justifications invoke bad actors like terrorists and cybercriminals, but the result has been a weakening of global cybersecurity and consumer trust. Tech firms variably cooperate or push back in an effort to reinforce consumer trust and comply with countervailing privacy and data protection laws.

Will all this surveillance stop online gun trafficking? It is too early to tell, but insofar as arms traffickers are cautious, the results might be lackluster even with expanding state surveillance. When anonymized markets have been shuttered, they have usually been replaced by improved services. Development continues on distributed peer-to-peer markets powered by strong encryption and crypto-currency. Projects like *OpenBazaar* seek to normalize anonymous peer-to-peer crypto-currency transactions. Consumers increasingly use encrypted VPNs and messaging applications, and major platforms increasingly adopt encryption or forswear data retention. Just as illegal weapon buyers circumvent registries and background checks by utilizing trusted suppliers, web-based weapons traffickers may become similarly cautious. In 2011, investigators sponsored by the City of New York tried to acquire guns illegally from 125 online sellers. They found that 62 percent of sellers they contacted were willing to sell guns illegally (City of New York 2011). However, a more recent Government Accountability Office investigation (2017) made 79 attempted purchases (seven on "Dark Web" platforms, and 72 on mainstream "surface web" platforms). Only two dark web purchases were successful, while all surface web attempts were unsuccessful. The caution exhibited by weapons traffickers and elaborate nature of trafficking investigation makes it difficult to arrest savvy traffickers online or off. Ultimately, many traffickers need only be introduced online before migrating to higher-trust channels to complete transactions.

Attempts to restrain digital gun files have had little effect so far. Under the 2018 injunctions, it is still technically illegal to post firearm code, but it's still fairly easy to find. S.1831, or the 3D-Printed Gun Safety Act of 2019, would criminalize distribution of digital firearm code "over the Internet or by means of the World Wide Web." This and similar legislation would resurrect Defense Distributed's ITAR takedown without relying on ITAR. However, the legislation stops short of declaring digital gun files illegal, and permits offline generation and sharing. Short of total prohibition on digital gun design (which might indeed be struck down and virtually unenforceable), DIYers will continue to have space to design firearms, discuss their products, and trade code through encrypted applications and physical media.

Some gunhackers are embracing this model. As mainstream social networks push gunhackers off-platform, they've migrated to friendlier platforms and encrypted chat servers. After Twitter, Reddit, and YouTube deplatformed many firearm tutorials, some producers migrated to Gunstreamer, PornHub, and other hosting sites. GitHub and the blockchain-based Spee.ch host firearm code. Even if removed from Spee.ch, the designs could theoretically remain accessible through the blockchain. When shooed from Reddit and Twitter, Deterrence Dispensed moved to the encrypted chat service Keybase, where they are now the fourth-largest user group with around 2,000 members. Despite publication restrictions, gunhackers continue to innovate. Even with throttled digital fabricators, encryption backdoors, endemic cybersurveillance, and the subsequent weakening of consumer privacy and private sector security, DIY experimenters and illicit gun traffickers may still find a way. If all else fails, they might just devolve to analog as craft gunmakers have done for centuries.

Forensic Alteration

> People are picking up the shell casings out here, simply just to make
> our job that much more difficult. Very frustrating.
> —Det. Scott Russ, Louisville Kentucky Homicide Unit
> (speaking at a murder scene) ("Lost Highway/Out for Murda,"
> *The First 48*, A&E, Season 9 Episode 16, January 28, 2010)

Firearm forensics has advanced since its nineteenth-century origins. Even
in its early days, the discipline reflected some desire for data repositories.
Forensic pioneers compiled reference books on the rifling striations left
on projectiles by common firearms. By the early twentieth century, investigators could identify the make and model of common guns with only a
recovered bullet. By the 1920s, comparison microscopes matched recovered bullets to *specific* guns (if recovered). *Tool mark analysis* strengthened
weapon matching by comparing the signatures left on spent cartridges by
firing pins, breech faces, and ejectors. Since cartridge cases are frequently
recovered, tool mark analysis was an important supplement. With incre-
mental improvements, firearm forensics has relied on these methods for
several decades. Recent developments involve the creation of forensic
databases, giving investigators broader abilities to match guns to offenses
across time and space.

Crime guns are frequently used in multiple crimes. Recovering forensic evidence from the same weapon at multiple scenes, or in the hands of
a seemingly unrelated offender, can narrow the field of suspects and identify repeat offenders. It's becoming easier for police to share forensic data
with repositories like the National Integrated Ballistic Information Network (NIBIN) and counterparts in other countries. NIBIN is a powerful
tool, but its full potential has not yet been met. Under-resourcing slows
the service, and local agency participation has been uneven. An evaluation found that local detectives rarely rely on NIBIN, since the system's
results often arrive after investigations are cleared by other means
(National Institute of Justice 2019).

Debate occasionally turns to whether forensic databases should collect
data retroactively on crime guns, or preemptively on *all* guns. NIBIN is
not without detractors in the gun rights and criminal defense communities. Firearm forensics is not as precise as DNA evidence, and NIBIN
searches frequently include duplicate matches. Investigators must determine which matches make sense in context. Expanding forensic databases to *all* guns would increase the potential for false matching as the
dataset becomes noisier.

Expanding data collection to all guns requires data collection during commercial manufacture. Serial number tracing systems provide some precedent for this. Serial numbers (and gun registries based on them) are established data infrastructures, though they don't contain forensic information except the serial itself. When a commercial firearm is recovered by police, registries and serial number tracing systems can identify the gun's most recent legal possessor or purchaser. This process is painstaking in America because dealer sales records are not allowed to be databased. The GCA mandated serialization of commercial firearms, and initially contained provisions for a Title I firearms registry as well. However, the registry was quashed over concerns that it would be used for general confiscation. Two decades later, the 1986 Firearm Owner's Protection Act (FOPA) prevented consolidation of sales records into a national database, as gun rights supporters feared the growing power of databases to form a consolidated national registry.

Consequently, BATFE does not retain records for Title I sales unless they are traced for investigative purposes. However, the records exist. They are kept by licensed dealers for 20 years, and investigators can review them. Maintaining decentralized paper records instead of a centralized database may sound silly to those unfamiliar with American gun politics, but the distinction is important to gun rights supporters and BATFE staff alike. Exceptions do allow BATFE to keep some tracing records. BATFE retains records for guns reported stolen, seized from felons, recovered from crime scenes, suspected of diversion, recorded in "multiple firearm sales reports," or sold by dealers who've had their books inspected or who've gone out of business. Through these exceptions, they've built an expanding (but far from comprehensive) in-house tracing infrastructure without technically creating a registry. Similar tensions apply to *universal background checks*. Currently, background check records are not permanently retained, as this might constitute a feared "backdoor registry." Despite these limitations, BATFE maintains its National Tracing Center, where specialists review warehouses of sales records kept on file, and make calls or dispatch agents to review dealer records that aren't on file. Given these data management challenges, BATFE has pieced together a fairly effective tracing system. Most queries are successful if the serial number is intact.

But it's not always intact. Defacement can obliterate serials. Unsurprisingly, defacement of a commercial gun is often an indicator of trafficking (Braga et al. 2012). When traffickers deface commercial firearms, they make it harder to identify the retail dealer or purchaser. This insulates straw buyers who purchase retail guns to resell illegally. If a gun-toting criminal is arrested, an obliterated serial prevents detectives from tracing to the straw buyer. If everybody keeps their mouth shut and no other evidence is found, detectives will have a hard time finding the traffickers.

International treaties and most national laws require firearm serialization. The UN Protocol on Small Arms and International Tracing Instrument requires firearms to be uniquely marked. Markings must be on an "essential or structural component of the weapon where the component's destruction would render the weapon permanently inoperable and incapable of reactivation" (United Nations General Assembly 2015). In practice, this usually means the frame or receiver. Some signatories don't enforce the requirements, and illegally made guns usually contain no serials unless they are phony. Serial numbers can be removed with hand files or power tools. Benefits may vary. Most countries criminalize defacement, so anyone caught with defaced guns could be charged. Additionally, serial number recovery has been a success for forensic science: acid etching and heat treating can recover defaced serials, and newer techniques like electron backscatter diffraction are frequently successful even when defacement appears thorough.

An obviously defaced firearm can't be legally resold, and police will notice the alteration. As U.S. marshal Mike Smith told me, "Filing the serial is a lot like John Dillinger scraping off his fingerprints. Sure, you've got no fingerprints, but now you're the only guy in the world without fingerprints" (Interview 2015). Nevertheless, thorough defacements are unrecoverable, and some jurisdictions report significant numbers of defaced guns. Defacement incentives may be greater in jurisdictions that maintain registries and tracing systems, as it separates trafficked guns from these supply-side data infrastructures.

By default, no illegally made weapon appears in any registry or serial number tracing system. Rarely, false markings are observed on counterfeit guns. More rarely, police encounter identical guns with identical serials, suggesting replication. Increasing availability of precision engraving, etching, and laser cutting tools may improve phony serialization in the future. At that point, hacked registry data may prove valuable to gun counterfeiters.

Serialization has never been perfect. Homemade ghost guns don't have serials. However, many guns produced abroad, or made before the GCA, don't have traceable serials either. Sometimes, guns have valid serials, but the manufacturing or retail records can't be found, making the gun equally untraceable as if it had no serial at all. Likewise, tracing may not support trafficking charges if the legal purchaser can provide an innocent explanation for how the gun ended up in the wrong hands. Serial numbers and registries make large-scale trafficking harder, but when traffickers and gun criminals are aware that weapons can be traced through serials and registries, they may deface the serials, steal guns, smuggle unregistered guns from elsewhere, make guns, or file phony theft or loss reports so straw buyers can't be held responsible when the guns are used in crimes.

This seemed to be the case in Canada. Criminologist Gary Mauser contends that during the years 2003–2010 when Canada maintained its now-scrapped long gun registry, only 1 percent of crime guns could be traced through the registry. The registry had no influence on homicide (which declined more in the United States during the same period), and apparently wasn't responsible for solving any gun crimes (Mauser n.d., 11). Similar criticisms undermined New Zealand's registry, which was abandoned in the 1970s but resurrected after the Christchurch Mosque shootings. However, it is unclear that the terrorist responsible for that massacre would have been deterred by registration since he bought the weapons legally and did not expect to escape. A few American jurisdictions have introduced, scrapped, and sometimes reintroduced registries. Gun rights supporters invariably criticize them as ineffectual and potentially confiscatory, while gun control supporters argue that they would be more effective if expanded and properly resourced.

Universal ballistic databases try to extend forensic data infrastructures to all guns. A universal ballistics database requires that all guns be test-fired before sale, and their bullets striae and casing imprints collected. If the gun is used in crime, recovered bullets or casings tie the gun to the scene, while tracing and registration tie the gun to whoever legally bought or registered it. Theoretically, *microstamping* would provide greater investigative convenience by requiring guns to stamp a serial number onto spent cases. Either way, police could identify the legal purchaser or registrant based only on a recovered casing. This sounds pretty good, but like many issues in gun regulation, the science, politics, and practicalities are disputed.

Gun control advocates argue that these technologies are sufficiently developed to apply them to all guns, supporting investigations without an unacceptable false hit rate. Gun rights advocates insist that universal forensic infrastructures would generate unacceptable false hit rates, require unmanageable compliance costs, and the systems could be bypassed with simple techniques. Gun control advocates argue that industry has dragged its feet on development of microstamping even as the technology is increasingly viable. Industry advocates reply that microstamping is far from ready, and would provide little investigative benefit.

Today, the only state that requires microstamping is California, though similar legislation has been passed in Washington, D.C., and discussed in several states and Congress. Some jurisdictions have attempted supply-side ballistic databases, but with poor results. In the 2000s, Maryland spent $5 million on a supply-side ballistic database, while New York spent $5 million per year on its database. Neither system was credited for any convictions. Both were scrapped.

Microstamping is proposed as a more reliable solution. 2018's *Pena v. Lindley* outlines the arguments in detail. In that case, California mandated microstamping for all new handgun designs. Gun rights advocates sued, arguing that no commercial manufacturer has developed a reliable microstamping system. By their argument, the law was a de facto ban on new handgun models in California, thereby violating the Second Amendment. The Federal Appellate Court for the Ninth Circuit disagreed, upholding the law because it permits residents to buy many grandfathered models that aren't microstamped. Perversely, the practical result was to guarantee that handguns continue to be sold in California, but *none* are microstamped.

While advocates debate supply-side forensics, DIY methods provide many bypasses. Supply-side databases only cover commercial guns. Shotgun pellets provide limited forensic data, and usually can't be traced back to the weapon that fired it. Revolvers don't eject cases, and barrels can be altered with hand files. Firing pins, ejectors, and breech faces can be altered or swapped. Barrels can be replaced, and barrel replacements can also change a firearm's caliber. Preventing these simple circumventions would require tracking systems for all barrels, firing pins, and other easily altered or swapped components. Crude homemade guns are unrifled. This confounds striation analysis, but the rarity of un-striated handgun bullets would indicate a DIY gun, and the idiosyncrasies of craft gunmaking may actually increase the prospects for forensic matching between projectiles and firearms. Ammunition is particularly difficult to trace. DIY methods might defeat ammunition tracing. *Reloaders* could defeat a database by fabricating cartridges, reusing cartridges, or defacing markings. Even unsophisticated criminals could use revolvers and shotguns, pick up spent cartridges, or "salt" crime scenes with cartridges from unrelated guns. Writing for the NRA, firearm forensic examiner C. Rodney James (2008) claimed there are at least 50 methods to bypass supply-side databases of guns and ammunition.

The desire for universal forensic databasing is understandable. Ideally, these tools would make it impossible to shoot a gun without leaving evidence that identifies the shooter. When focused only on crime guns, these resources hold great potential. Problematically, advocates continue to argue whether the technology is reliable enough to apply to all guns, while real-life deployments as *universal* forensic infrastructures have produced lackluster results. Meanwhile, DIY gunmaking and alterations provide plausible circumventions. Though DIY products are intrinsically harder to trace, there is some hope of applying forensic techniques to homemade guns. Weapons researcher N.R. Jenzen-Jones and his company Armament Research Services (ARES) are working on something along these lines: software that can assist forensic matching of individual DIY guns, or DIY guns produced from known "families," to recovered projectiles or cases (Interview 2018). Tools like these may soon match homemade crime guns to crime scenes (assuming the gun is recovered), much as existing techniques already do with commercial firearms.

Hacking "Smart Guns"

Smart guns include features that ensure only authorized users can fire them. Smart guns might dis-incentivize gun theft because stolen guns would be useless. Self-defenders couldn't be shot with their own gun. Accidents and suicides by unauthorized users might be reduced. These benefits are attractive, but a number of challenges must be overcome. DIY techniques create problems and solutions for smart guns.

For market viability, smart guns must be as reliable as conventional firearms. Many buyers would also resist any networked firearm technology that enables third-party tracking or control. Police, military, and armed citizens may be suspicious of technologies that could allow an adversary, technical failure, or natural hazard to disable the firearm. For defensive, sporting, or hunting applications, user-authentication must involve no delay. Some users are skeptical of firearms with integral electronics (which firearms are already reliable without). A few police agencies have expressed interest, while reiterating that smart guns must be as reliable as conventional variants. The President of the International Association of Chiefs of Police stated there are "plenty of agencies interested in beta testing the technology," but that "[a smart gun] can't be 99% accurate, it has to be 100% accurate. It has to work every single time" (Rosenwald 2015).

Progress has been made, but meeting the standards of clientele remains challenging. The NRA and NSSF have both stated they don't oppose smart guns, but they have challenged proposals to mandate them in lieu of conventional guns (as a poorly considered but now-rescinded New Jersey law once did). A 2016 NRA-ILA statement reads:

Gun control supporters advocate laws to prohibit the sale of firearms that do not possess "smart" technology, as a way to prohibit the manufacture of traditional handguns, raise the price of handguns that would be allowed to be sold and, presumably, to embed into handguns a device that would allow guns to be disabled remotely. The NRA doesn't oppose the development of "smart" guns, nor the ability of Americans to voluntarily acquire them. However, NRA opposes any law prohibiting Americans from acquiring or possessing firearms that don't possess "smart" gun technology.

Larry Keane of the NSSF expressed similar sentiments: "If people think there's a market for these products, then the market should work. People should be allowed to build what they think is a better mousetrap. The firearms industry has never been opposed to the research and development of this technology" (Rose 2014).

If preconditions of reliability and protection from third-party interference can be met, smart guns may prove marketable. While some consumers are skeptical, others who would not buy conventional firearms might find smart guns appealing. Estimated consumer interest in smart guns depends on who conducts the survey. The Johns Hopkins Bloomberg School of Public Health found that a majority of Americans would consider purchasing smart guns, whereas the NSSF conducted a survey indicating lower demand (Benham 2016; Bazinet 2013). In 2013, the Violence Policy Center, a gun control advocacy group, cautioned that smart guns are attractive to non-gun owners and might increase gun ownership, and public investments in the technology should therefore be discouraged.

The United States has wide legal space for experimentation. This usually catches headlines when applied provocatively. For example, a teenager received media attention for mounting a remotely operated pistol on an aerial drone. Authorities investigated, concluding no laws were broken. He then designed another drone with a flamethrower and posted a video of his drone-roasted Thanksgiving turkey. This story combines several elements of a technologic moral panic: youth, weapons, and drones. However, the legal space for this experimentation enables other youth to apply their ingenuity differently. Another teenager was lauded for designing a fingerprint-activated smart gun, for which he received a $50,000 research grant. He used some of his funding to buy a 3D-printer to complete his smart gun designs.

The primary smart gun user-authentication methods are biometrics and radio frequency identification (RFID). It's not easy to design a biometric firearm that shoots immediately under varying conditions. RFID allows for rapid use, but it has drawbacks. Transmissions could theoretically be jammed or scanned, and if the gun is in close proximity to the authorized user (as in an entangled or contested scenario), it might be fired by the adversary. Smart guns include electronics, which are less-reliable than conventional mechanisms. Even if all new firearms were "smart," a billion "dumb" guns would not disappear, nor would the tools to make them.

Universal smart gun standards may backfire given the ease with which hackers undermine other electronic security standards. The same capabilities that enable a teenager to design a printable smart gun, may also allow an experienced hacker to jailbreak the weapon in hours. Even encryption may not secure stolen smart guns: hackers might just remove the electronics. A mandated standard could exacerbate the problem: many digital devices are hackable, and smart guns convert mechanical items to digital devices. Smart guns have already been hacked. In 2015, *Wired's* Andy Greenberg reported on a smart rifle that a hacker could remotely disable or retarget, and a clever hacker from Colorado demonstrated that the first-generation Armatrix smart gun could be unlocked with a cheap magnet.

If smart gun standards are universal, one successful hack might invalidate the security of *every* smart gun overnight. Commercial manufacturers have been hesitant to invest: developing the technology is expensive and politically contentious, yet manufacturers run the risk of investing millions in smart guns only to be embarrassed by gunhacking videos within days of product release. Open space for competitive experimentation would produce more resilient smart gun designs. The open source movement can contribute to smart guns as a consumer option, while also invalidating top-down standards. If hundreds of open source engineers have creative freedom to design and test smart guns in different technical directions, viable smart guns will probably arrive sooner.

Note

1. The actor who played the Soup Nazi sued for unauthorized use of his image. Serbu had to stop making the shirts.

CHAPTER EIGHT

Enter the Tech Vigilantes: Surveillance Capitalism and "Corporate Gun Control"

I think large intermediaries will be under more pressure to remove and deplatform content. The problem with creating "public interest" standards when your audience is the entire planet, it's very difficult to know what the "community standards" should be. Every government across the board will want a piece of the action.
—Adam Thierer, Mercatus Center at George Mason University
(Interview 2018)

I don't think that they anticipated being censored. The libertarian types have been blindsided by the extent to which the tech platforms proved to be illiberal. They have business risks they need to mitigate. If that means your Second Amendment or First Amendment rights get trampled, they don't care!
—Jon Stokes, technology and firearms journalist
(Interview 2018)

Privacy concerns have long been a fulcrum in America's toxic gun politics. A repurposing of gun registries (or permanent background check records) for confiscation is a nightmare scenario for gun rights activists, and fear of gun registration has undoubtedly fueled the popularization of homemade guns in America. Registries have sometimes served as confiscation infrastructures abroad, and have served limited confiscations (and proposed confiscations) in America—a reality that gun rights supporters belabor and gun control supporters dismiss. Irrespective of their potential benefits, distrust of gun registration has undermined its adoption in America. An unknown but nontrivial portion of home gunmaking reflects this dynamic, as unregistered ghost guns fulfill a desire to keep firearm ownership private.

Yet, for all the toxicity the registry fight has brought, gun registries are practically antiquated. The registry debate bypasses an increasingly relevant reality: the tech sector knows more about most citizens than the government does. Harvard professor Shoshanna Zuboff (2019) calls this the Age of Surveillance Capitalism, in which privacy is subsumed in an overarching surveillance market. A tedious story of our lives is recounted in our emails, online transactions, social media activity, court and criminal records, property records, search queries, GPS data, travel history, cloud documents, exercise activities, browser histories, and smart device usage. To varying degrees, all of these can be logged. Zuboff describes this public-private surveillance infrastructure as essentially amoral. The system wants your data, and the system is getting it. It is still largely up to journalists, civil libertarians, and consumer watchdogs to raise privacy concerns. The tech sector vacuums ever-growing swaths of consumer data, and governments periodically demand (or appropriate) access to it. Citizens must campaign for privacy on platforms that can shut down disfavored speech with a keystroke.

The expansive scope of surveillance capitalism holds potential to become history's greatest tool for crime-fighting *and* repression. Gun registries contain few datapoints: serial number, name and address of the registrant, and a few other details. Registries don't know who possesses the gun at any moment, and most don't record ammunition or accessories. Registries can increase accountability when registered guns disappear suspiciously, but they don't record illegal transactions because illegal transactors don't report them. Registries don't know if you're making guns, nor your levels of training and practice, or what guns you want in the future. Registries only know what the retailer discloses on initial sale, or what the registrant chooses to disclose later.

A tech-sector registry could combine probabilistic forecasts of what users have and what users *might* do. A state registry doesn't know if somebody spends most of their time making anonymous threats, researching targets, making weapons, or watching extremist media. Yet, unless the user is privacy-conscious, their internet service providers probably know. Even security-conscious users can be surveilled by intelligence agencies, private hacking companies, or proficient cybercriminals. Gun registries (and other lawful data repositories) are skewed toward compliant populations. Even among compliant users, a registry doesn't know who has recently suffered mental health crises elevating their risk of harm, nor can it forecast probable targets. Not only do technology services collect a spectrum of useful data for such forecasting, they are under increasing pressure to harness it.

Location data and social networks do provide granular insights on violence risk. Back in the 1970s, a study of 10,000 Philadelphia youth found that 51 percent of the population's crime was attributable to a 6 percent subpopulation. A 2015 study found most crime in several U.S. cities was concentrated in less than 5 percent of their areas (Weisburd 2015). The United Kingdom's *Guardian* found 26 percent of America's gun homicides occurred in locations containing only 1.5 percent of the population (Aufrichtig 2017). Research shows 85 percent of shootings occurred within preexisting social networks (Papachristos, Braga, and Hureau 2012), and 70 percent of Chicago's gunshot injuries were perpetrated by 6 percent of the population (Papachristos, Wildeman, and Roberto 2015). A 2018 study of 20+ U.S. cities found less than 1 percent of their populations responsible for more than 50 percent of shootings. Not only is violence connected to high-risk social networks, but most violence is committed by a minority of *that* minority. For example, networks containing only 0.15 percent of the population were responsible for 53 percent of shootings in Minneapolis (Lurie, Acevedo, and Ott 2018).

With expansive access to user data, tech platforms could support granular interventions. They've already begun. Facebook's AI monitors users and their contacts to flag those at risk of suicide. Human reviewers then dispatch police for wellness checks. In November 2017, Facebook's Global Head of Safety stated that the company triggered about 3,500 wellness checks in the prior year (Kaste 2018). Eventually, algorithms could flag individuals for violent crime, prostitution, drug trafficking (or use), or weapon violations. Algorithmic risk assessments might incorporate object recognition and content analysis tools to determine whether a user owns guns. *Imagga* and similar applications can search through social media postings and identify firearms. However, effectiveness would require access to all content (including "private" and encrypted content). Unless user data collection is universally mandated, privacy-oriented users could move to platforms that do not retain or view user data. Even the NRA has gotten wise to this possibility, warning members to avoid posting photos of their guns with serial numbers visible, lest the images be data-mined for a backdoor registry (Luebbert 2019).

The prospect of a technology sector applying its omniscience at the front lines of public safety is fraught with complications. Private platforms are less constrained by free speech, due process, transparency, or search and seizure boundaries that apply to liberal governments. Yet, even liberal governments regularly gain lawful (and occasionally unlawful) access to user data. Numerous tech firms and hacking companies have generated controversy for violating user privacy or compromising liberal values to service repressive governments.

Algorithmic harm reduction remains a black box of proprietary methods and undiscovered liabilities. As Ian Barnett and John Torous (2019) wrote in the *Annals of Internal Medicine*, in testing its suicide-prevention programs on users, Facebook may be engaged in "clinical research" requiring greater transparency, credentials, informed consent, and disclosure of outcomes. Predictive policing (aka *precrime*) methods can forecast crime patterns and hotspots, but its ethics and accuracy are debatable when singling out individuals. Applying predictive analytics to individuals carries risk of chilling speech and commerce, incorrectly placing users under investigation, or supporting criminal charges based on opaque methods.

Nevertheless, when the status quo fails to prevent outrageous violence, calls for tech sector intervention understandably gain ground. Some are calling for greater leveraging of private sector surveillance technologies and user data access. In 2014, the ACLU discovered that the DEA intended to deploy, or had deployed, license plate readers at legal gun shows (U.S. Department of Justice Drug Enforcement Administration 2014). A 2018 proposal in the Illinois legislature called for police review of social media accounts before granting firearm licenses (Blakley 2019), and a 2019 Illinois proposal (SB337) would require 24-hour license plate recognition at licensed firearm dealers. A 2018 New York bill (S9197) would require firearm applicants to submit to reviews of their Facebook, Snapchat, Twitter, and Instagram accounts, and their last three years of Google, Yahoo, and Bing searches.

In addition to opposition by gun rights and civil liberties groups, it is unclear that these measures would effectively combat gun crime or trafficking. Privacy-oriented platforms and search engines limit data retention. Few crime guns are acquired at gun shows, and known offenders are already disqualified from retail purchasing. Nevertheless, traffickers could bypass license plate readers by calling a taxi with a burner phone and paying with cash, or simply *walking in*. The use of more potent surveillance technologies like facial recognition at firearm retailers would require massive deployments that are increasingly challenged as unacceptable when applied to other types of crime. Likewise, current regulations already prevent known offenders from purchasing at retailers, ensuring that the surveillance would primarily track legal buyers.

Mainstream tech platforms face pressure to share information for public safety, but they are also pressured to protect user privacy. Will tech companies be required to preserve user data for public safety review? Are platforms liable if they send police to a user's home in error? Can the government deem a firearm applicant suspicious because she doesn't use social media? In the age of surveillance capitalism, divesting from social media is a subversive act.

Meanwhile, corporations are embroiled in a proxy-war over firearms in the marketplace and online sharing of firearms information. In 2015, Walmart pulled "military-style" firearms from its shelves, and in 2018 raised its required age for long guns to 21 from the federal standard of 18. In 2019, it phased out some ammunition. After the Parkland shooting, Citibank threatened to cancel the accounts of firearm businesses unless they adopted sales policies more restrictive than required by federal law. In 2019, Dick's Sporting Goods pulled guns from 125 locations, contributing to an "accelerated decline" in its hunting business. However, in a country with tens of thousands of independent firearm retailers, disarmament by big-box stores is largely symbolic. Many American gun stores have little need to appeal to nonfirearm customers and are less vulnerable to pressure campaigns.

Gun retailers are more dependent on the financial, e-commerce, and social media sectors. In 2019, e-commerce firm Salesforce banned business clients from selling a variety of semiautomatic guns, 10+ round magazines, 3D-printed guns, gun blueprints, and other legal items (Salesforce 2019). In 2018, bookkeeping behemoth Intuit/QuickBooks cancelled the transactions of a firearms training academy, claiming violations of their prohibition on "online gun sales." These sales entailed customers ordering products from the academy's licensed store. The order would be shipped to a licensed retailer in the recipient's state, where the recipient would pass a background check for receipt. These transactions are legal under federal law, don't bypass background checks, and represent a significant portion of retail gun sales. If payment processors boycott these sales, legal firearms commerce would take a hit.

Some elected officials have proposed divestment from hedge funds, pension funds, or public contracting with vendors connected to the firearms industry. In 2019, the San Francisco Board of Supervisors passed a unanimous but unconstitutional resolution declaring the NRA a "domestic terrorist organization," and declaring their intention to reject contractors with relationships with the NRA. A similar Los Angeles ordinance required city contractors to disclose any connections with the NRA. Financial investigations have focused on the NRA directly. In 2019, New York Attorney General Letitia James launched a probe of the organization's finances, with potential to suspend the NRA's nonprofit status. The NRA resisted with a series of lawsuits. However, some revelations about the NRA's finances have indeed caused internal rifts, as former president Oliver North accused CEO Wayne LaPierre of cronyism and financial mismanagement, members at the NRA's 2019 conference brought a failed motion to oust LaPierre, and the organization cut ties with its public relations firm Ackerman McQueen.

Others have suggested banks and payment processers surveille gun owners directly. In 2018, *New York Times* columnist Andrew Ross Sorkin observed that at least eight American mass shooters ran up credit debts on gun transactions over a period of 11 years. The article suggested financial surveillance to identify suspicious purchasing patterns. A 2019 congressional proposal, the "Gun Violence Prevention Through Financial Intelligence Act," would begin feasibility processes along these lines. In some respects, financial surveillance is plausible. Google alone claims to have access to 70 percent of Americans' credit and debit transactions. However, there are procedural questions. Who decides what legal transactions should be flagged? Hunters, firearm trainers, police and security professionals, collectors, "preppers," and competitive shooters may make innocent transactions that reviewers deem suspicious, particularly if the reviewers are unfamiliar with these subcultures. If an algorithm is looking for ammunition purchases in "assault weapon" calibers, will it disregard identical purchases for bolt-action rifles? Do corporate reviewers determine which legal buyers to flag for police? Will there be a toll-free hotline for lawsuits?

Additionally, can enough data be analyzed? Much payment data is nongranular. Some retailers resist sharing stock keeping unit (SKU) data, as it could be damaging if leaked or exploited. In fact, a 2019 European Commission investigation focused on Amazon.com's ability to exploit its access to merchant data to stifle competition. It may be possible to require retailers to collect and share more granular data, but this entails compliance costs, business risks, and legal challenges.

None of these complications compare to the unfavorable sociomathematics of the *base rate fallacy*. Security analysts periodically cite this fallacy as a drawback of broad security regimes. Simplified, the base rate fallacy is a failure to account for aggregate true positive and false positive rates when applied to samples in which true positives are rarer than false positives. When profiling rare threats, base rate errors result in many more false positives than true positives even as the profile appears anecdotally accurate. This might be acceptable if false positives impose no harm. However, false positives in security and policing often harm those who've been singled out while wasting resources and reducing the profile's credibility. Writing for the moderate gun rights blog *OpenSourceDefense.org*, software engineer Kareem Shaya (2018) applies this logic to Ross Sorkin's profiling concept. Assuming unrealistically low false positive and negative rates of 1 percent, if 25 million Americans make gun-related credit card purchases per year, and four are mass shooters, in most years the profiling system will catch all shooters, but will also generate 250,000 false positives. The profile would be wrong in 99.9984 percent of cases.

Similar arithmetic could undermine red flag legislation. Assuming every state receives only two tips from concerned citizens per day, that's 36,500 annual tips. The highest estimate of mass shootings in America is one per day in 2015 and this estimate may be overinclusive (Ingraham 2015). *Mother Jones* estimated seven mass fatality public shootings in 2015 under more conservative definitions (Follman, Aronsen, and Pan 2019). Nevertheless, if we double the highest estimate, we get 730 annual incidents for the system to prevent. So, about 2 percent of tips would identify a genuine threat, and 35,770 nonthreats would be investigated. Let's assume the system is pretty smart: firearm recovery teams are dispatched to 99 percent of real threats, but only 1 percent of false threats. This system would seize guns from 722 authentic threats and 357 nonthreats, while missing seven real shooters. Even assuming artificially low error rates, every tip would have a 98 percent probability of error, and 1/3 of seizures would be incorrect. Worse, this assumes all tips are made in good faith. If red flag laws provide for anonymous submissions without penalty for intentional falsehood, some people will file false complaints hoping that police will harass the targets of their personal beefs. Street gangs might file tips against rivals, forcing police to become their enforcers.

Profiling difficulties are *worse* for home gunmaking. The system would need to identify all possible components, while also identifying a vast range of tools, materials, and media. Hardware stores, gun retailers, digital tool suppliers, industrial equipment manufacturers, and even libraries and bookstores would need to be surveilled to produce a high-confidence forecast of who is making guns. The active failure rate could prove extreme, and the system would suffer a critical vulnerability: it is legal to buy firearms, tools, and media with cash.

Beyond financial services and big-box retailers, the fight over information is heating up. As DIY gunmaking and modification have been increasingly enabled by digital media, gun rights advocates have criticized social media companies for "deplatforming": essentially censoring, demonetizing, or reducing the search availability of firearms content that is technically legal, but undesirable to platform administrators for cultural reasons or due to liability concerns. "I think it's [deplatforming] totally real, and it's driven by liability concerns, and it's rational," said Jon Stokes. Stokes is in a unique position to comment: he's a cofounder of *Ars Technica*, and also a prominent technology and firearms journalist.[1] Stokes went on: "People say, 'I don't want to get deplatted by my service providers. It's an existential business risk. I know some of these people, tech execs. I definitely don't think most of them want to take away peoples' rights, but they're dealing with a market demand for tyranny. I don't think they know what to do with it" (Interview 2018).

Deplatforming also impacts smaller-scale users and content providers. After the government settled with Defense Distributed, the Second Amendment Foundation reposted the files. The federal government didn't stop them, but users quickly found that Twitter and Facebook wouldn't permit the URL to be shared despite its prior publication in mainstream media and its federal legality. In following months and years, Amazon Web Services, YouTube, Shopify, Reddit, and other platforms narrowed the scope of firearms information that could be shared, posted, or monetized. Much of this deplatformed content related to DIY gunmaking, modification, or maintenance (though YouTube did somewhat relax its guidelines since).

It's clear that the internet is becoming less the open platform of the 1990s and early aughts. *Freedom House's* internet freedom reports reflect a decade of declining global internet freedom. Authoritarian regimes use prohibitions on fake news to censor legitimate journalism, while conservatives, libertarians, and progressives accuse big tech of deplatforming alternative views in the guise of neutral restrictions on hate speech, misinformation, or term-of-service violations. Tech sector "neutrality" is unconvincing to most Americans. In a 2018 Pew Research poll, 72 percent of Americans (85 percent of conservatives and 62 percent of liberals) believed online platforms censor political speech that the *company* finds disagreeable Smith 2018). Meanwhile, authentic incitement and disinformation periodically generates nasty consequences.

In 2019 alone, the online forum 8chan hosted manifestos by the New Zealand Mosque shooter, the Poway Synagogue shooter, and the El Paso gunman. In response, web infrastructure company Cloudflare pulled service from 8chan. After white nationalists held a rally in Charlottesville Virginia in 2017, Cloudflare refused service to the neo-Nazi website *The Daily Stormer*. In a company email, Cloudflare CEO Matthew Prince defended the decision while acknowledging the ethical quandary, saying "Literally, I woke up in a bad mood and decided someone shouldn't be allowed on the internet. No one should have that power" (Conger 2017).

Prince also acknowledged deplatforming's flipside: shutting down a website doesn't necessarily eliminate the activity. Prince later said that banning 8chan "would make the job of law enforcement and controlling hate groups online harder" (Roose 2019). Deplatformed activities may only migrate to other services or *go dark*, where researchers and law enforcement are harder pressed to track them. 2018's FOSTA-SESTA legislation foreshadowed the problem. By making platforms liable for commercial sex activity even if it occurs against their own policies, FOSTA resulted in the shutdown of websites that had purposely (or inadvertently) facilitated prostitution. However, before FOSTA, some of the same platforms were lauded by police and sex workers' advocates for removing illegal content and assisting investigations of authentically predatory activity. With several mainstream personals websites shuttered by FOSTA, sex workers argued they were being pushed into the more dangerous underworld. Yet, as long as any competition exists in technology services, disfavored speech may find a home. FOSTA-SESTA didn't prevent sex workers from discreetly continuing even on popular platforms like Instagram. The Daily Stormer and 8chan both went back online with different infrastructure services.

The government of New Zealand pursued brute force censorship: after the Christchurch Mosque shooting, New Zealand's Chief Censor prohibited the attacker's smarmy white supremacist manifesto,[2] threatening 14 years imprisonment for possessing or sharing it. This is a rather more censorious response than the post-9/11 years, when mainstream publishers reprinted al-Qaeda manifestoes to assist the public in understanding a violent enemy's worldview. While censoring extremist material is meant to reduce social contagion, it also toys with authoritarian practices. If this policy were broadly adopted, the citizens of free countries would depend on governments and media intermediaries to present only *official* narratives on the motivations behind political violence.

While many surveillance, censorship, and deplatforming proposals could provide ways to identify suspicious activity, discourage illegal gun-making or trafficking, and perhaps even undermine the role of firearms in the legitimate economy, they are also a species of technologic vigilantism. In America, many "corporate gun control" initiatives do not target activities that courts or legislatures have declared illegal. Rather, they undermine legal activity that is disfavored within liberal segments of corporate culture. Agreement on new lines of speech, commerce, and consumer privacy has proven elusive. Pressures to politicize banking and reign-in the toxic effects of open web platforms are strengthening. Yet, many consumers and civil libertarians are uncomfortable with new lines being drawn not by courts or legislatures, but an ascendant technology oligarchy. This is more than an abstract: insofar as media standards are restrictive toward nonleft views, they may backfire politically. Indeed, psychologists have demonstrated that "politically correct" communication norms pushed independent voters toward Donald Trump instead of Hillary Clinton (Conway, Repke, and Houck 2017).

Where do we draw the lines in a public square dominated by large technology platforms, particularly when activities are legal but disfavored within the culture of big tech? Conversely, even many civil libertarians hesitate to defend the worst ugliness unleashed in the online space. As Stokes acknowledged, "Even I couldn't publicly complain about the deplatforming of Gab [social media site and magnet for white nationalists] after the Pittsburgh synagogue shooting, it was such a toxic swamp" (Interview 2018). At any rate, Gab is back online.

Uncertainty in the new standards of speech and commerce have caused concern among firearm retailers, consumers, content providers, and supportive legislators. The sense of a corporativist conspiracy against gun rights is growing among conservatives. Writing for *The National Review*, David French (2018) wrote that corporate gun control may be "as great a danger to gun rights as it is to the culture of free speech in this nation." Referring to the notorious conspiracy theorist and internet troll, conservative journalist Stephen Gutowski described the deplatforming of firearms content as "far more aggressive than anything we've seen with Alex Jones" (Twitter Post, August 8, 2018).[3] When YouTube demonetized and censored a variety of legal firearm content, a few firearm channels migrated to that bastion of free speech: porn sites.

Others have taken vigilante stands to undermine gun control. In a takeoff on American "sanctuary cities" which limit local cooperation with federal immigration authorities, the Second Amendment "sanctuary county" movement has grown. In Second Amendment sanctuaries, police or elected officials deprioritize enforcement of gun laws they believe to be unconstitutional. Alaska, Idaho, Montana, Wyoming, and Kansas have passed some equivalent of Second Amendment sanctuary legislation. More than half the counties of Washington, Colorado, New Mexico, and Illinois, about a third of counties in Nevada and Oregon, and a smattering of counties in other states have declared themselves sanctuaries. When New York passed the SAFE Act in 2013, a majority of counties passed protest resolutions, and the New York State Sheriff's Association joined a lawsuit against several provisions.

Some conservatives propose penalizing financial institutions for usurping the powers of public regulators. George Mason University's Brian

Knight observed that Citi and Bank of America both received federal bailouts in 2008, and that banks rely on government-provided services, market advantages, and legal protections. He cautioned against politicized banking: "When banks use government-provided market power to force social change, they are effectively acting as a private regulator. However, we did not deputize banks as social regulators, and it's possible that any number of 'controversial' organizations—Planned Parenthood, adult entertainment shops, fast-food restaurants—would lose access to financial services if we allow it to become the norm" (Knight 2018).

In 2019, Republican Senators Kevin Cramer and John Kennedy introduced the Freedom Financing Act, which would penalize banks for refusing clients engaged in legal firearms commerce. Some executives have expressed reservations about deplatforming legal activities. During a congressional oversight hearing, Wells Fargo CEO Timothy Sloan said, "We just don't believe that it is a good idea to encourage banks to enforce legislation that does not exist" (U.S. Congress 2019). Visa spokeswoman Amanda Pires quoted: "We do not believe Visa should be in the position of setting restrictions on the sale of lawful goods or services" (Sorkin 2018).

Other gun rights measures try to counteract the specter of surveillance by healthcare providers. The NY SAFE Act of 2013 includes provisions for healthcare workers to report patients who may pose a threat to self or others. The patient's records are reviewed for signs of gun ownership, and registered weapons may be seized. However, the New York State Psychiatric Association objected, observing that the law omitted standards of seriousness and imminence imposed by the national patient privacy legislation HIPAA (New York State Psychiatric Association n.d.). Meanwhile, a dozen U.S. states have passed physician *gag laws* to prevent doctors from inquiring about patients' gun ownership. However, these laws have been challenged on the basis that they violate the First Amendment rights of physicians to constructively discuss firearm safety with patients outside of any confiscatory program.

These dynamics reflect a capture of security policy within a totalizing zero-sum politics. In America, many sociopolitical issues have become seemingly intractable within a framework of diametrically opposed cultural views. With an immoderate and uncivil political duopoly, national elections have become referenda on which half of the population should fear the cultural preferences of the other half. With only two parties and an increasing focus on social engineering as the spoils of electoral victory, even moderates are pressured toward partisanship. Civil persuasion is eclipsed by binary mass mobilization. Two sides are allowed. Pick *one*.

Gun policy (and ghost guns themselves) reflect America's erosion in sociopolitical trust. Gun rights advocates don't trust that universal background checks or registries wouldn't be turned toward confiscation. Gun control advocates insist that confiscation would be absurd, while lauding confiscation abroad and occasionally proposing it at home. Citing research and cases of malfeasance, some gun control advocates reject carry licensing as a contributor to crime. Meanwhile, studies by the famously progun economist John Lott (2010) suggests that licensed carriers are particularly law-abiding (241–48). Consequently, blue jurisdictions make carry permits unobtainable even for well-qualified citizens, while red jurisdictions pass laws allowing residents to carry guns with no training or licensing whatsoever. In restrictive jurisdictions, the sight of a nonuniformed citizen carrying a handgun can set off lockdowns and tense police contacts. In looser jurisdictions, millions carry concealed weapons without incident, and gun rights activists carry ARs into coffee shops as a political statement.

This is a capture of political power to create opposing sociocultural bubbles, each hoping to prevail nationally. Coherent national policies are elusive, and partisans continually provide reasons for their adversaries to question the stability of valued rights. Those who feel vulnerable learn a perverse lesson: government and tech may be your friend today, but could become your enemy later. In a culture war, rights become ammunition. When the Obama administration sought a path to legal citizenship for undocumented youth, it offered registration under the "Deferred Action for Childhood Arrivals" (DACA) program. By registering employment records, biometric data, and family information, these youth gained protections from deportation and could proceed toward citizenship. Yet, the Trump administration later threatened to suspend DACA, raising fears that the DACA registry would fuel a deportation list. Similar fears have undermined state programs encouraging undocumented drivers to get training, permitting, and car insurance.

After the Trump administration appointed a conservative Supreme Court majority, a flurry of red state legislatures threatened to virtually eliminate legal abortion. Meanwhile, blue state legislatures tried to expand abortion rights, while Planned Parenthood built clinics directly across restrictive states' borders. During the COVID-19 crisis, some liberal jurisdictions shuttered firearm businesses under emergency powers, while some conservative jurisdictions shuttered abortion clinics. Each faction argued that the civil liberties they were disrupting were inessential in times of emergency. There is even a DIY angle in the culture war over abortion. As legislators argue over clinics, safe and effective abortifacient drugs have popularized. Some women get the drugs online or through informal networks. In this framework of cultural conflict, DIY becomes a method to render disagreeable regulation irrelevant. Instead of endlessly debating irreconcilable positions, DIYers find ways to *do it anyway*. In a statement worthy of Cody Wilson, the general counsel of a prochoice health advocacy group was quoted in 2019: "Self-managed abortion is going to play a bigger role, no matter what happens with *Roe*" (North 2019).

As of this writing, 33 U.S. states permit medical or recreational cannabis. More than half of Americans have tried it, and some studies associate legalization with neutral effects or reductions in crime (Smith et al. 2014; Lu et al. 2019; Dragone et al. 2019). Nevertheless, when honorably discharged veterans disclosed employment with licensed cannabis companies, the Veterans Administration denied them benefits (Kopp 2019). When citizens in Honolulu, Hawaii, legally registered their firearms and medical cannabis, they received warnings that their gun rights were rescinded due to unlawful drug use under federal law (which, as of this writing, does not recognize state cannabis legalization). By this logic, it's worthwhile to threaten citizens who trust government enough to register legal guns and legal cannabis in a country where felons get unregistered guns with ease, and high schoolers get illegal marijuana more readily than alcohol.

Broad data collection can protect public safety, but it can also be leveraged to repress populations, prosecute culture wars, or enable incredible granularity in petty harassment. In an America with historically low faith in mainstream institutions, millions resist mandatory disclosure of private activities. The popularization of ghost guns illustrates that firearms activity is no exception. In public safety, the impulse toward data collection is strong. Yet privacy-invading policies can backfire in an environment of insufficient political trust. If citizens are penalized for compliance as soon as the *other* side wins an election, we can't be surprised when some lose trust in the institutions collecting their data. A broadening surveillance and censorship regime carries political, economic, and cultural costs, but its benefits are not guaranteed. As citizens acclimate to surveillance culture, many will limit personal disclosures for fear of penalty. Meanwhile, serious adversaries may keep quiet on social media, stick to cash and crypto-currency, use privacy-oriented devices and applications, and share little with the tech sector, physicians, police, or government. The dazzling light of big data surveillance shines ever brighter. Yet, serious criminals and others we are correct to worry about, can still hide in the shadows cast by billions of innocent users.

Notes

1. More recently, Stokes became an editor of *OpenSourceDefense.org*

2. Which admitted that he'd chosen guns to aggravate political tensions in America. You'll have to take my word for it. I won't cite the manifesto because (a) it's detestable, and (b) I want this book to be saleable to the fine citizens of New Zealand.

3. Alex Jones was subsequently banned from many platforms as well.

CHAPTER NINE

Uninventing the Wheel: Weapons and Crime Control in a Postindustrial Age

> The struggle between "for" and "against" is the mind's worst disease.
> —Sent-ts'an, Third Zen Patriarch (attributed)

In a postindustrial world, it doesn't matter how loudly we proclaim the belief that guns are categorically good or bad for society. In a postindustrial world, *guns are here*. This admittedly reductionist statement doesn't render all weapons policy obsolete. To the contrary, it begs an evaluation of how weapons policy can maintain relevance given the numeric challenge posed by centuries of industrial gunmaking, and the techno-regulatory challenges posed by the neoartisanal moment.

The greatest ambitions of DIY provocateurs overlap the greatest *fears* of concerned journalists and gun control supporters, but neither has fully materialized. Technology hasn't enabled push-button gunmaking, nor have traditional gun laws been completely invalidated. Instead, we're left with recourse to speculation of the type that predominates in a fearful and polarized political culture. Speculation that the historically long-standing and very American practice of independent gunmaking will be so transformed by technology and partisan politics that it will spitefully push every boundary, cleverly undermine the spirit of every law, and gleefully watch the machinery of gun control sputter.

Speculation that DIY methods will enable violent actors to get guns, as if this were not longstanding practice. Speculation that the new sorcerer-artisans will make unregistered, undetectable, untraceable, unstoppable weapons to defeat our security talismans. Speculation that a diverse global phenomenon motivated by desires for autonomy, innovation, and personal security within the law and outside of it, can be controlled by a few legislative changes. Speculation that technologic disruptions can be nudged away by a benevolent technocratic oligarchy. Speculation too, that to regulate DIY gunmaking portends the earliest stage in the end of liberty, a crucial salvo in the inevitable war against gun rights in America, followed by shaming, boycotts, surveillance, censorship, registration, confiscation, and a slide to tyranny over one of the world's largest, freest, and best-armed populations. It's not speculative that the neoartisanal moment poses a different kind of challenge than our regulatory pantomimes have prepared us for.

DIY gunmaking tells us that the social outcomes of guns will not become easier to control by regulating industrial supply. Registration and background checks are supply-side regulatory layers. These layers have benefits, and America's background check system should be improved rather than jettisoned. Several notorious active shooters passed background checks they should have failed, but lapses prevented the system from doing its job. Legislators have tried to improve the system with bills like the Fix NICS Act of 2017. However, trafficking routes around regulatory layers. Registries and point-of-sale regulations struggle to impact trafficking because commercial regulatory layers don't eliminate (and may incentivize) alternate procurement channels like smuggling, theft, straw purchase, staged thefts and losses, defacement, registry noncompliance, and off-books manufacture.

These channels interact with legal supply chains to varying degrees. Yet they separate guns from legal chains-of-custody, undermining many crime-fighting benefits that registries and background checks are meant to provide. It's difficult to combat all channels simultaneously, and traffickers adapt. In America, it's impractical to expect registries or background checks alone to cut the supply of illegal guns enough to sustainably reduce homicides. Few offenders acquire guns through controlled channels. Regulatory differentials are easily exploited, and America's federalist framework generates many differentials across states and regions. For maximum effectiveness, supply-side tactics must be national in scope, crafted more restrictively than is politically achievable, and accompanied by much more robust enforcement at any rate.

Homemade guns are an overlay on this complex scenario. They have caused fewer problems than illicit commercial guns, but they undermine hope that doubling down on traditional regulation will solve all the world's gun problems. Regardless of one's orientation toward the contradictory schools of thought in gun policy research, it's ultimately a Sisyphean exercise to relitigate nonstarters. Guns are here. It's too late to eliminate or even track them all. The strictest controls achievable in America will not alter this reality. We can decry the volume of commercial guns as an irresponsible oversupply driven by media sensationalism and industry lobbyists, or we can celebrate America's longstanding, innovative, and largely law-abiding firearm culture. Either way, the guns are still here.

Nevertheless, the last three decades have seen U.S. homicide rates decline to half their post–World War II peaks. Concurrently, the number of firearms doubled, and many gun laws were loosened. This book doesn't endorse arguments that more guns categorically generate more or less crime, but violence can clearly decline even as more firearms circulate and some laws are relaxed. DIY invites us to consider what effective *crime control* looks like in a world saturated with firearms, and where more people can make guns if they want them. For the sake of argument, let's assume ghost guns can't be stopped overnight by a few legislative tweaks. How should we approach weapons policy in a postindustrial world where the supply of firearms is increasingly difficult to control?

Deemphasize Registration

Gun prohibition then, is not the same as banning DDT or leaded gasoline. It is more like banning fire.
—Nicholas Johnson, professor, Fordham University School of Law (Johnson 2008, 846)

Why do the Poles pour motor oil on their flower beds? To keep the guns from rusting.
—Soviet joke

Registering more than a fraction of guns in America (or a majority in many countries), will remain impossible. Fewer crime guns are retailed in jurisdictions with registries, but the benefits are undermined by smuggling (Webster, Vernick, and Hepburn 2001). National registration will probably remain nonviable, and many jurisdictions will never pass registries. Where registries exist, compliance lags. DIY adds complexity: even if many thousands of straw purchases and tens of thousands of trafficked guns per year can be reduced, illegal makers can supplement these illicit channels.

Quality controls focused on behavior are ultimately more important than attacking gun supply. Well-crafted red flag laws are a move in this direction. Another solution would be universal background checks with protections against data retention, or perhaps national licensing without registration. Graduated licensing might classify different types of firearms by (clearly imperfect) gradations of capability. A basic license might entitle any American who passes a background check to exercise the rights outlined in *Heller* (which include access to semiautomatic hand-guns and other common defensive firearms). Training and vetting could authorize endorsements for hunting, higher-capacities, and concealed carry.

Assault weapons (aka modern sporting rifles) are the most tactically useful civilian arms. Though this may change in coming years, courts have ruled that these rifles *can* be banned. However, they are very popular, and access to militarily useful weapons was central to the country's militia history. Instead of banning America's most popular rifle, a militia endorsement reflecting a higher degree of training, vetting, and civic responsibility could enable licensees to own (or make) as many semiauto rifles as they wish (and in virtually any configuration or magazine capacity), provided they meet standards modestly consistent with some modernized iteration of an *unorganized militia*. The entire system would be *shall-issue*: no applicant would be denied upon meeting modest requirements.

Any licensee's rights would apply nationally, thus exempting gun rights from the minefield of state and local laws. Owners could transfer firearms to any appropriately licensed recipient. Nothing would be banned, and qualified citizens could carry firearms in *more* jurisdictions than currently allowed (as some "blue" jurisdictions reject permits from other jurisdictions). The role of militia licensing as an extension of national security might exclude those who belong to violent extremist groups, or those who are legitimately watchlisted, though these classifications must be handled with serious care.

National shall-issue licensing would trade some of the privacy and ease of access that currently applies in looser jurisdictions, and replace it with a straightforward system that protects the rights of licensees in all jurisdictions while providing improved mechanisms to connect firearm activities to the qualifications and trustworthiness of individuals. Problematically, the line between licensing and registration relies on legal boundaries preventing police from harassing citizens, searching properties, or confiscating guns based only on a citizen's licensee status. However, even if a general confiscation were attempted, it could not succeed at recovering more than a fraction of licensees' guns because the system wouldn't retain information about specific guns. These safeguards against *general* confiscation are essential to make licensing or universal background checks politically agreeable.

However, gun rights supporters will argue that national licensing is unconstitutional and unnecessary. We already have an increasingly integrated system of background checks, state licensing, and searchable criminal record databases. In most jurisdictions, police can quickly check whether an individual has records rendering gun possession illegal. In that sense, we are already building the data infrastructure of national licensing, we just don't have the licenses. Furthermore, national licensing suffers the deficiencies of any one-size-fits-all solution in a megasociety: it would be difficult to legislate to the satisfaction of "pro" and "anti" factions, expensive to implement, and probably wouldn't produce major reductions to routine gun crime (which is disproportionately committed by illegal users who wouldn't get licensed anyway).

In America, the closest analog to national licensing is universal background checks, which are opposed by many gun rights advocates, though supported by a majority of gun owners (Pew Research Center 2018). Universal background checks (UBCs) extend to private transactions. Private transactors would need to visit a licensed retailer, pay a fee, provide information about themselves and the transferred firearm, and wait for federal clearance to conduct the transaction. Because background checks record the make, model, and serial number of the gun, the difference between universal background checks and *national registration* hinges on data retention. If retained temporarily, it's a background check. If retained permanently, it's a "backdoor registry." UBCs wouldn't stop illegal manufacturing or transfers. Some research suggests universal background checks might not seriously dent gun crime or trafficking. Several studies indicate little or no impact on crime (Kagawa et al. 2018; Crifasi et al. 2018; Castillo-Carniglia et al. 2019). One metastudy (RAND Corporation 2008) found moderate evidence that dealer background checks decrease homicide and suicide, but found the evidence in favor of private-seller background checks "inconclusive" (53–54). Meanwhile, most felons bypass background checks by getting guns through informal contacts (Alper and Glaze 2019). Even if UBCs were passed nationally, they would probably continue to do so.

If we want universal background checks to seriously impact illegal trade, the system must perform as a national registry. Instead of relitigating this battle to the detriment of political trust, gun control advocates should support improved nonconfiscatory systems focused on modest standards for gun ownership and greater enforcement against trafficking and violence. This would replace threatened bans and confiscations with standardized training and vetting requirements scaled to the rights being exercised, and selective seizures of individuals' guns only under clear legal protections. While some gun rights advocates will never trust these programs, and some gun control advocates will never resist broadening them beyond their promised scope, panic purchasing may be subdued, *some* tragedies may be averted, and stability may enter the gun policy conversation.

Don't Fixate on Supply Controls

> There wouldn't be any evidence of DIY firearms until one showed up. People would be buying machine tools, but so what? Lots of people buy machine tools, you can't do anything about it! I don't think it's possible to combat. How would you do it? Are you going to send inspectors to machine tool producers or sellers of the materials? Forget about it.
> —Julius Wachtel, criminologist and BATFE supervisor (ret.)
> (Interview 2016)

> Our results have been disappointing because supply-side rules depend, ultimately, on cutting the inventory close to zero. And that, in America, is a problem.
> —Nicholas Johnson, professor, Fordham University
> School of Law (Johnson 2008, 842)

Gun control can never prevent all DIY gunmaking. Broad tracking systems on components, tools, and information would be costly and controversial. Few supply-chain regulations would produce more than political backlash. Gun control advocates have recommended extending background check, serialization, or registry requirements to partially finished components. This is the approach endorsed by Nick Suplina of Everytown. Suplina and most gun control advocates want to preserve, if not expand, the supply-side tracking paradigm established in 1968: "I don't want to lay this at the feet of the hobbyists, but there's nothing about the interest in the mechanics and construction of your own firearm that needs to be connected to untraceable firearms that circumvent federal law" (Interview 2019). For anyone who already supports universal background checks or gun registration, this approach sounds eminently reasonable.

However, decades of worry that these tracking systems would be used for confiscation, and numerous domestic proposals for (and foreign implementations of) precisely the confiscations they fear, has left gun rights advocates with deep distrust of gun tracking systems. Strong gun rights supporters believe it entirely legitimate to resist these tracking infrastructures in order to render general confiscation infeasible. Meanwhile, gunhackers and traffickers undermine these tracking systems for fun and profit. Applying these laws in America will invite tenacious challenges by gun rights advocates. They may chill the popularization of ghost guns among casual consumers, but I suspect it would also incentivize the illegal component trade, encourage makers to adjust designs for exemption, and motivate skilled DIYers to develop more components from scratch. Police may struggle to enforce the requirements, and retailers, hobbyists, and criminals alike will find creative circumventions. That gun control advocates desire these laws is understandable, but they may come at significant political cost with no guarantee of practical success.

Some digital toolmakers will limit their products' abilities to fabricate firearm designs. This may chill casual experimentation, but it won't stop serious gunhackers or traditional home gunmakers. Controls on materials are less promising. Censorship is a slippery slope, particularly if the information is constitutionally legal. The surveillance and censorship needed to suppress gunmaking information could delegitimize liberal governance of cyberspace while industrious DIYers develop new designs. This might never be fully outlawed under the First and Second Amendments, nor enforceable if it were. Gunhackers will continue improving and sharing designs through privacy-oriented applications. Even if all methods of online sharing were shuttered, peer-to-peer sharing and physical data smuggling would continue. Only invasive cybersurveillance and encryption-busting searches of all digital storage devices in parcels, luggage, and travelers' pockets can hope to halt these transfers of firearms data. This regime would be incompatible with liberal governance, and still fail to halt all sharing of digital gun designs.

In America, perhaps the simplest legal adjustment would be to establish a clearer definition of "commercial" activity. Current law allows any citizen who is not prohibited from owning guns to make any number of unregistered and unserialized firearms provided they are not "engaged in the business." Total criminalization of personal gunmaking would be controversial and would face constitutional challenges. However, by naming a specific volume of activity that qualifies as *commercial*, amateur gunmakers and collectors could continue on a small scale without fear, high-volume makers with commercial ambition could be held to reasonable commercial requirements, and police would have a clearer standard for charging unlicensed commerce.

Guns can be made with general use technology. Controlling general use technology involves many trade-offs, and unsuccessful controls lose credibility. Tight restrictions on commercial firearms may incentivize illicit production, while restrictions only on homemade guns would have minor impacts on crime. Modest legal tweaks could make it easier to target large-scale trafficking. However, attempts to stop illegal gunmaking through supply-side controls on tools, materials, components, or information are likely to prove quixotic so long as illicit weapons remain in demand.

Focus on Violence and Illegal Demand

Other countries have guns and they don't have the crime. At the end of the day it's still more a social and behavioral issue than a technology issue.

—Greg Moser, State of Colorado counterterrorism coordinator (ret.) (Interview 2015).

Most adult men in Switzerland have a rifle, and there's been one mass shooting in its history. It's because the culture is different. I think you need to build consumer and technology cultures that are healthy! At the moment, American culture is not moving in that direction.

—Jonathan Poritz, cryptographer/computer science professor (Interview 2019)

Tactics focused on high-risk individuals and underlying contributors to violence are less divisive than controls on broad swaths of legal gun owners. As Harvard's Thomas Abt (2019) argues, targeted violence reduction programs are also cost-effective. Wider measures like economic development, healthcare, or gun control should be structured as components in violence prevention (198–200). If policies aren't tailored to reduce *violence*, they shouldn't be prioritized over investments that clearly *do* reduce violence.

By interrupting violent scenarios and supporting conflict resolution, violence reduction programs can achieve excellent results. The Cure Violence program was associated with 41–73 percent fewer shootings in Chicago neighborhoods (Skogan et al. 2008). In New York City, the program correlated with 37–50 percent reductions to gun injury in two communities. In Philadelphia, the program was linked to a 30 percent reduction in shootings. When implemented in Trinidad and Tobago, the program was associated with a 45 percent violent crime reduction. New York City is America's most-policed metropolis. A study of Cure Violence deployments there found three outreach workers could reduce homicides within test communities by 24 percent, while it would require a 150 percent increase in NYPD staffing over 20 years for similar results ("Scientific Evaluations" 2019). Abt argues that violence prevention programs could be offered throughout American cities for $30,000 per homicide prevented, leading to annual reductions around 10 percent. Each prevented murder would save $10 million in social costs (205–08).

Even with these investments, some violent crime and weapons trafficking will continue. Concentrated enforcement is another tool. Project Safe Neighborhoods is a Department of Justice program that coordinates police and prosecutors at the federal, state, and local levels. Under this program, police and prosecutors target the most violent offenders, most prolific traffickers, and most dangerous hotspots. Where applied, concentrated enforcement has reduced violent crime by 4–20 percent (McGarrell et al. 2009, 140–41, 184).

We don't know what serious enforcement would accomplish because its rarely been tried. In the world's most armed country, BATFE maintains a staff just over 5,000—about half the size of the LA County Sheriff's Office. BATFE's budget is around $1.2 billion, less than half that of the Drug Enforcement Administration. A 2003 report by the Americans for Gun Safety Foundation claimed that 20 of 22 major federal gun laws were rarely enforced (Kessler 2003). The report observed that 420,000 firearms were stolen between 2000 and 2002, yet only 524 federal gun theft charges were filed. Prosecutors in 38 states pursued no charges for selling guns to minors, yet youths under 17 committed 93,000 gun crimes and are disproportionately victims of it. In 2000 alone, more than 2,500 defaced guns (aka, commercially bought guns rendered into ghost guns by traffickers using simple tools) were recovered in just seven cities. Yet between 2000 and 2002, only 259 prosecutions for possession of defaced guns were pursued *nationwide*.

Federal gun crime prosecutions subsequently declined during the Obama administration, and enforcement hasn't become much more effective since. It's illegal for prohibited persons to "lie and try" on background check forms, but a 2018 report found 112,000 denials in 2017 resulted in only 12,700 investigative referrals, and only 12 prosecutions by June 2018 (U.S. Government Accountability Office 2018). BATFE staff periodically complain that countertrafficking is under-resourced. Criminology professor and former BATFE Special Agent Julius Wachtel explained, "Gun trafficking is not a major program in ATF." He continued, "Sometimes when I was in [state], I was the only agent in the state . . . because enforcement is so elaborate, you can only do the biggest cases. We generally didn't touch a case unless we had more than 1500 guns diverted" (Interview 2016).

Meanwhile, the background check system continues to prohibit non-violent felons, legal cannabis users, and legal residents who aren't shown to be dangerous. As ACLU legal director Louise Melling wrote, "the categories of people that federal law currently prohibits from possessing or purchasing a gun are overbroad, not reasonably related to the state's interest in public safety, and raise significant equal protection and due process concerns" (Melling 2018). Fortunately for gun buyers who are technically prohibited, a 2004 Justice Department report explains that ATF chose not to recover weapons from most prohibited buyers because "Special agents did not consider most of the prohibited persons who had obtained guns to be dangerous and therefore did not consider it a priority to retrieve the firearm promptly" (U.S. Department of Justice Office of the Inspector General 2004, iii). Meanwhile, BATFE's reputation still suffers from the Ruby Ridge and Waco debacles of the 1990s, periodic accusations of entrapment, and the controversial "Fast & Furious" gunwalking scandal in which Mexican cartels were allowed to purchase more than 2,000 guns, but less than half were recovered. Ultimately, rather than defanging BATFE, it should be better-resourced and its claws sharpened for the missions most Americans expect of it: spearheading multi-agency counter-trafficking and violent gun offender enforcement. If concentrated multiagency enforcement gets results, why not provide for it in every major city?

However, the idea of narrowly targeting dangerous individuals instead of broadly targeting "weapons," is complicated by available tactics. Stop-and-frisk tactics are rightly criticized as a street dragnet focused on minority males. They drive negative police contacts and produce more petty arrests than serious charges. When the New York Civil Liberties Union (2012) analyzed New York City's stop & frisk program at its height in 2011, it found only 1.9 percent of stops recovered weapons (typically knives), and only 1 in 3,000 stops recovered illegal guns. Though marketed as an initiative to recover illicit guns, civil libertarians and minority rights advocates criticized the program's practical focus on penalizing petty cannabis possession and charging citizens (including blue collar tradespeople) with felonies under obscure laws that prohibited common utility knives. Likewise, when defendants are caught with firearms in commission of nonviolent crimes, draconian penalties can be stacked to create sentences in excess of the danger. In America, it's possible for drug dealers who are caught with a gun (but never use it) to receive greater penalties than murderers who didn't use a gun.

Meanwhile, some jurisdictions fail to seriously penalize repeat weapons offenders. Federal prosecutors infrequently charge weapons-only offenses given their tedium and cost. Nevertheless, it makes little sense to overcriminalize nonviolent and technical offenses, or harass citizens in weapon dragnets, while freeing repeat offenders to quickly acquire guns again. Police paramilitarization is surely necessary in some scenarios and is tempting when any suspect might be armed. However, one recent study found that paramilitarization failed to reduce crime or enhance officer safety, but did degrade the reputation of police (Mummolo 2018); another found paramilitarization to render police use-of-force more likely (Delehanty et al. 2017).

Recent decades have seen greater tactical, technical, and legal capabilities extended to police, yet the national homicide clearance rate in 2016 was the lowest on record: 59 percent (Hargrove, Rosselet, and Witzig 2018). Many major cities suffer dismal clearance rates. In 2017, Chicago's homicide clearances hovered around 17 percent. This is *worse* than it sounds: Chicago considers a murder "cleared" if a suspect is identified—even if never arrested or convicted. In 2016, clearance rate for all shootings in Chicago were around 5 percent (Kapustin et al. 2017). Unsolved homicides are contagious, and public support is crucial to solving them. Unfortunately, public cooperation lags in many cities as perceptions of police prejudice and inability to protect witnesses have raised barriers to cooperation.

Race and class profiling, and perceptions of police prejudice and unaccountability (whether fair or not), undermine the relationships needed to stop this cycle. While sometimes vaguely defined or poorly implemented, *targeted* methods like *focused deterrence, problem-oriented* policing, *intelligence-led* policing, and *community-based* policing can build community relationships, leverage local pressures, and identify serious offenders and hotspots while catching fewer innocents in the middle. Illegal gun carrying is encouraged by drug trafficking culture. One BJS study found that between 25.7 and 44.6 percent of homicides in test cities related to drug trafficking (U.S. Department of Justice 1994, 4). Harvard economist Jeffrey Miron (2004) argued that drug legalization could reduce homicides by at least 25 percent (51). While violent markets must be suppressed, sustainable solutions won't derive from supply-side gun or drug controls, but through evidence-based education, treatment, and legalization programs that reduce illegal demand and the harms of a violent drug trade.

Failures in supply-side policy are often rebranded as *success denied* through insufficient resourcing. Yet, supply-side controls on high-demand products often prove ineffective. In 2016, researchers evaluated cocaine control tactics between 2000 and 2008. Direct attacks on supply (like spraying defoliants or deploying special operators) cost $940,000 per kilo prevented from reaching American consumers. Meanwhile, coca farmers increased production efficiency by 35 percent. Border and highway interdiction cost $175,000 per kilo: more than five times the drug's street value. During the same period, the number of users increased and street prices declined by 11 percent. Demand reduction was more effective. Addiction treatment prevented consumption for $12,500–$68,705 per kilo, and addiction prevention stopped consumption for $8,250 per kilo (Mejia and Restrepo 2016). Many policing tactics have improved, but they can't defeat economics. Too often, the costs of supply-side enforcement are the *costs of pretending.*

Censorship is a slippery slope. However, if media wants to contribute to a constructive debate while minimizing contagion effects, voluntary guidelines to reduce sensationalism and provide moderate coverage of gun debate might reduce copycatting and panic buying. Dozens of studies support media contagion effects with regard to suicide, and media organizations have already developed voluntary guidelines to reduce suicide contagion. Numerous studies demonstrate connections between media sensationalism and active shootings. Instead of censoring information about guns, perhaps media platforms should consider halting the practice of awarding mass murderers with the types of attention they seek.

Environmental and healthcare initiatives can also reduce violence. Counties with higher lead exposure suffer up to 400 percent higher homicide rates (Stretesky and Lynch 2001). Research correlates lead exposure with aggravated assault (Mielke and Zahran 2012), and probability of arrest (Wright et al. 2008). Reduced lead exposure may have accounted for an astounding 56 percent decline in violent crime (Reyes 2007). Healthcare access also improves outcomes. Studies suggest that suicides may be reduced by 5 percent when insurers cover mental healthcare equally to physical healthcare (Lang 2013), and expanding access to SSRI medications may reduce suicide by 5 percent (Ludwig, Marcotte, and Norberg 2009). A detailed study on the relationships between socioeconomic conditions and gun violence found that institutional social capital (i.e. public trust in institutions) was associated with a 17 percent reduction in gun homicide, upward social mobility correlated with a 25 percent decrease in gun homicide, but greater poverty and more males living alone were correlated with 26 percent and 12 percent higher homicide rates (Kim 2019).

Attacking the underlying causes of illegal demand and use might actually work better for guns than for drugs. Whereas drugs are quickly consumed, guns can be kept for decades. Illegal guns address insecurity within populations whose desire for them outstrips the perceived risk of illegal possession. Without the insecurity generated by endemic (and unsolved) drug-related violence, illegal weapon demand might be reduced. Without the sociopolitical insecurity generated by media sensationalism and confiscatory proposals, some *legal* demand might be reduced. Insofar as violence can be reduced through other methods, gun control has become a band-aid slapped onto much deeper societal wounds that remain undertreated. Sustainable transformation requires investment in violence prevention, physical and mental healthcare, education and economic opportunity, improved police-community relations, re-earning of public trust in media and government, and a sustained attack on the sociopolitical, institutional, cultural, environmental, and systemically prejudicial factors that burn within high-violence enclaves of America and around the world. Concurrently, policymakers should establish improved red flag processes and provide the resources to investigate every violent weapons offense and gun trafficking network with the seriousness they deserve. Robust efforts along these lines would surely translate to violence reduction.

The success of *nongun* policy in reducing crime should encourage a holistic approach. In the United States and other nations, significant populations have been economically disadvantaged, subject to racial, class, or cultural prejudice, and underserved by public services. Many of the same individuals are situated where drug trafficking is the most approachable profession, normalized violence bolsters weapon demand, a combination of drug abuse and overpenalization of drug use undermines employment and family intactness, gangs act *in loco parentis*, and cultures of casual violence and unaccountable criminality have evolved after generations under these conditions. Illegal guns make this *worse*, but do we expect gun control to do the job of reforming the entire spectrum of disadvantage? America's gun control debate often reflects envy of other wealthy nations, but America still contains considerable populations living under conditions more akin to Brazil than to Norway. Is it surprising that these disadvantaged Americans suffer violence at rates more similar to Brazilians than Norwegians? In the end, perhaps it doesn't matter so much whether illegal guns are made in a factory or a basement workshop. By addressing a spectrum of contributing variables, we can reduce demand for illegal guns while also decreasing the likelihood that they'll be *used*.

Improve Technology and Research

Improved weapons screening can help safeguard vulnerable locations while stemming the still-unachieved specter of totally undetectable guns.

However, it's unwise to assume that facilities are *secure* simply because they employ weapons screening. To stop serious threats, screening must be accompanied by physical security, planning and training, and effective counterforce. Weapons screening without these components will be vulnerable to attackers who don't respect the norms of a security badge or velvet rope. If screening prevents off-duty officers and legal licensees from carrying weapons yet fails to stop attackers, it will be criticized as security theater irrespective of advancements in technology.

Gunshot detection systems (GDSs) triangulate the location of gunshots. Developed for combat counter-sniper roles, these tools can provide widespread coverage in urban areas. With Shotspotter or other GDSs, police can respond faster and collect more forensic evidence. In some high-crime neighborhoods, up to 80 percent of gunshots go unreported. GDSs enable modeling of shooting patterns even when nobody calls police. This improves hotspot policing and encourages collection of forensic evidence from more shootings. When police analyze bullets and casings not only from reported shootings but from *all* shootings, it can provide valuable investigative connections. Crime gun forensic databases like NIBIN are promising resources, and should be improved without increasing their noise-to-signal ratio by expanding them to all retail firearms.

Research on homemade weapons is difficult. DIY gunmaking is often clandestine and in many jurisdictions illegal. Even many legal consumers select DIY because they value privacy. We don't know how many unfinished frames are sold. Police data collection on homemade weapons has been haphazard until recently, and may not be representative. It may never be possible to reliably track homemade weapons, but improved data collection would help contextualize the issue. Some 80 percent retailers disclose sales numbers; others don't. Requiring disclosure would put the role of "80%" builds in context and wouldn't require disclosing data on legal recipients. If retailers are concerned that disclosure would reveal damaging information to competitors, the reporting could be anonymized. Problematically, it may be difficult to compel disclosure from retailers who only sell unfinished parts but not legally defined *firearms*, and these numbers obviously won't include *illegal* component trafficking.

Data collection on DIY seizures has been sparse and nonstandardized. Some countries don't track DIY, others track it imprecisely. BATFE collects data through its tracing procedures, compiling state-level data on seized frames, receivers, "any other weapons," and other categories that provide limited insight. Media reporting is often inaccurate, but can provide some insight into general trends and high-profile cases.

Problematically, not all seized crime items appear in reporting, nor are all items listed in reporting "crime" items. Some countries gather data, but don't make it available to researchers. Collecting, improving, standardizing, and publishing data is necessary to place the DIY phenomenon in context.

Encourage Less-Lethal Alternatives

> I think the law will adapt to less-lethal weapons. Nonlethal weapons that are effective, is an idea that has been coming for a long time. Sometimes the law adjusts wrong, but I think the biggest thing is that if somebody really developed a nonlethal weapon as effective as firearms, we would want law to accommodate that.
> —Adam Winkler, Constitutional Law professor, UCLA School of
> Law (Interview 2019)

Technology can provide alternatives to *lethal* violence. Guns, blades, and batons easily produce fatal injuries. Martial artists can apply a spectrum of force from harmless to deadly, but even skilled fighters are fortunate to survive against an armed attacker or multiple opponents. Firearms are reliable, portable, discriminate, intimidating, concealable, effective between inches to thousands of yards, can penetrate obstructions, and rapidly incapacitate. Unfortunately, to produce rapid incapacitation, firearms must seriously damage the body. Firearm injuries reliably stop aggressive threats, but they are severe. Modern trauma care reduces mortality, and the majority of gunshots are nonfatal. Yet, even nonfatal gunshots frequently produce costly recoveries and disabilities. Because guns rely on rapid infliction of serious injury, the threshold between an incapacitating and fatal shooting is slim.

In the defensive space, perhaps the most-needed *Star Trek* technology isn't replication, but the *phaser*, a gunlike weapon set to kill when needed, but usually set to *stun*. Unfortunately, it's difficult to engineer weapons that provide the defensive benefit of firearms without serious injury. For generations hence, firearms will continue to represent a plausible deadly threat, and counterforce by firearm will continue to be part of the solution. Yet, the ethics, law, and politics of force would be positively altered by a weapon that does what guns do without *doing what guns do*. The imperfection of less-lethal weapons is evidenced by the fact that police don't deploy them against deadly threats without lethal backup. However, future research may produce effective nonlethal incapacitating weapons. What technologies might apply?

Obviously, there are less-lethal firearm munitions. Rubber, bean bag, pepper, or electro-shock rounds operate through blunt force (and sometimes, chemical or electro-shock effects). They can be lethal, and anyone who has been hit by one will testify they wouldn't care to repeat the experience. However, they're not as reliable as a penetrating munition. Conducted energy devices (CEDs) like Axon's Taser are an option, but they're short-ranged, can't penetrate heavy clothing, and provide few shots. An evaluation of police taser deployments found failure to stop the threat in 20–40 percent of cases (American Public Media 2019b). In rare cases, Tasers contribute to fatal injuries. Nevertheless, they're a viable alternative in some scenarios. Restrictive jurisdictions have sometimes prohibited CEDs while permitting real guns. Cases like 2016's *Caetano v. Massachusetts* established stun guns and other "bearable" arms as constitutionally protected. While the public good might be poorly served if untrained people carried Tasers everywhere, it's illogical to discourage less-lethal alternatives in jurisdictions full of real guns.

Chemical agents like pepper spray can be effective. However, they are only useful at short range and have little effect unless shot toward the face. They are relatively safe but can contribute to death if a subject has respiratory problems. Pepper sprays can deter attacks, but may also enrage attackers if it fails to incapacitate them. One evaluation of police pepper spray deployments found significantly *higher* rates of officer injury than with use of CEDs (National Institute of Justice 2019). Pepper spray is often deployed when combatants are in close quarters or entangled, it may blow back on the defender, and sometimes escalates the fight if it fails. In some countries, citizens purchase pneumatic *gas guns*. These shoot chemical pellets at longer range. However, they are much less effective than firearms, and their gunlike designs can often be illegally converted to fire live ammunition. Gas guns are popular in some countries, but uncommon in America.

High-powered microwave (HPM) devices are a futuristic option: they heat exposed skin at a distance, producing debilitating pain. However, they are too large, their energy requirements are prohibitive, effectiveness degrades in rainy weather, they can't penetrate all clothing, and they only debilitate adversaries within the beam. Long range acoustic devices (LRADs) project sound at long distance, producing intolerable pain. However, they may not reliably incapacitate, and attackers can wear earplugs. Other possibilities include sticky foam, slippery chemicals, netguns, psychoactive gases, nauseating malodorants, electrified water cannons, electro-lasers, pulsed energy projectiles, networked drone swarms, and dazzling lasers that temporarily (or permanently) blind an adversary. In an homage to *Star Trek*, one Department of Defense project is called the PHASR rifle.

Some technologies include the range, reliability, and rapid effect of firearms. However, none are yet practical for personal use. We are learning to build weapons reminiscent of Star Trek's phaser, but we haven't developed the miniaturized electronics or power sources to convert them into practical personal weapons. The implication for harm reduction is to ensure that the law provides oversight without chilling development of practical and ethical options for self-defense.

(Non)Necessity Is the Mother of (Un)Invention: How Guns Are Like Wheels

> You don't need a ghost gunner or 3D-printer or CNC machine. There are people in caves in Afghanistan making automatic firearms. They've found gunmaking plants in Australia, Canada, and the UK. They're everywhere. They will always be everywhere. As long as there's demand for firearms there will be supply.
> —Dan Zimmerman, managing editor, *The Truth about Guns* (progun blog) (Interview 2018)

> What are you going to do? Are you going to take all these DIY people and put them in jail? Can you imagine the *machine shop* in that place?
> —Michael Heidrick, maker (Interview 2015)

These recommendations will fail to please all, or even most readers. Doctrinaire gun control supporters might think this approach insufficiently restrictive, too dismissive of research favored by their faction, too soft on industry, and too deferential to legal gun culture and the gun rights position. Doctrinaire gun rights supporters might think these recommendations too restrictive, too dismissive of research favored by their faction, too willing to speculate on security problems that haven't fully manifested, and too deferential to the gun control position. This derives from a false dichotomy that solidified over a century of supply-side gun control in America. As controlling the *harms* of guns became linked to controlling the *supply* of guns, centers of gravity in research, fundraising, and advocacy shifted toward attacking or defending *guns*. Both sides of that debate have arguments of merit, but tunnel vision on the social outcomes of gun supply tends to bypass demand and use. We argue more often about regulating *supply* because to argue about *demand* would reveal longstanding failures of policy, trust, and social welfare for which both of America's mainstream political parties bear responsibility.

Technologic adoptions can't be explained without demand. Consider the wheel. For a long time, historians debated the wheel's inevitability. The wheel has entered mythology as an invention so simple that any civilization without it must have been primitive. As western historians came to appreciate the ingenuity of nonwestern civilizations, it became harder to argue that wheel-less cultures were backward. Many civilizations were capable of making wheels, but *didn't*. Historians have tried to explain why advanced civilizations rejected an easily replicated technology. Perhaps some societies lacked domestic animals to pull carts, or just never discovered wheels. Maybe geographic conditions were unfavorable. These theories would explain why numerous complex civilizations arose without wheeled vehicles. Yet, there were exceptions. Some civilizations adopted wheels with humans pulling the carts. The ancient Egyptians had good geography for the wheel, but didn't adopt wheeled transport for more than a millennium after learning of it. Meanwhile, civilizations with poorer geographies adopted the wheel earlier.

Wheel-historian Richard Bulliet (2016) suggests another explanation: some societies *just didn't think they needed it*. By Bulliet's argument, rather than assuming the wheel was so universally beneficial that any civilization without it must have suffered some deficiency, we should ask why preindustrial civilizations would want it in the first place (49). As it turns out, many preindustrial societies could handle typical transport needs without wheeled carts, and typical military needs without wheeled chariots. Perhaps the wheel wasn't so universally helpful that every civilization would choose to reorganize around it.

Cultural, economic, and political factors played roles in how societies made, used, and regulated firearms, but nations that industrialized earlier generally ended up with more gun manufacturing and more commercial firearms. These nations got more guns because their regimes and populations wanted them. Industrialization led to more guns, but also coincided with massive improvements in science, education, literacy, security, justice, opportunity, political rights, social tolerance, health, economic choice, and quality of life which, barring outliers, outstripped the social costs of more weapons becoming available. As Harvard psychology professor Steven Pinker (2011) observes, enlightenment values, scientific method, and industrialization coincided with tremendous reductions in violence and insecurity, a connection he laments "may be the most significant and least appreciated development in the history of our species" (692). Industrialization made the global gun, but also enabled societies to prevent violence more effectively. Wherever drug trafficking, war, corruption, state ineffectiveness, and insecurity rule, so do weapons traffickers. This is only natural and occurs even in disadvantaged enclaves of wealthy nations.

Today, we are in the early stages of a redistribution in arms-making capacity. Industrial gunmaking continues, but attempts to control social outcomes through controls on commercial manufacture will be increasingly challenged by a return to neoartisanal modes of production. Few societies were able to suppress artisanal weapons. Those that did relied on isolation from international trade, censorship, controls on markets, labor, tools, and materials, surveillance, broad restrictions on weapon making and ownership, and authoritarian enforcement methods. Can similar controls arrest the rise of DIY gunmaking today? To some degree, they can, but only with trade-offs so significant they ought to give us pause.

More often, preindustrial regimes attacked the sociolegal permissibility and use of weapons. This approach predominated longer than supply-side control. By leveraging tools, technology, and information, dangerous traffickers and harmless hobbyists will become increasingly capable of circumventing legacy controls. In this undistant future, only an illiberal clampdown incorporating invasive surveillance, tight restrictions, broad censorship, and aggressive enforcement could hope to stop motivated traffickers from making their own weapons. Yet, by leveraging new technologies and tactics, restoring civility to public discourse, and refocusing on the conditions that drive illegal demand and use, we stand to make great gains against gun violence. This doesn't require a massive expansion to gun laws, nor does the neoartisanal moment render all gun control obsolete. Instead, the rise of ghost guns invites a number of awkward but ultimately constructive adjustments to how we approach gun policy.

We must acknowledge the numerical challenge that lies behind the modern "gun problem," and admit that even if gun *rights* don't win, the *technology behind guns* did. We must acknowledge the value that guns hold for many millions of people and restore a sense of trust and pragmatic compromise to gun policy debate. We must acknowledge that America's status quo is unacceptable to many citizens on both sides of the gun divide, and that the negative role of guns has come to dominate the conversation not only due to media hype or gun control advocacy, but because many people are negatively impacted by gun violence or the fear of it. We must better account for the dynamics of gun trafficking, and reform our policy repertoires to effectively target high-risk individuals while minimizing political toxicity. We must acknowledge the very human reasons that people want guns urgently enough to make, buy, and keep them illegally. Most importantly, we must admit that the simplistic binary we call gun politics can never address the complexity of a postindustrial world.

Bibliography

ABC News. 2014. "Homemade Guns: Legal, Unregistered and Can Kill." April 22, 2014. https://abcnews.go.com/GMA/video/homemade-guns-legal-un registered-kill-23437165.

ABC Radio Australia. 2008. "Crocodiles Enjoy Gun-Free Solomon Islands." http://www.radioaustralia.net.au/international/2008-09-19/crocodiles -enjoy-gunfree-solomon-islands/22648.

Abel, Pete. 2000. "Manufacturing Trends, Globalizing the Source." In *Running Guns: The Global Black Market in Small Arms*, edited by Lora Lumpe. New York: Zed Books.

Abt, Thomas. 2019. *Bleeding Out: The Devastating Consequences of Urban Violence— And a Bold New Plan for Peace in the Streets.* New York: Basic Books.

Aguirre, Katherine, Robert Muggah, Jorge Restrepo, and Michael Spagat. 2006. "Illegal Arms Trafficking and Manufacturing." In *Small Arms Survey 2006: Unfinished Business*, edited by Katherine et al. Aguirre. Geneva: Small Arms Survey.

Aisch, Gregor, and Josh Keller. 2015. "How Gun Traffickers Get around State Gun Laws." *The New York Times*, November 13, 2015. https://www.ny times.com/interactive/2015/11/12/us/gun-traffickers-smuggling-state -gun-laws.html.

Allen, Douglas W., and Peter T. Leeson. 2015. "Institutionally Constrained Tech-nology Adoption: Resolving the Longbow Puzzle." *The Journal of Law & Economics* 58 (3): 683–715.

Alper, Mariel, and Lauren Glaze. 2019. "Source and Use of Firearms Involved in Crimes: Survey of Prison Inmates, 2016." Special Report NCJ 251776. U.S. Department of Justice, Office of Justice Programs, Bureau of Justice Statistics.

Alpers, Philip. 2005. "Gun-Running in Papua New Guinea: From Arrows to Assault Weapons in the Southern Highlands." Small Arms Survey Spe-cial Report No. 4. Geneva: Graduate Institute of International and Devel-opment Studies.

Alpers, Philip. 2016. "The Truth about Gun Ownership after Port Arthur." *ABC News* (Australia), April 28, 2016. https://www.abc.net.au/news/2016-04 -28/alpers-the-truth-about-gun-ownership-after-port-arthur/7365790.

Alpers, Philip, Robert Muggah, and Conor Twyford. 2004. "Trouble in Paradise: Home-Made Firearms." In *Small Arms Survey 2004: Rights at Risk*, edited by Peter Batchelor and Keith Krause, 277–308. Geneva: Graduate Institute of International and Development Studies.

Alpers, Philip, Amelie Rossetti, and Mike Picard. 2020. "Guns in Australia: Proportion of Households with Firearms." Sydney School of Public Health, The University of Sydney. https://www.gunpolicy.org/firearms/compare years/10/proportion_of_households_with_firearms.

American Public Media. 2019a. "APM Survey: Americans Views on Key Gun Policies. Part 2: Knowledge of Gun-Related Deaths." APM Research Lab. https://www.apmresearchlab.org/gun-related-deaths.

American Public Media. 2019b. "When Tasers Fail." APM Reports. May 9, 2019. https://www.apmreports.org/when-tasers-fail.

Arizmendi, Clint, Ben Pronk, and Jacob Choi. 2014. "Services No Longer Required? Challenges to the State as Primary Security Provider in the Age of Digital Fabrication." *Small Wars Journal* 22 (11). https://small warsjournal.com/jrnl/art/services-no-longer-required-challenges-to-the -state-as-primary-security-provider-in-the-age.

"Assembly Floor Analysis. California AB61: Gun Violence Restraining Orders." 2019. Track Bill, September 2019. https://trackbill.com/bill/california -assembly-bill-61-gun-violence-restraining-orders/1609327/.

Aufrichtig, Aliza. 2017. "Mapping US Gun Murders at a Micro Level: New Data Zooms in on Violence." *The Guardian*, March 20, 2017. https://www.the guardian.com/world/2017/mar/20/mapping-gun-murders-micro-level -new-data-2015.

Australian Government. 2011. "Container Examination Facilities." Australian Customs and Border Protection Service. https://web.archive.org/web /20180328073659/https://www.homeaffairs.gov.au/Factsheets/Docu ments/ceffactsheetjuly2011.pdf.

Australian Government, Australian Institute of Criminology. 2015. "Homicide Statistics." Australian Institute of Criminology, July 7, 2015. https://web .archive.org/web/20160401000000*/http://www.aic.gov.au/statistics /homicide.html.

Australian National Audit Office. 2014. "Screening of International Mail." Performance Audit Report Auditor-General Report No. 42 of 2013–14. Australian National Audit Office. https://www.anao.gov.au/work/performance -audit/screening-international-mail.

Avendano, Charlie. 2011. "Taking Risks with Peace in Burundi: Ignoring Good Practice in Civilian Disarmament." Ottawa: Peacebuilding Centre Press.

Bajekal, Naina, and Vivienne Walt. 2015. "How Europe's Terrorists Get Their Guns." *Time*, December 7, 2015. https://time.com/how-europes-terrorists -get-their-guns/.

Baker, Jeanine, and Samara McPhedran. 2007. "Gun Laws and Sudden Death: Did the Australian Firearms Legislation of 1996 Make a Difference?" *The British Journal of Criminology* 47 (3): 455–69.

Batchelor, Peter. 2001. "Small Arms, Big Business: Products and Producers." In *Small Arms Survey 2001: Profiling the Problem*, edited by Peter Batchelor and Keith Krause, 7–59. Geneva: Graduate Institute of International and Development Studies.

Batchelor, Peter. 2003. "Chapter 1. Workshops and Factories: Products and Producers." In *Small Arms Survey 2003: Development Denied*, edited by Peter Batchelor and Keith Krause, 9–56. New York: Oxford University Press.

Baum, Dan. 2013. "How to Make Your Own AR-15." *Harper's Magazine*, June 2013. http://harpers.org/archive/2013/06/how-to-make-your-own-ar-15/6/.

Bazinet, Mike. 2013. "Americans Skeptical of 'Smart Guns'; Oppose Their Legislative Mandate, National Poll Finds." National Shooting Sports Foundation, November 13, 2013. https://www.nssf.org/americans-skeptical-of -smart-guns-oppose-their-legislative-mandate-national-poll-finds/.

Beletsky, Leo, and Corey S. Davis. 2017. "Today's Fentanyl Crisis: Prohibition's Iron Law, Revisited." *International Journal of Drug Policy* 46: 156–59.

Benham, Barbara. 2016. "Survey: Most Americans Support Smart Guns." Johns Hopkins Bloomberg School of Public Health, January 21, 2016. https:// hub.jhu.edu/2019/06/10/smart-guns-personalized-firearms-unlikely-to -boost-gun-safety/.

Benson, Ragnar. 2000. *Guerrilla Gunsmithing: Quick and Dirty Methods for Fixing Firearms in Desperate Times*. Boulder, CO: Paladin Press.

Berman, Eric, and Jonah Leff. 2008. "Light Weapons: Products, Producers, and Proliferation." In *Small Arms Survey 2008: Risk and Resilience*, edited by Eric G. Berman, Keith Krause, Emile LeBrun, and Glenn McDonald, 6–41. Cambridge and New York: Cambridge University Press.

Berman, Eric G., and Louisa N. Lombard. 2008. "Weapons Generated within CAR: Indigenous Production." In *The Central African Republic and Small Arms: A Regional Tinderbox*, edited by Eric G. Berman and Louisa N. Lombard, 65–69. Geneva: Small Arms Survey, the Graduate Institute of International and Developmental Studies.

Barnett, Ian, and John Torous. 2019. "Ethics, Transparency, and Public Health at the Intersection of Innovation and Facebook's Suicide Prevention Efforts." *Annals of Internal Medicine* 170 (8): 565–66.

Bhattacharya, Asitesh. 2006. "Gunpowder and Its Applications in Ancient India." In *Gunpowder, Explosives, and the State: A Technological History*, by Brenda J. Buchanan, 42–50. Burlington, VT: Ashgate Publishing.

Blakley, Derrick. 2019. "New Gun Bill Would Require Buyers To Reveal Social Media History." CBS Chicago, February 6, 2019. https://chicago.cbslocal .com/2019/02/06/gun-law-bill-social-media-illinois-background-foid/.

Boothroyd, Geoffrey. 1970. *The Handgun*. New York: Crown Publishers.

Borelli, Frank. 2016. "Editor's Blog: Smart Guns Aren't Smart." Officer.Com, May 2, 2016. http://www.officer.com/blog/12201635/why-smart-guns-arent-smart.

Brady Campaign to Prevent Gun Violence. 2015. "The Brady Campaign State Scorecard." Crimadvisor. https://lawcenter.giffords.org/scorecard/.

Braga, Anthony A., and Rod K. Brunson. 2015. "The Police and Public Discourse on 'Black-on-Black' Violence." New Perspectives in Policing. Harvard Kennedy School and National Institute of Justice. https://www.ncjrs.gov/pdffiles1/nij/248588.pdf.

Braga, Anthony A., Garen J. Wintemute, Glenn L. Pierce, Philip J. Cook, and Greg Ridgeway. 2012. "Interpreting the Empirical Evidence on Illegal Gun Market Dynamics." *Journal of Urban Health* 89 (5): 779–93.

Bricknell, Samantha. 2008. "Criminal Use of Handguns in Australia." Trends and Issues in Crime and Criminal Justice No. 361. Australian Institute of Criminology. https://aic.gov.au/publications/tandi/tandi361.

Bricknell, Samantha, and Australian Institute of Criminology. 2012. "Firearm Trafficking and Serious and Organised Crime Gangs." Research and Public Policy Series No. 116. Canberra: Australian Institute of Criminology. https://aic.gov.au/publications/rpp/rpp116.

Brunner, John. 1968. *Stand on Zanzibar.* Garden City, NY: Doubleday.

Bucci, Nino. 2016. "As Many as 600,000 Illegal Guns in Australia." *The Age (Australia)*, October 21, 2016. https://www.theage.com.au/national/victoria/as-many-as-600000-illegal-guns-in-australia-20161020-gs74ay.html.

Bughin, Jacques, Jeongmin Seong, James Manyika, Michael Chui, and Raoul Joshi. 2018. "Notes from the Frontier: Modeling the Impact of AI on the World Economy." Discussion Paper. McKinsey Global Institute.

Bulliet, Richard W. 2016. *The Wheel Inventions & Reinventions.* New York: Columbia University Press.

Burges, William. 1865. *Art Applied to Industry: A Series of Lectures.* Oxford and London: John Henry and James Parker.

Burghardt, Henry D. 1919. *Machine Tool Operation.* New York: McGraw-Hill Book Company, Inc.

Burnett, John. 2012. "Law-Abiding Mexicans Taking Up Illegal Guns." Weekend Edition Saturday. National Public Radio. https://www.npr.org/2012/01/28/145996427/mexican-community-takes-taboo-stance-on-guns.

Burns, R. D. 1993. "Arms Control in Antiquity." In *Encyclopedia of Arms Control and Disarmament.* New York: Scribner's.

California State Auditor. 2016. "The CalGang Criminal Intelligence System: As the Result of Its Weak Oversight Structure, It Contains Questionable Information That May Violate Individuals' Privacy Rights." 2015–130. California State Auditor Report. Sacramento, CA: California State Auditor.

Callahan, Molly. 2019. "The Story behind the Data on Mass Murder in the United States." News @ Northeastern, August 13, 2019. https://news.northeastern.edu/2019/08/13/the-story-behind-the-data-on-mass-murder-in-the-united-states/.

Camiel, Deborah. 2013. "3-D Printed AR-15s Aimed at Gun Control." *CNBC*, April 22, 2013. https://www.cnbc.com/id/100661606.

Carlson, Jennifer. 2018. *Citizen-Protectors: The Everyday Politics of Guns in an Age of Decline*. Oxford: Oxford University Press.

Carlson, Khristopher, Joanna Wright, and Hannah Donges. 2015. "In the Line of Fire: Elephant and Rhino Poaching in Africa." In *Small Arms Survey 2015: Weapons and the World*, edited by Glenn McDonald, Emile LeBrun, Anna Alvazzi del Frate, Eric G. Berman, and Keith Krause, 7–36. Geneva: Graduate Institute of International and Development Studies.

Castillo-Carniglia, Alvaro, Rose M. C. Kagawa, Magdalena Cerdá, Cassandra K. Crifasi, Jon S. Vernick, Daniel W. Webster, and Garen J. Wintemute. 2019. "California's Comprehensive Background Check and Misdemeanor Violence Prohibition Policies and Firearm Mortality." *Annals of Epidemiology* 30 (February): 50–56.

CBS News. 2018. "3D-Printed Gun: Cody Wilson Says 'Debate Is Over.'" CBS News, August 1, 2018. https://www.cbsnews.com/news/3d-printed-gun -cody-wilson-says-gun-access-fundamental-human-right/.

Chan, Andy, and Jason Payne. 2017. "Homicide in Australia: 2008–09 to 2009– 10 National Homicide Monitoring Program Annual Report." Monitoring Reports No. 21. Canberra: Australian Institute of Criminology. https://aic .gov.au/publications/mr/mr21.

Chapman, S., P. Alpers, K. Agho, and M. Jones. 2006. "Australia's 1996 Gun Law Reforms: Faster Falls in Firearm Deaths, Firearm Suicides, and a Decade without Mass Shootings." *Injury Prevention* 12 (6): 365–72.

Chenoweth, Erica. 2013. "The Success of Nonviolent Civil Resistance." Presented at the TEDx, Boulder, CO, November. https://www.nonviolent-conflict .org/resource/success-nonviolent-civil-resistance/.

City of New York. 2011. "Point, Click, and Fire: An Investigation of Illegal Online Gun Sales." New York: City of New York.

Collingridge, David. 1982. *The Social Control of Technology*. London: Frances Pinter.

Conger, Kate. 2017 "Cloudflare CEO on Terminating Service to Neo-Nazi Site: 'The Daily Stormer Are Assholes.'" Gizmodo. https://gizmodo.com/ cloudflare-ceo-on-terminating-service-to-neo-nazi-site-1797915295.

Conway, Lucian Gideon, Meredith A. Repke, and Shannon C. Houck. 2017. "Donald Trump as a Cultural Revolt Against Perceived Communication Restriction: Priming Political Correctness Norms Causes More Trump Support." *Journal of Social and Political Psychology* 5 (1): 244–59.

Cook, Philip J., and Jens Ludwig. 2006. "Aiming for Evidence-Based Gun Policy." *Journal of Policy Analysis and Management* 25 (3): 691–735.

Cook, Philip J., Jens Ludwig, Sudhir Alladi Venkatesh, and Anthony A. Braga. 2007. "Underground Gun Markets." *The Economic Journal* 117 (524): F588–618.

Cook, Philip J., Susan T. Parker, and Harold A. Pollack. 2015. "Sources of Guns to Dangerous People: What We Learn by Asking Them." *Preventive Medicine, Special Issue on the Epidemiology and Prevention of Gun Violence* 79 (October): 28–36.

Corbett, Jonathan. 2012. "$1B of TSA Nude Body Scanners Made Worthless By Blog — How Anyone Can Get Anything Past The Scanners." *Professional Troublemaker*, March 6, 2012. https://professional-troublemaker.com /2012/03/06/1b-of-nude-body-scanners-made-worthless-by-blog-how -anyone-can-get-anything-past-the-tsas-nude-body-scanners/.

Cornell, Saul, and Nathan DeDino. 2004. "A Well Regulated Right: The Early American Origins of Gun Control." *Fordham Law Review* 73 (2): 487–528.

Costello, Tom, and Alex Johnson. 2015. "TSA Chief Out After Agents Fail 95 Percent of Airport Breach Tests." *NBC News*, June 1, 2015. https://www.nbc news.com/news/us-news/investigation-breaches-us-airports-allowed -weapons-through-n367851.

Cramer, Clayton E. 2018. *Lock, Stock, and Barrel: The Origins of American Gun Culture*. Santa Barbara, CA: Praeger.

Crifasi, Cassandra K., Molly Merrill-Francis, Alex McCourt, Jon S. Vernick, Garen J. Wintemute, and Daniel W. Webster. 2018. "Association between Firearm Laws and Homicide in Urban Counties." *Journal of Urban Health* 95 (3): 383–90.

Crosby, Alfred W. 2010. *Throwing Fire: Projectile Technology through History*. Cambridge: Cambridge University Press.

Delehanty, Casey, Jack Mewhirter, Ryan Welch, and Jason Wilks. 2017. "Militarization and Police Violence: The Case of the 1033 Program." *Research & Politics* 4 (2): 1–7.

Dick, James. 2013. "The Gunpowder Shortage." *Journal of the American Revolution*, September. https://www.revolutionarywarjournal.com/gunpowder/.

Dick, Philip K. 2011. *A Scanner Darkly*. Boston: Mariner Books.

Dragone, Davide, Giovanni Prarolo, Paolo Vanin, and Giulio Zanella. 2019. "Crime and the Legalization of Recreational Marijuana." *Journal of Economic Behavior & Organization* 159 (March): 488–501.

Duer, Ben. 1942. *World War II Work Incentive Poster Printed and Displayed on Factory Floor by Douglas Aircraft Company*. Poster. https://www.pbs.org /wgbh/roadshow/appraisals.

Duwe, Grant. 2007. *Mass Murder in the United States: A History*. Jefferson, NC: McFarland.

Dyer, Gwynne. 1985. *War*. New York: Crown.

Edelman, Adam. 2015. "Low Assault-Weapon Registration Stats Suggest Low Compliance with Gov. Cuomo's Landmark SAFE Act Gun Control Law." *New York Daily News*, June 23, 2015. https://www.nydailynews.com/news /politics/ny-safe-act-weapons-registry-numbers-released-article-1.2267730.

Fabio, Anthony, Jessica Duell, Kathleen Creppage, Kerry O'Donnell, and Ron Laporte. 2016. "Gaps Continue in Firearm Surveillance: Evidence from a Large U.S. City Bureau of Police." *Social Medicine* 10 (1): 13–21.

Fairleigh Dickinson University. 2013. "Beliefs about Sandy Hook Cover-up, Coming Revolution, Underlie Divide on Gun Control." Public Mind Poll. http://publicmind.fdu.edu/2013/guncontrol/.

Farago, Robert. 2015. "Strewth! Australian Police Seize 3D Printed Guns!" The Truth about Guns, February 2015. http://www.thetruthaboutguns.com /2015/02/robert-farago/struth-australian-police-seize-3d-printed-guns/.

Federal Aviation Administration. 2019. "UAS Sightings Report." February 15, 2019. https://www.faa.gov/uas/resources/public_records/uas_sightings _report/.

Federal Bureau of Investigation. 2015. "FBI Uniform Crime Report: Murder." Data. 2015 Crime in the United States. https://ucr.fbi.gov/crime-in-the -u.s/2015/crime-in-the-u.s.-2015/offenses-known-to-law-enforcement /murder/murdermain_final.

Fjestad, S. P. 2013. *Blue Book of Gun Values*. Minneapolis, MN: Blue Book Publications.

Follman, Mark, Gavin Aronsen, and Deanna Pan. 2019. "US Mass Shootings, 1982–2019: Data from Mother Jones' Investigation." *Mother Jones*, August 31, 2019. https://www.motherjones.com/politics/2012/12/mass-shootings -mother-jones-full-data/.

Fox, James Alan, and Emma E. Fridel. 2018. "The Three R's of School Shootings: Risk, Readiness, and Response." In *The Wiley Handbook on Violence in Education: Forms, Factors, and Preventions*, edited by Harvey Shapiro. New York: Wiley/Blackwell Publishers.

Frasetto, Mark. 2013. "Firearms and Weapons Legislation up to the Early 20th Century." Available at SSRN: https://papers.ssrn.com/abstract=2200991.

French, David. 2018. "Corporate Gun Control Might Be the Worst Threat to Gun Rights." National Review, August 21, 2018. https://www.nationalreview .com/2018/08/corporate-gun-control-worst-threat-gun-rights/.

Friedman, Jeffrey A. 2019. "Priorities for Preventive Action: Explaining Americans' Divergent Reactions to 100 Public Risks." *American Journal of Political Science* 63 (1): 181–96.

Gallup. 2018. "Indicators of News Media Trust." A Gallup/Knight Foundation Survey. https://www.knightfoundation.org/reports/indicators-of-news -media-trust.

Gandhi, Mahatma, and Dennis Dalton. 1996. *Mahatma Gandhi: Selected Political Writings*. Indianapolis, IN: Hackett Pub. Co.

Garcia, Mary Lynne. 2013. "Introduction to Vulnerability Assessment." In *Effective Physical Security*. 4th ed., edited by Lawrence J Fennelly. Waltham, MA: Butterworth-Heinemann.

Gardner, Tony. 2011. "Leeds 'Home Gunsmith' Dies before Trial." *Yorkshire Evening Post*, May 31, 2011. http://www.yorkshireeveningpost.co.uk/news /latest-news/top-stories/leeds-home-gunsmith-dies-before-trial -1-3378343.

Gartenstein-Ross, Daveed, and Daniel Trombly. 2012. "The Tactical and Strategic Use of Small Arms by Terrorists." Foundation for Defense of Democracies. Washington, DC: FDD Press.

Gordon, Amanda. 2011. "Questions on Large Capacity Magazines." OLR Research Report. https://www.cga.ct.gov/2011/rpt/2011-R-0158.htm.

Gottfried, Jeffrey, and Elizabeth Grieco. 2019. "Nearly Three-Quarters of Repub-
    licans Say the News Media Don't Understand People like Them." Pew
    Research Center: FactTank, January 18, 2019. https://www.pewresearch
    .org/fact-tank/2019/01/18/nearly-three-quarters-of-republicans-say-the
    -news-media-dont-understand-people-like-them/.
Gould, Chandre, Guy Lamb, Gregory Mthembu-Salter, Steven Nakana, and
    Dennis Rubel. 2004. "Country Study: South Africa." In *Hide and Seek:
    Taking Account of Small Arms in Southern Africa*, edited by Guy Lamb and
    Chandre Gould. Pretoria: Institute for Security Studies.
Gramlich, John, and Katherine Schaeffer. 2019. "7 Facts about Guns in the U.S."
    Pew Research Center, October 22, 2019. https://www.pewresearch.org
    /fact-tank/2018/12/27/facts-about-guns-in-united-states/.
Greenberg, Andy. 2015. "This App Lets Anyone 3D Print 'Do-Not-Duplicate'
    Keys." Wired, August 4, 2015. https://www.wired.com/2015/08/this-app
    -lets-anyone-3-d-print-do-not-duplicate-keys/.
Greener, W. W. 2016. *Gun and Its Development*. 9th ed. New York: Skyhorse
    Publishing.
Grunewald, Scott. 2015. "The Shuty Hybrid 3D Printed 9mm Pistol Raises Ques-
    tions About 3D Printed Gun Control." Blog. *3DPrint.Com*, August 19,
    2015. https://3dprint.com/89919/shuty-hybrid-3d-printed-pistol/.
Guo, Xiao. 2006. "Illegal Trade in Guns Problem for Poorer Regions." *China
    Daily*, June 13, 2006. https://www.chinadaily.com.cn/china/2006-06/13
    /content_616018.htm.
Haaretz. 2013. "Israeli TV Program Sneaks 3-D Printed Pistol into Knesset with-
    out Being Detected." June 4, 2013. https://www.haaretz.com/.premium
    -plastic-3-d-gun-slips-past-knesset-guards-1.5291141.
Hamm, Mark, and Ramon Spaaij. 2017. "Lone Wolf Terrorism in America: Using
    Knowledge of Radicalization Pathways to Forge Prevention Strategies,
    1940–2013." Ann Arbor, MI: Inter-university Consortium for Political
    and Social Research.
Hargrove, Thomas K., Rachael Rosselet, and Eric W. Witzig. 2018. "Are Murders
    Worth Solving?" Murder Accountability Project. http://www.murderdata
    .org/2018/01/are-murders-worth-solving-new-analysis.html.
Harrison, David. 2009. "£80 Starting Pistol Prompts Surge in Gangland Shoot-
    ings." *The Telegraph*, October 24, 2009. https://www.telegraph.co.uk
    /news/uknews/law-and-order/6422397/80-starting-pistol-prompts-surge
    -in-gangland-shootings.html.
Hays, G. H., and N. R. Jenzen-Jones. 2018. "Beyond State Control: Improvised
    and Craft-Produced Small Arms and Light Weapons." Small Arms Survey.
    Geneva: Graduate Institute of International and Development Studies.
Hemenway, David. 1997. "Survey Research and Self-Defense Gun Use: An Expla-
    nation of Extreme Overestimates." *Journal of Criminal Law and Criminol-
    ogy* 87 (4): 1430–45.
Herald Sun. 2016. "Authorities Seize Guns and Drugs in Border Blitz." Febru-
    ary 21, 2016. http://www.heraldsun.com.au/news/victoria/authorities

-seize-guns-and-drugs-in-border-blitz/news-story/d34a6c11b02614028
8df56895eebfa66?nk=24f26a5c169cc254f5db70eb8bff3760-14680
49726.

Holsinger, Bruce. 2015. "The Medieval Roots of Our DIY Gun Culture." Slate Magazine, May 7, 2015. https://slate.com/news-and-politics/2015/05/medieval
-roots-of-our-diy-gun-culture-people-have-been-making-their-own-guns
-since-the-late-middle-ages.html.

Hounshell, David A. 1984. *From the American System to Mass Production, 1800–
1932: The Development of Manufacturing Technology in the United States.* Baltimore: Johns Hopkins University Press.

Howard, Alun. 2005. "National Gun Law Guidelines Consultation: Analysis of
Specific National Gun Laws." Unpublished IANSA Working Paper. International Action Network on Small Arms.

"Identification of Firearms." *Code of Federal Regulations*, title 26 (1958): 53.
https://books.google.com.

"Illegal Firearm Manufacturing and Trafficking (Fabricación y Tráfico Ilícitos de
Armas)." 2006. National Report of Guatemala on Its Implementation of
the Programme of Action to Prevent, Combat and Eradicate the Illicit
Trade in Small Arms and Light Weapons in All Its Aspects (UNPoA).
http://www.poa-iss.org/PoA/PoA.aspx.

Ingraham, Christopher. 2015. "We're Now Averaging More than One Mass
Shooting per Day in 2015." *Washington Post*, August 26, 2015. https://
www.washingtonpost.com/news/wonk/wp/2015/08/26/were-now
-averaging-more-than-one-mass-shooting-per-day-in-2015/.

Insall, Roger. 2001. "People Investigation: The IRA Ghost Gun Investigation; It
Looks like a Plastic Toy but It Can Shoot Real Bullets and Is Almost Invisible to x-Rays." *The People*, August 12, 2001. https://www.thefreelibrary
.com/PEOPLE+INVESTIGATION%3A+THE+IRA+GHOST+GUN+INVE
STIGATION%3B+It+looks+like+...-a077122462.

International Crisis Group. 2010. "Illicit Arms in Indonesia." International Crisis
Group, Asia Briefing No. 109.

Ismay, John, Thomas Gibbons-Neff, and C. J. Chivers. 2017. "How ISIS Produced Its Cruel Arsenal on an Industrial Scale – The New York Times."
New York Times, December 10, 2017. https://www.nytimes.com/2017/12
/10/world/middleeast/isis-bombs.html.

Jacobs, James B. 2002. *Can Gun Control Work?* Oxford: Oxford University
Press.

Jakarta Post. 2013. "Most Armed Robbers Use Homemade Guns: Police." *The
Jakarta Post*, April 7, 2013. https://www.thejakartapost.com/news/2013
/04/17/most-armed-robbers-use-homemade-guns-police.html.

James, C. Rodney. 2008. "Why Microstamping and Bullet Serialization Won't
Work." NRA-ILA, August 1, 2008. https://www.nraila.org/articles/2008
0801/why-microstamping-and-bullet-serializat.

Jang, S. Mo. 2019. "Mass Shootings Backfire: The Boomerang Effects of Death
Concerns on Policy Attitudes." *Media Psychology* 22 (2): 298–322.

Jashinsky, Jared Michael, Brianna Magnusson, Carl Hanson, and Michael Barnes. 2016. "Media Agenda Setting Regarding Gun Violence before and after a Mass Shooting." *Frontiers in Public Health* 4: 1–6.

Jefferson, Thomas, and Julian P. Boyd. 1971. *The Papers of Thomas Jefferson. Vol. 18.* Princeton, NJ: Princeton University Press.

Jenzen-Jones, N. R. 2014. "Producers of Small Arms, Light Weapons and Their Ammunition." Small Arms Survey Research Notes No. 43. https://www .files.ethz.ch/isn/182840/SAS-Research-Note-43.pdf.

Jenzen-Jones, N. R. 2015. "Small Arms and Additive Manufacturing: An Assessment of 3D-Printed Firearms, Components, and Accessories." In *Behind the Curve: New Technologies, New Control Challenges*, edited by Benjamin King and Glen McDonald, 43–75. Occasional Paper of the Small Arms Survey. Geneva: Graduate Institute of International and Development Studies.

Jetter, Michael, and Jay K. Walker. 2018. "The Effect of Media Coverage on Mass Shootings." IZA DP No. 11900. IZA Institute of Labor Economics.

Johnson, Nicholas. 2008. "Imagining Gun Control in America: Understanding the Remainder Problem." *Wake Forest Law Review* 43: 854–55.

Johnston, Jennifer, and Andrew Joy. 2016. "Mass Shootings and the Media Contagion Effect." Paper presented at the annual American Psychological Association meeting, Denver, CO.

Johnston, Trevor, Troy D. Smith, and J. Luke Irwin. 2018. "Additive Manufacturing in 2040." Santa Monica, CA: Rand Corporation.

Kagawa, Rose M. C., Alvaro Castillo-Carniglia, Jon S. Vernick, Daniel Webster, Cassandra Crifasi, Kara E. Rudolph, Magdalena Cerdá, Aaron Shev, and Garen J. Wintemute. 2018. "Repeal of Comprehensive Background Check Policies and Firearm Homicide and Suicide." *Epidemiology* (Cambridge, Mass.) 29 (4): 494–502.

Kalmoe, Nathan P., and Lilliana Mason. 2019. "Lethal Mass Partisanship: Prevalence, Correlates, & Electoral Contingencies." *NCAPSA American Politics Meeting.* https://www.dannyhayes.org/uploads/6/9/8/5/69858539/kalmoe ___mason_ncapsa_2019_-_lethal_partisanship_-_final_lmedit.pdf.

Kapustin, Max, Nathan Hess, Jen Ludwig, Marc Punkay, Kimberley Smith, Lauren Speigel, and David Welgus. 2017. "Gun Violence in Chicago 2016." Chicago: University of Chicago Crime Lab.

Karp, Aaron. 2007. "Completing the Count: Civilian Firearms." In *Small Arms Survey 2007: Guns and the City*, edited by Eric G. Berman, Keith Krause, Emile LeBrun, and Glen McDonald, 39–72. Cambridge: Cambridge University Press.

Karp, Aaron. 2013. "Unregistered Ownership." Legacies in War in the Company of Peace: Firearms in Nepal Issue Brief No. 2. Geneva: Small Arms Survey.

Karp, Aaron. 2018. "Estimating Global Civilian- Held Firearms Numbers." Briefing Paper. Small Arms Survey. Australia: Australian Government Department of Foreign Affairs and Trade.

Kassem, Ramzi. 2016. "I Help Innocent People Get Off Terrorism Watch Lists. As a Gun Control Tool, They're Useless." *Washington Post*, June 28, 2016. https://www.washingtonpost.com/posteverything/wp/2016/06/28/i-help -innocent-people-get-off-terror-watch-lists-as-a-gun-control-tool-theyre -useless/.

Kaste, Martin. 2018. "Facebook Increasingly Reliant on A.I. To Predict Suicide Risk." *NPR All Things Considered*, November 17, 2018. https://www.npr .org/2018/11/17/668408122/facebook-increasingly-reliant-on-a-i-to -predict-suicide-risk.

Kerley, David, and Jeffrey Cook. 2017. "TSA Fails Most Tests in Latest Under-cover Operation at US Airports." *ABC News*, November 9, 2017. https:// abcnews.go.com/US/tsa-fails-tests-latest-undercover-operation-us-air ports/story?id=51022188.

Kessler, Jim. 2003. "The Enforcement Gap: Federal Gun Laws Ignored." A Study of Federal Gun Prosecutions from FY 2000-FY2002. Americans for Gun Safety Foundation. http://content.thirdway.org/publications/10/AGS _Report_-_The_Enforcement_Gap_-_Federal_Gun_Laws_Ignored.pdf.

Khan, Igtidar Alam. 2006. "The Indian Response to Firearms, 1300–1750." In *Gunpowder, Explosives, and the State: A Technological History*, edited by Brenda J. Buchanan, 51–66. Ashgate Publishing.

Kim, Daniel. 2019. "Social Determinants of Health in Relation to Firearm-Related Homicides in the United States: A Nationwide Multilevel Cross-Sectional Study." *PLOS Medicine* 16 (12): e1002978.

King, Benjamin. 2015. "From Replica to Real: An Introduction to Firearms Con-versions." Small Arms Survey Issue Brief 10. Geneva: Graduate Institute of International and Development Studies.

Kleck, Gary. 2018. "What Do CDC's Surveys Say About the Frequency of Defen-sive Gun Uses?" Available at SSRN: https://papers.ssrn.com/sol3/papers .cfm?abstract_id=3194685.

Klieve, Helen, Michael Barnes, and Diego De Leo. 2008. "Controlling Firearms Use in Australia: Has the 1996 Gun Law Reform Produced the Decrease in Rates of Suicide with This Method?" *Social Psychiatry and Psychiatric Epidemiology* 44: 285–92.

Knight, Brian. 2018. "Are Banks That Engage in Political Activism Really 'Private'?" *The Hill*, June 20, 2018, Opinion. https://thehill.com/opinion/finance /393236-are-banks-that-engage-in-political-activism-really-private.

Kopel, David B. 1992. *The Samurai, the Mountie, and the Cowboy: Should America Adopt the Gun Controls of Other Democracies?* Buffalo, NY: Prometheus Books.

Kopel, David B. 2016. "Background Checks for Firearms Sales and Loans: Law, History, and Policy." *Harvard Journal on Legislation* 53: 303–67.

Kopp, Emily. 2019. "Veterans Are Being Denied This GI Bill Benefit If They Work in Cannabis." *Roll Call*, June 3, 2019. https://www.rollcall.com/news /congress/veterans-denied-gi-bill-benefit-if-they-work-in-cannabis.

Lal, Rollie. 2007. "Japanese Trafficking and Smuggling." In *Transnational Threats: Smuggling and Trafficking in Arms, Drugs, and Human Life*, edited by Kimberley L. Thachuk and Marion Eugene Bowman. Westport, CT: Praeger Security International.

Landau, Les. 1998. "Counterpoint." Television Show. *Star Trek Voyager.* https://www.startrek.com/database_article/star-trek-voyager-synopsis.

Lang, Matthew. 2013. "The Impact of Mental Health Insurance Laws on State Suicide Rates." *Health Economics* 22 (1): 73–88.

Lankevich, George J. 2002. *New York City A Short History.* New York and London: New York University Press.

Lankford, Adam. 2013. "A Comparative Analysis of Suicide Terrorists and Rampage, Workplace, and School Shooters in the United States from 1990 to 2010." *Homicide Studies* 17 (3): 255–74.

Lankford, Adam. 2018. "Do the Media Unintentionally Make Mass Killers into Celebrities? An Assessment of Free Advertising and Earned Media Value." *Celebrity Studies*, January. https://doi.org/10.1080/19392397.2017.1422984.

Larabee, Ann. 2015. *The Wrong Hands: Popular Weapons Manuals and Their Historic Challenges to a Democratic Society.* Oxford: Oxford University Press.

Lee, Wang-Sheng, and Sandy Suardi. 2010. "The Australian Firearms Buyback and Its Effect on Gun Deaths." *Contemporary Economic Policy* 28 (1): 65–79.

Leering, Raoul. 2017. "3D Printing: A Threat to Global Trade." Economic and Financial Analysis. ING. https://www.ingwb.com/insights/research/3d-printing-a-threat-to-global-trade.

Leigh, A., and C. Neill. 2010. "Do Gun Buybacks Save Lives? Evidence from Panel Data." *American Law and Economics Review* 12 (2): 509–57.

Lekakis, George. 2015. "Spike in Gun Crimes Reveals Nation's Secret Gun Problem." *The New Daily* (Australia), November 10, 2015. https://thenewdaily.com.au/news/national/2015/11/10/australias-secret-gun-problem-exposed/.

Lidin, Olof G. 2004. *Tanegashima: The Arrival of Europe in Japan.* Copenhagen: NIAS Press.

Lipson, Hod, and Melba Kurman. 2013. *Fabricated : The New World of 3D Printing.* Indianapolis, IN: John Wiley and Sons.

"Lost Highway/Out for Murda." 2010. Television Show. *The First 48.* A&E. https://www.aetv.com/shows/the-first-48.

Lott, John R. 2010. *More Guns, Less Crime Understanding Crime and Gun Control Laws, Third Edition.* Chicago: University of Chicago Press.

Lott, John R. 2018. "Concealed Carry Permit Holders Across the United States: 2018." Available at SSRN: https://papers.ssrn.com/abstract=3233904.

Lu, Ruibin, Dale Willits, Mary K. Stohr, David Makin, John Snyder, Nicholas Lovrich, Mikala Meize, Duane Stanton, Guangzhen Wu, and Craig Hemmens. 2019. "The Cannabis Effect on Crime: Time-Series

Analysis of Crime in Colorado and Washington State." *Justice Quarterly* October: 1–31.

Ludwig, Jens, Dave E. Marcotte, and Karen Norberg. 2009. "Anti-Depressants and Suicide." *Journal of Health Economics* 28 (3): 659–76.

Luebbert, L. A. 2019. "Be Mindful of Serial Numbers When Posting Your Gun Photos Online." America's First Freedom. October 28, 2019. https://www .americas1stfreedom.org/articles/2019/10/28/be-mindful-of-serial -numbers-when-posting-your-gun-photos-online/.

Lurie, Stephen, Alexis Acevedo, and Kyle Ott. 2018. "The Less Than 1%: Groups and the Extreme Concentration of Urban Violence." PowerPoint presented at the American Society of Criminology, November 14. https://cdn.theatlantic. com/assets/media/files/nnsc_gmi_concentration_asc_v1.91.pdf.

Magliocca, Nicholas R., Kendra McSweeney, Steven E. Sesnie, Elizabeth Tell-man, Jennifer A. Devine, Erik A. Nielsen, Zoe Pearson, and David J. Wrathall. 2019. "Modeling Cocaine Traffickers and Counterdrug Inter-diction Forces as a Complex Adaptive System." *Proceedings of the National Academy of Sciences* 116 (16): 7784–92.

Margolin, Josh. 2013. "Exclusive: After Westgate, Interpol Chief Ponders 'Armed Citizenry.'" ABC News, October 21, 2013. https://abcnews.go.com/Blotter /exclusive-westgate-interpol-chief-ponders-armed-citizenry/story?id= 20637341.

Matthews, Sam. 2014. "Q&A With A Deep Web Arms Dealer." Vocativ, February 24, 2014. https://www.vocativ.com/tech/bitcoin/q-deep-web-arms-dealer/.

Mauser, Gary. n.d. "The Canadian Long-Gun Registry: A Preliminary Evalua-tion." https://www.sfu.ca/~mauser/papers/long-gun/The-LGR.pdf.

McGarrell, Edmund F., Natalie Kroovand Hipple, Nocholas Corsaro, Timothy S. Bynum, Heather Perez, Carol A. Zimmermann, and Melissa Garmo. 2009. "Project Safe Neighborhoods—A National Program to Reduce Gun Crime: Final Project Report." Submitted to the National Institute of Jus-tice. Michigan State University.

McPhedran, Samara. 2016. "A Systematic Review of Quantitative Evidence about the Impacts of Australian Legislative Reform on Firearm Homicide." *Aggression and Violent Behavior* 28 (May): 64–72.

McQuaid, Hugh. 2014. "Police: About 50,000 Assault Rifles Registered By Con-necticut Gun Owners," *CT News Junkie*, January 17, 2014. http://www .ctnewsjunkie.com/archives/entry/police_register_about_50000_assault _rifles/.

McTague, Robert & Thomas Ricks. 2017. "Some Thoughts on How We Might Get from Where We're at Now to a Second Civil War." *Foreign Policy*, October 10, 2017. https://foreignpolicy.com/2017/10/10/some-thoughts-on-how -we-might-get-from-where-were-at-now-to-a-second-civil-war/.

Mejia, Daniel, and Pascual Restrepo. 2016. "The Economics of the War on Illegal Drug Production and Trafficking." *Journal of Economic Behavior and Orga-nization* 126 (June): 255–75.

Melling, Louise. 2018. "The ACLU's Position on Gun Control." American Civil Liberties Union, March 26, 2018. https://www.aclu.org/blog/civil -liberties/mobilization/aclus-position-gun-control.

Mielke, Howard W., and Sammy Zahran. 2012. "The Urban Rise and Fall of Air Lead (Pb) and the Latent Surge and Retreat of Societal Violence." *Environment International* 43 (August): 48–55.

Mines, Keith, and Thomas Ricks. 2017. "Will We Have a Civil War? A SF Officer Turned Diplomat Estimates Chances at 60 Percent." *Foreign Policy*, March 10, 2017. https://foreignpolicy.com/2017/03/10/will-we-have-a-civil-war -a-sf-officer-turned-diplomat-estimates-chances-at-60-percent/.

Miron, Jeffrey A. 2004. *Drug War Crimes: The Consequences of Prohibition.* Oakland, CA: Independent Institute.

Mowery, Keaton, Eric Wustrow, Tom Wypych, Corey Singleton, Chris Comfort, Eric Rescorla, J. Alex Halderman, Hovav Shacham, and Stephen Checkoway. 2014. "Security Analysis of a Full-Body Scanner." In *Proceedings of the 23rd USENIX Security Symposium*, 369–84. San Diego, CA.

Mtonga, Robert, and Gregory Mthembu-Salter. 2004. "Country Study: Zambia." In *Hide and Seek: Taking Account of Small Arms in Southern Africa*, edited by Chandre Gould and Guy Lamb. Pretoria: Institute for Security Studies.

Mummolo, Jonathan. 2018. "Militarization Fails to Enhance Police Safety or Reduce Crime but May Harm Police Reputation." *Proceedings of the National Academy of Sciences* 115 (37): 9181–86.

"Muzeum Karla Zemana." 2016. Muzeum Karla Zemana. http://www.muzeum karlazemana.cz/.

Mwakasungula, Undule, and David Nungu. 2004. "Country Study: Malawi." In *Hide and Seek: Taking Account of Small Arms in Southern Africa*, edited by Chandre Gould and Guy Lamb. Pretoria: Institute for Security Studies.

National Academies of Sciences, Engineering, & Medicine. Division on Engineering and Physical Sciences; Computer Science and Telecommunications Board; Committee on Law Enforcement and Intelligence Access to Plaintext Information. 2018. *Decrypting the Encryption Debate: A Framework for Decision Makers.* Washington, DC: National Academies Press.

National Firearms Act: Hearings Before the Committee on Ways and Means, 73rd Cong., 2nd sess. (Washington, DC, Government Printing Office: 1934) (statement of Homer Cummings U.S. Attorney General) 21–22.

National Institute of Justice. 2014. "Opening the Black Box of NIBIN." National Institute of Justice. July 1, 2014. nij.ojp.gov/media/video/23911.

National Institute of Justice. 2019. "Pepper Spray: Research Insights on Effects and Effectiveness Have Curbed Its Appeal." *NIJ Journal* 281. https://nij .ojp.gov/topics/articles/pepper-spray-research-insights-effects-and -effectiveness-have-curbed-its-appeal.

National Public Radio. 2018. "The Science in Science Fiction." *Talk of the Nation.* NPR. https://www.npr.org/2018/10/22/1067220/the-science-in-science -fiction.

New York Civil Liberties Union. 2012. "New NYCLU Report Finds NYPD Stop-and-Frisk Practices Ineffective, Reveals Depth of Racial Disparities." New York Civil Liberties Union, May 9, 2012. https://www.nyclu.org/en/press-releases/new-nyclu-report-finds-nypd-stop-and-frisk-practices-ineffective-reveals-depth-racial.

New York State Psychiatric Association. n.d. "The SAFE Act: Guidelines for Complying." New York State Psychiatric Association. https://www.nyspsych.org/index.php?option=com_content&view=article&id=73:the-safe-act--guidelines-for-complying&catid=41:safe-act&Itemid=140.

New York Times. 1953. "Bronx Boy Slain; Zip Gun is Sought: Conference Earlier in the Day Discusses Ways to Combat Use of Homemade Pistol." December 20, 1953. https://archive.nytimes.com/.

Noack, Rick. 2016. "It's Impossible to Monitor All Terror Suspects. These Charts Show Why." *Washington Post*, June 15, 2016. https://www.washingtonpost.com/news/worldviews/wp/2016/06/15/its-impossible-to-monitor-all-terror-suspects-these-charts-show-why/.

North, Anna. 2019. "A Boom in At-Home Abortions Is Coming." Vox, July 9, 2019. https://www.vox.com/the-highlight/2019/7/1/18638649/abortion-pill-internet-misoprostol-mifepristone.

NRA-ILA. 2015. "Stop Obama's Planned Gag Order on Firearm-Related Speech." June 5, 2015. https://www.nraila.org/articles/20150605/stop-obamas-planned-gag-order-on-firearm-related-speech.

NRA-ILA. 2016. "Smart' Guns/Personalized Firearms." 2016. https://www.nraila.org/.

NRA-ILA. 2019. "Pennsylvania AG Targets Partially-Manufactured Receivers, Gun Owners." December 23, 2019. https://www.nraila.org/articles/20191223/pennsylvania-ag-targets-partially-manufactured-receivers-gun-owners?utm_source=email&utm_medium=email&utm_campaign=ila_alert.

O'Neill, Kevin. 2012. "Is Technology Outmoding Traditional Firearm Regulation? 3D Printing, State Security, and the Need for Regulatory Foresight in Gun Policy." Available at SSRN: http://papers.ssrn.com/sol3/papers.cfm?abstract_id=2186936.

Ouimet, Jason. 2020. "Trump Administration Completes Pro-Gun Regulatory Reform." *America's 1st Freedom*, January 21, 2020. https://www.americaslstfreedom.org/articles/2020/1/21/trump-administration-completes-pro-gun-regulatory-reform.

Paoli, Giacomo Persi. 2010. "The Method Behind the Mark: A Review of Firearm Marking Technologies." Small Arms Survey Issue Brief No. 1. Geneva: Graduate Institute of International and Development Studies.

Papachristos, Andrew V., Anthony A. Braga, and David M. Hureau. 2012. "Social Networks and the Risk of Gunshot Injury." *Journal of Urban Health: Bulletin of the New York Academy of Medicine* 89 (6): 992–1003.

Papachristos, Andrew V., Christopher Wildeman, and Elizabeth Roberto. 2015. "Tragic, but Not Random: The Social Contagion of Nonfatal Gunshot

Injuries." *Social Science & Medicine, Special Issue: Social Networks, Health and Mental Health* 125 (January): 139–50.

Pape, Robert Anthony. 2006. *Dying to Win: The Strategic Logic of Suicide Terrorism.* New York: Random House Trade Paperbacks.

Pardo, Bryce, Jirka Taylor, Jonathan P. Caulkins, Beau Kilmer, Peter Reuter, and Bradley D. Stein. 2019. "The Future of Fentanyl and Other Synthetic Opioids." Santa Monica, CA: Rand Corporation.

Parker, Kim, Juliana Horowitz, Ruth Igielnik, and Baxter L Oliphant. 2017. "America's Complex Relationship with Guns." Pew Research Center Social & Demographic Trends, June 22, 2017. https://www.pew socialtrends.org/2017/06/22/americas-complex-relationship-with-guns/.

Partridge, Emma. 2014. "Police Pop Pen-Gun Syndicate." *The Sydney Morning Herald,* September 27, 2014. https://www.smh.com.au/national/nsw /police-pop-pengun-syndicate-20140927-10mgve.html.

Patrick, Brian Anse. 2013. *The National Rifle Association and the Media: The Motivating Force of Negative Coverage.* London: Arktos.

Paudel, Lekh Nath. 2014. "The Highway Routes: Small Arm Smuggling in Eastern Nepal." Small Arms Survey, Nepal Armed Violence Assessment, Issue Brief No. 4. Geneva: Small Arms Survey.

Pearce, Brian. 2016. "The History of Handloading: Not Just a Fad Anymore." Load Data, April 7, 2016. https://loaddata.com/Article/LoadDevelopment /The-History-of-Handloading-Not-Just-a-Fad-Anymore/448.

Perrin, Noel. 1979. *Giving up the Gun: Japan's Reversion to the Sword, 1543–1879.* Boston: David R. Godine.

Pew Research Center. 2018. "Gun Policy Remains Divisive, But Several Proposals Still Draw Bipartisan Support." Pew Research Center U.S. Politics & Policy, October 18, 2018. https://www.people-press.org/2018/10/18/gun -policy-remains-divisive-but-several-proposals-still-draw-bipartisan -support/.

Pew Research Center. 2019a. "Partisan Antipathy: More Intense, More Personal." Pew Research Center U.S. Politics & Policy, October 10, 2019. https:// www.people-press.org/2019/10/10/partisan-antipathy-more-intense -more-personal/.

Pew Research Center. 2019b. "Public Trust in Government: 1958–2019." Pew Research Center U.S. Politics & Policy, April 11, 2019. https://www .people-press.org/2019/04/11/public-trust-in-government-1958-2019/.

Phillips, Janet, Malcolm Park, and Catherine Lorimer. 2007. "Firearms in Australia: A Guide to Electronic Resources." Parliament of Australia, August 9, 2007. https://www.aph.gov.au/About_Parliament/Parliamentary _Departments/Parliamentary_Library/pubs/BN/0708/FirearmsAustralia.

Pinker, Steven. 2011. *The Better Angels of Our Nature: Why Violence Has Declined.* New York: Penguin Books.

Pliny, and H. Rackham. 1938. *Natural History.* Cambridge, MA: Harvard University Press.

Porfiri, Maurizio, Raghu Ram, Shinnosuke Nakayama, James Macinko, and Rifat Sipahi. 2019. "Media Coverage and Firearm Acquisition in the Aftermath of a Mass Shooting." *Nature Human Behaviour* 3 (9): 913–21.

Portnoy, Erica. 2019. "Why Adding Client-Side Scanning Breaks End-To-End." Electronic Frontier Foundation. November 1, 2019. https://www.eff.org /deeplinks/2019/11/why-adding-client-side-scanning-breaks-end-end -encryption.

Post, Jerrold, Farhana Ali, Schuyler Henderson, Steven Shanfield, Jeff Victoroff, and Stevan Weine. 2009. "The Psychology of Suicide Terrorism." *Psychiatry* 72: 13–31.

RAND Corporation. 2008. "The Science of Gun Policy: A Critical Synthesis of Research Evidence on the Effects of Gun Policies in the United States." Research Reports RR-2088-RC. https://www.rand.org/pubs/research _reports/RR2088.html.

Reuter, Peter, and Jenny Mouzos. 2003. "A Massive Buyback of Low-Risk Guns." In *Evaluating Gun Policy: Effects on Crime and Violence*, edited by Philip J. Cook and Jens Ludwig. Washington, DC: Brookings Institution Press.

Reyes, Jessica Wolpaw. 2007. "Environmental Policy as Social Policy? The Impact of Childhood Lead Exposure on Crime." Working Paper 13097. National Bureau of Economic Research.

Ricks, Thomas E. 2017. "Will We Have a 2nd Civil War? You Tell Me." *Foreign Policy*, March 7, 2017. https://foreignpolicy.com/2017/03/07/will-we-have -a-2nd-civil-war-you-tell-me/.

Rios, Billy. 2015. "Pulling Back the Curtain on Airport Security: Can a Weapon Get Past TSA?" YouTube, March 17. https://www.youtube.com/watch?v= hbqVNlwfjxo.

Robertson, Doug. 2011. "Guns Black Market Booming." *The Advertiser* (Australia), December 20, 2011. https://www.pressreader.com/australia/the-adve rtiser/20111221/282291022076725.

Rodgers, Dennis, and Jose Luis Rocha. 2013. "Turning Points: Gang Evolution in Nicaragua." In *Small Arms Survey 2013: Everyday Dangers*, edited by Emile LeBrun, Glenn McDonald, Anna Alvazzi del Frate, Eric Berman, and Keith Krause. Cambridge: Cambridge University Press.

Roose, Kevin. 2019. "Why Banning 8chan Was So Hard for Cloudflare: 'No One Should Have That Power.'" *New York Times*, August 5, 2019. https://www .nytimes.com/2019/08/05/technology/8chan-cloudflare-el-paso.html.

Ropeik, David. 2018. "School Shootings Are Extraordinarily Rare. Why Is Fear of Them Driving Policy?" *Washington Post*, March 9, 2018. https://www .washingtonpost.com/outlook/school-shootings-are-extraordinarily-rare -why-is-fear-of-them-driving-policy/2018/03/08/f4ead9f2-2247-11e8 -94da-ebf9d112159c_story.html.

Rose, Joel. 2014. "A New Jersey Law That's Kept Smart Guns Off Shelves Nationwide." *NPR*, June 24, 2014. https://www.npr.org/sections/alltechconside

red/2014/06/24/325178305/a-new-jersey-law-thats-kept-smart-guns-off
-shelves-nationwide.

Rosenwald, Michael. 2015. "Renewed Push for Smart Guns Could Trigger a New
Furor over the Technology." *Washington Post*, October 22, 2015. https://
www.washingtonpost.com/local/renewed-push-for-smart-guns-could
-trigger-a-new-furor-over-the-technology/2015/10/21/156451a4-7813
-11e5-a958-d889faf561dc_story.html.

Roth, Randolph. 2002. "Guns, Gun Culture, and Homicide: The Relationship
between Firearms, the Uses of Firearms, and Interpersonal Violence."
The William and Mary Quarterly 59 (1): 223–40.

Safi, Michael, and Nick Evershed. 2015. "Australia Is Now World's Sixth-Largest
Arms Importer." *The Guardian*, April 3, 2015. https://www.theguardian.com
/australia-news/2015/apr/03/australias-arms-imports-surge-after-costly.

Sageman, Marc. 2008. *Leaderless Jihad: Terror Networks in the Twenty-First Century*. Philadelphia: University of Pennsylvania Press.

Salesforce. 2019. "Acceptable Use and External-Facing Services Policy." April 11,
2019. https://c1.sfdcstatic.com/content/dam/web/en_us/www/documents
/legal/Agreements/policies/ExternalFacing_Services_Policy.pdf.

Sanfelice, Laura Quadarella. 2017. *Why We Are under Attack: Al Qaeda, the Islamic
State, and the "Do-It-Yourself" Terorism*. Rome, Italy: Aracne Editrice.

Schaeffer, Katherine. 2019. "Share of Americans Who Favor Stricter Gun Laws
Has Increased since 2017." Pew Research Center, October 16, 2019.
https://www.pewresearch.org/fact-tank/2019/10/16/share-of-americans
-who-favor-stricter-gun-laws-has-increased-since-2017/.

Schneier, Bruce. 2018. *Click Here to Kill Everybody: Security and Survival in a
Hyper-Connected World*. New York: W.W. Norton & Company.

Schroeder, Matt. 2016. "Dribs and Drabs: The Mechanics of Small Arms Trafficking from the United States." Small Arms Survey Issue Brief No. 17.
Geneva: Graduate Institute of International and Development Studies.

Schwab, Klaus, and Richard Samans. 2016. "Preface." World Economic Forum—
The Future of Jobs. http://wef.ch/1PqcasD.

"Scientific Evaluations." 2019. Cure Violence. http://cureviolence.org/.

Scott, Kellie. 2015. "Cases of Arson-Homicide in Australia Almost Double in 20
Years, Australian Institute of Criminology Shows." *ABC News* (Australia),
October 10, 2015. https://www.abc.net.au/news/2015-07-03/arson-homi
cides-on-the-rise-in-australia-institute-criminology/6592448.

Shapiro, Josh. 2019. Commonwealth of Pennsylvania Office of Attorney General,
Receivers Legal Opinion Letter to Colonel Robert Evanchick. December
16, 2019. https://www.attorneygeneral.gov/wp-content/uploads/2019/12
/19.12.16-Receivers-Legal-Opinion.pdf.

Shaya, Kareem. 2018. "Base Rate Neglect and Andrew Ross Sorkin's Credit Card
Surveillance System." Open Source Defense, December 28, 2018. https://
opensourcedefense.org/blog/base-rate-neglect-and-andrew-ross-sorkins
-credit-card-surveillance-system.

Shulgin, Alexander. 1975. "Drugs of Abuse in the Future." *Clinical Toxicology* 8 (4): 405–56.

Silva, Jason R., and Emily Ann Greene-Colozzi. 2019. "Fame-Seeking Mass Shooters in America: Severity, Characteristics, and Media Coverage." *Aggression and Violent Behavior* 48 (September): 24–35.

Silver, James, Andre Simons, and Sarah Craun. 2018. "A Study of the Pre-Attack Behaviors of Active Shooters in the United States between 2000 and 2013." Federal Bureau of Investigation, U.S. Department of Justice. https://www.fbi.gov/file-repository/pre-attack-behaviors-of-active -shooters-in-us-2000-2013.pdf/view.

Singer, Peter W. 2010. *Wired for War: The Robotics Revolution and Conflict in the Twenty-First Century.* New York: Penguin Books.

Skogan, Wesley G, Susan M. Hartnett, Natalie Bump, and Jill Dubois. 2008. "Evaluation of CeaseFire-Chicago." Chicago: Northwestern University.

Small Arms Survey 2007. 2007. Cambridge: Cambridge University Press.

Smith, Aaron. 2018. "Public Attitudes Toward Technology Companies." Pew Research Center Internet & Technology, June 28, 2018. https://www.pew internet.org/2018/06/28/public-attitudes-toward-technology-companies.

Smith, Philip H., Gregory G. Homish, R. Lorraine Collins, Gary A. Giovino, Helene R. White, and Kenneth E. Leonard. 2014. "Couples' Marijuana Use Is Inversely Related to Their Intimate Partner Violence over the First 9 Years of Marriage." *Psychology of Addictive Behaviors: Journal of the Society of Psychologists in Addictive Behaviors* 28 (3): 734–42.

Snead, Jason, and John-Michael Seibler. 2016. "Purposeless Regulation: The FAA Drone Registry." Report Government Regulation. The Heritage Foundation, February 2, 2016. https://www.heritage.org/node/10747/print -display.

Snow, Deborah. 2014. "Customs Gets $88m to Upgrade Screening of Mail and Cargo." *The Sydney Morning Herald*, January 23, 2014. https://www.smh .com.au/politics/federal/customs-gets-88m-to-upgrade-screening-of -mail-and-cargo-20140122-3196p.html.

Sorkin, Andrew Ross. 2018. "How Banks Unwittingly Finance Mass Shootings." *New York Times*, December 24, 2018. https://www.nytimes.com/inter active/2018/12/24/business/dealbook/mass-shootings-credit-cards.html.

Spitzer, Robert. 2015. *Guns Across America: Reconciling Gun Rules and Rights.* Oxford: Oxford University Press.

State of New York Attorney General. 2019. "Ghost Gun Cease and Desist Letter." September 23, 2019. https://ag.ny.gov/sites/default/files/ghost_gun_cease _and_desist_letter.pdf.

Stephens, Alain. 2019. "Ghost Guns Are Everywhere in California." The Trace, May 17, 2019. https://www.thetrace.org/2019/05/ghost-gun-california -crime/.

Stoakes, Emanuel. 2019. "New Zealand Is Trying to Buy Back the Military-Style Weapons It Banned in April. It's Not so Easy." *Washington Post*, June 30,

2019. https://www.washingtonpost.com/world/asia_pacific/new-zealand
-is-trying-to-buy-back-the-assault-style-weapons-it-banned-in-april-its
-not-so-easy/2019/06/30/c3e49844-9365-11e9-956a-88c291ab5c38
_story.html.

Stokes, Jon. 2016. "No, the Gun Industry Is Not 'Secretly Pulling' for Hillary." *All
Outdoor*, February 20, 2016. http://www.alloutdoor.com/2016/02/20/no
-the-gun-industry-is-not-secretly-pulling-for-hillary/.

Stratfor. 2011. "Mexico's Gun Supply and the 90 Percent Myth." *Stratfor Worldview*, February 10, 2011. https://worldview.stratfor.com/article/mexicos
-gun-supply-and-90-percent-myth.

Stretesky, Paul B., and Michael J. Lynch. 2001. "The Relationship Between Lead
Exposure and Homicide." *Archives of Pediatrics & Adolescent Medicine* 155
(5): 579–82.

Sullum, Jacob. 2016. "The FBI Distributes Child Pornography to Catch People
Who Look at It." Hit & Run Blog: Reason, August 31, 2016. https://reason
.com/blog/2016/08/31/the-fbi-distributes-child-pornography-to-.

The Sun Daily. 2013. "KDN Sets New SOP to Address Lost Firearms." October 23,
2013. http://www.thesundaily.my/news/863786.

Tallman, Mark. 2017. "Making Crimes? Technology, Law, and DIY Firearms."
Dissertation. Denver: University of Denver.

Thornton, Mark. 2007. *The Economics of Prohibition*. Salt Lake City: University of
Utah Press.

Thruvision. 2018. "Thruvision TAC Data Sheet V.1.3." Thruvision: Global People
Screening Solutions, July 2018. http://thruvision.com/wp-content/
uploads/2018/11/1810-TV-TAC8-Datasheet-v1.3.pdf.

Tirone, Daniel C., and James Gilley. 2015. "Printing Power: 3-D Printing and
Threats to State Security." *Journal of Policing, Intelligence and Counter Terrorism* 10 (2): 102–19.

Towers, Sherry, Andres Gomez-Lievano, Maryam Khan, Anuj Mubayi, and Car-
los Castillo-Chavez. 2015. "Contagion in Mass Killings and School
Shootings." *PLOS ONE* 10 (7): e0117259.

Tuccille, J. D. 2013. "How Government Officials Doom Gun Registration Laws."
Reason.Com, December 11, 2013. https://reason.com/2013/12/11/how
-government-officials-sealed-the-doom/.

United Nations General Assembly. 2015. "International Instrument to Enable
States to Identify and Trace, in a Timely and Reliable Manner, Illicit Small
Arms and Light Weapons." A/CONF.192/15. http://www.poa-iss.org
/CASAUpload/Members/Documents/1@International%20Tracing
%20Instrument.pdf.

United Nations Office on Drugs and Crime. 2012. "Firearms within Central
America." Transnational Organized Crime in Central America and the
Caribbean. https://www.unodc.org/documents/toc/Reports/TOCTA
SouthAmerica/English/TOCTA_CACaribb_firearmssmuggling_within
_CAmerica.pdf.

United Nations Security Council. 2008. "Small Arms Report of the Secretary-General." S/2008/258. http://www.poa-iss.org/DocsUpcomingEvents/S-2008-258.pdf.

U.S. Bureau of Alcohol, Tobacco, Firearms and Explosives. 2013. "What Is ATF Doing in Regards to People Making Their Own Firearms? | Bureau of Alcohol, Tobacco, Firearms and Explosives." ATF Mission Areas, Firearms. Last Reviewed May 14, 2015. https://www.atf.gov/firearms/qa/what-atf-doing-regards-people-making-their-own-firearms.

U.S. Bureau of Alcohol, Tobacco, Firearms and Explosives. 2015. "ATF Releases U.S. Firearms Crime Gun Trace Data for 2014." News Release. ATF Bureau of Alcohol, Tobacco, Firearms and Explosives, July 23, 2015. https://www.atf.gov/news/pr/atf-releases-us-firearms-crime-gun-trace-data-2014.

U.S. Bureau of Justice Statistics. 2012. "About 1.4 Million Guns Stolen During Household Burglaries and Other Property Crimes from 2005 Through 2010." Bureau of Justice Statistics, November 8, 2012. https://www.bjs.gov/content/pub/press/fshbopc0510pr.cfm.

U.S. Bureau of Justice Statistics and Marianne Zawitz. 1995. "Guns Used in Crime." Bureau of Justice Statistics Selected Findings. https://www.bjs.gov/content/pub/pdf/GUIC.PDF.

U.S. Congress. House Committee on Financial Services. *Holding Megabanks Accountable: An Examination of Wells Fargo's Pattern of Consumer Abuses.* 116th Cong. March 12, 2019.

U.S. Department of Homeland Security. 2016. "Patron Screening Best Practices Guide: Commercial Facilities Sector-Specific Agency." https://www.cisa.gov/publication/patron-screening-guide.

U.S. Department of Justice. 1994. "Drug-Related Crime." Fact Sheet NCJ-149286. Drugs & Crime Data Center & Clearinghouse. https://www.bjs.gov/content/pub/pdf/DRRC.PDF

U.S. Department of Justice. n.d. "OJJDP Program—Profile 19: Getting Guns Off the Streets, New York City Police Department—New York, NY." Office of Juvenile Justice and Delinquency Program. https://ojjdp.ojp.gov/sites/g/files/xyckuh176/files/pubs/gun_violence/profile19.html.

U.S. Department of Justice, Bureau of Alcohol, Tobacco, and Firearms. 1977. "Concentrated Urban Enforcement Program, Rpt on Program Effectiveness in Urban Law Enforcement." (inserted material) before the U.S. Senate, Subcommittee on Treasury, U.S. Postal Service, and General Government Appropriations. Treasury, Postal Service, and General Government Appropriations for FY78. Part 1; 838–49.

U.S. Department of Justice, Bureau of Alcohol, Tobacco, Firearms, and Explosives. 2017. "Firearms Commerce in the United States Annual Statistical Update 2017." https://www.atf.gov/resource-center/docs/undefined/firearms-commerce-united-states-annual-statistical-update-2017/download.

U.S. Department of Justice, Bureau of Alcohol, Tobacco, Firearms and Explosives, National Tracing Center. 2011. "ATF Firearms Tracing Guide: Tracing Firearms to Reduce Violent Crime." 3312.13. ATF Publication. https://www.atf.gov/file/58631/download.

U.S. Department of Justice Drug Enforcement Administration. 2014. "FOIA Request Response. Re: American Civil Liberties Union and ACLU of Massachusetts v. United States Department of Justice, et al." Case Number: 12-004477-F. FOI/Records Management Section. https://www.aclu.org/files/assets/33780-33791%202014.03.31%20response.pdf#page=4.

U.S. Department of Justice Office of the Inspector General. 2004. "Review of the Bureau of Alcohol, Tobacco, Firearms and Explosives' Enforcement of Brady Act Violations Identified Through the National Instant Criminal Background Check System." I-2004–006. https://oig.justice.gov/reports/ATF/e0406/final.pdf.

U.S. Government Accountability Office. 2017. "Internet Firearms Sales: ATF Enforcement Efforts and Outcomes of GAO Covert Testing." GAO-18-24. https://www.gao.gov/products/GAO-18-24.

U.S. Government Accountability Office. 2018. "Few Individuals Denied Firearms Purchases Are Prosecuted and ATF Should Assess Use of Warning Notices in Lieu of Prosecutions." GAO-18-440. https://www.gao.gov/assets/700/694290.pdf.

Vavreck, Lynn, John Sides, and Chris Tausanovitch. 2019. "What Is Voters' Highest Priority? There's a Way to Find Out." *New York Times*, December 5, 2019. https://www.nytimes.com/2019/12/05/upshot/impeachment-biggest-issue-voters-poll.html.

Violence Policy Center. 2013. "'Smart' Guns Backgrounder." http://www.vpc.org/fact_sht/Smart%20Gun%202013.pdf.

Violence Policy Center. 2015. "Criminal Use of the 50 Caliber Sniper Rifle." Regulating the Gun Industry, May 6, 2015. http://vpc.org/regulating-the-gun-industry/criminal-use-of-50-caliber/.

Volokh, Eugene. 2009. "Implementing the Right To Keep and Bear Arms for Self-Defense: An Analytical Framework and a Research Agenda." *UCLA Law Review* 56. https://www.uclalawreview.org/implementing-the-right-to-keep-and-bear-arms-for-self-defense-an-analytical-framework-and-a-research-agenda/.

Warmington, B. H. 1964. *Carthage*. Harmondsworth: Penguin Books.

Warner, Gordon, and Donn F. Draeger. 1982. *Japanese Swordsmanship: Technique and Practice*. New York: Weatherhill.

"Washington Post-ABC News Poll April 8–11, 2018." 2018. *Washington Post*, April 20, 2018. https://www.washingtonpost.com/politics/polling/washington-postabc-news-poll-april-811/2018/04/20/6bd4d6b6-3f09-11e8-955b-7d2e19b79966_page.html.

Watts, Sean. 2015. "Regulation-Tolerant Weapons, Regulation-Resistant Weapons and the Law of War." *International Law Studies* 91 (1): 540–621.

Webster, Daniel. W., Jon. S. Vernick, and L. M. Hepburn. 2001. "Relationship between Licensing, Registration, and Other Gun Sales Laws and the Source State of Crime Guns." *Injury Prevention* 7 (3): 184–89.

Weisburd, David. 2015. "The Law of Crime Concentration and the Criminology of Place." Criminology 53 (2): 133–57.

Witte, Griff, and Karla Adam. 2015. "Getting a Gun Legally in Europe May Be Hard, but Terrorists Have Little Trouble." *Washington Post*, February 19, 2015. https://www.washingtonpost.com/world/europe/getting-a-gun -legally-in-europe-may-be-hard-but-terrorists-have-little-trouble/2015 /02/19/9eb6bce2-b78b-11e4-bc30-a4e75503948a_story.html.

Wright, James David, Peter H. Rossi, Kathleen Daly, and Eleanor Weber-Burdin. 1983. *Under the Gun: Weapons, Crime, and Violence in America.* New York: Aldine Pub. Co.

Wright, John Paul, Kim N. Dietrich, M. Douglas Ris, Richard W. Hornung, Stephanie D. Wessel, Bruce P. Lanphear, Mona Ho, and Mary N. Rae. 2008. "Association of Prenatal and Childhood Blood Lead Concentrations with Criminal Arrests in Early Adulthood." *PLOS Medicine* 5 (5): e101.

Yancey, George. 2017. *Compromising Scholarship: Religious and Political Bias in American Higher Education.* Waco, TX: Baylor University Press.

Yousef, Hasin. 2018. "Sticking to One's Guns: Mass Shootings and the Political Economy of Gun Control in the U.S." Available at SSRN: https://papers .ssrn.com/abstract=3360831.

Yuill, Kevin. 2016. "Better Die Against Injustice than to Die Like a Dog: African-Americans and Guns, 1866–1941." In *A Cultural History of Firearms in the Age of Empire*, edited by Karen Jones, Giacomo Macola, and David Welch. London: Routledge.

Zimmermann, Philip R. 1995. *PGP Source Code and Internals.* Cambridge, MA: MIT Press.

Zuboff, Shoshana. 2019. *The Age of Surveillance Capitalism: The Fight for a Human Future at the New Frontier of Power.* London: Profile Books.

Interviews by Author

Alpers, Philip. 2016.
Arson & Explosive Investigator, Midsized Illinois City (Anonymous). 2016.
Australian criminologist (Anonymous). 2016.
Blackman, Joshua. 2015.
Broadhurst, Roderic. 2016.
Chenoweth, Christopher. 2016.
Chief of Detectives, Midwestern City (Anonymous). 2015.
Chief of Police, Midwestern City (Anonymous). 2015.
Cross, Dee. 2015.
Crumling, Mike. 2019.

Director, State Police Training Institute (Anonymous). 2016.

Duan, Charles. 2019.

Evans, Richard. 2016.

Faculty Member, University of Illinois Program in Arms Control & Domestic and International Security (Anonymous). 2015.

Haines, Fiona. 2016.

Heidrick, Michael. 2015.

Industrial Designer/Makerspace Administrator (Anonymous). 2015.

Jenzen-Jones, Nic. 2018.

Kingery, Max. 2016.

Leighton-Daly, Mathew. 2016.

Liebel, Steven. 2016.

Machinist and information security specialist (Anonymous). 2015.

Machinist and software developer (Anonymous). 2015.

Maker (Anonymous). 2015.

Malet, David. 2016.

Moser, Greg. 2015.

Narula, Abhishek. 2015.

NSW Criminal Intelligence Specialist (Anonymous). 2016.

O'Brien, Nick. 2015.

Poritz, Jonathan. 2019.

Presson, William. 2016.

Schroeder, William. 2015.

Security studies professor (Anonymous). 2015.

Serbu, Mark. 2019.

Shafer, Joseph. 2016.

Sheriff's Deputies (Two anonymous individuals). 2015.

Smith, Mike. 2015.

Smith, Montella. 2016.

Spitzer, Robert. 2018.

Staber, Tim. 2016.

Steele, Brett. 2016.

Stokes, Jon. 2018.

Suplina, Nicholas. 2019.

Thierer, Adam. 2018.

Trella, Lynn. 2016.

University Chief of Police (Anonymous). 2016.

Vizzard, William. 2016.

Wachtel, Julius. 2016.

Wanberg, John. 2016.

Warren, Ian. 2016.

West, Levi. 2015.

Wilson, Harry. 2019.

Winkler, Adam. 2019.

Zimmerman, Dan. 2018.

Index

The terms *DIY* and *homemade* are used interchangeably in the text, but for consistency in indexing, the term *DIY* is used for both in the index. Page numbers followed by *t* indicate tables.

About the Author

Dr. Mark A. Tallman, ABCP, CIPS, RSO, WFR is an assistant professor of homeland security and emergency management at the Massachusetts Maritime Academy. He previously instructed for Colorado State University's Center for the Study of Homeland Security and Center for Cybersecurity Education and Research. He was a project manager for the University of Denver's Program on Terrorism and Insurgency Research, and is executive director of a private security and emergency planning consultancy.